Once Upon Dickson

Woodruff's
CLEANERS
LAUNDRY

WHEELER'S DRIVE-IN

CO

Ken's
PIZZA PARLOR

The
D-Lux

LONE STAR HOTEL.

409 W. DICKSON
BULLS-EYE PUB
& PASTIME PARLOUR
"THE ONLY PUB IN TOWN"

GEORGE
Majestic Lounge

'SHUL

Poor Richard's

Chatter Box
BEAUTY SHOP

Home

the
library

Vickers
CLEANERS & DYERS

The
1st NATIONAL
BANK

KI

WINCHESTER'S

Brooks' TEXACO Statio

De Luxe Eat Shop

Once Upon Dickson

An Illustrated History, 1868–2000

BY ANTHONY J. WAPPEL
WITH ETHEL C. SIMPSON

Phoenix International, Inc. with the
University of Arkansas Libraries
Special Collections Department
Fayetteville

Published in cooperation with the University of Arkansas Libraries Special Collections Department.

Manufactured in the United States of America

12 11 10 09 08 5 4 3 2 1

Designed by Liz Lester

Inquiries should be addressed to:
Phoenix International, Inc.
17762 Summer Rain Road
Fayetteville, Arkansas 72701
Phone (479) 521-2204
www.phoenixbase.com

LIBRARY OF CONGRESS CATALOGING-IN-PUBLICATION DATA

Wappel, Anthony J., 1963–
Once upon Dickson : an illustrated history, 1868–2000 / by Anthony J. Wappel, with Ethel C. Simpson.
p. cm.
Includes bibliographical references and index.
ISBN 978-0-9768007-7-4 (alk. paper)
1. Dickson Street (Fayetteville, Ark.)—History--Pictorial works. 2. Fayetteville (Ark.)—History—Pictorial works. I. Simpson, Ethel C., 1937– II. Title.
F419.F3W37 2008
976.7'14—dc22

2008009979

To the generations of nameless and forgotten laborers,
students, professors, residents, and transients
who made Dickson Street . . . Dickson Street.

CONTENTS

FOREWORD BY THE AUTHOR

I first came to Fayetteville on May 16, 1986, to enroll in the graduate school of the University of Arkansas. On May 17 I found an apartment on North Duncan Avenue in one of Cathy Boyd's properties near the corner of West Dickson Street. I was fortunate to find something so close to the campus. Not only could I walk to school, I was close enough to walk—I didn't have a car for the first six years I lived in Fayetteville—to the IGA and Safeway supermarkets on College Avenue at least once a week to buy groceries and other necessities.

In order to avoid both traffic and the occasional persons shouting obscenities as they drove past, I tried to do my shopping on Saturday mornings. Dickson Street was always very peaceful at 7:00 and 8:00 A.M. and these early morning walks enabled me to reflect, as an armchair historian, upon the history of the street that I began to know quite well. Walking past partially demolished stone walls, old flower beds, and, in 1986, several abandoned buildings, I began to wonder how Dickson Street evolved and how it looked in earlier years. What were some of the first businesses on the street? Who were Dickson Street's residents?

In 1988, the year site preparation for the Walton Arts Center commenced, I began documenting the numerous businesses and families that occupied Dickson Street. I found that the earliest plat map of the Town of Fayetteville, dated 1835, showed the northern boundary to be an unnamed street running along what is now called Dickson. In addition to old city directories, telephone books, and tax records, I obtained information from advertisements in the yearbooks of the University of Arkansas and in Fayetteville's numerous newspapers. Fate, as well as cooperative employers, granted me the opportunity to conduct much of my research while working at the reference desk in the Special Collections department of the University of Arkansas Libraries. After finishing a block-by-block inventory of businesses and residents, I had to decide what to do with it. Rather than analyzing the information from a purely historical, social, or economic perspective, I decided to abstract the information I had gathered and write, as impartially as I could, a series of short biographies and histories of residents and businesses of Dickson Street's sixteen blocks.

The enormous quantity of information gathered while researching this project makes it impossible to do justice to all of Dickson Street's residents and businesses. I decided to limit this work to those who had occupied their spaces for at least fifteen years. Although I occasionally refer to earlier events, I chose 1868 as a starting point simply because the Washington County Tax Records began in that year and the development of the University of Arkansas and Dickson Street followed soon afterward. Also, the official ending date of this history is 2000, but I was able to insert later information where appropriate.

I apologize in advance for any oversights, and give warning that many dates are approximate and that some ownership history may be slightly askew. Some addresses or street numbers will appear off, but often when a building was demolished, the new building that replaced it was given a higher number than the earlier one had. I make no attempt to analyze why Dickson Street developed as it did. This is a job for economists, geographers and sociologists. Nor do I make an attempt to glamorize any time period. This can be left to personal reminiscences. Even as I was working on this history it was clear that, not for the first time, Dickson Street was changing rapidly; one of my aims was to preserve some trace of the people, structures, and events that have given the street its distinctive and memorable character. I did this for fun and hope the book brings back some pleasant memories for long-term residents and provides a glimpse into a part of Fayetteville's past for those just now becoming acquainted with it.

Tony Wappel

A NOTE FROM THE CO-AUTHOR

I preceded Tony to Fayetteville by more than twenty-five years, though I became a permanent resident only in 1969. Like him and thousands of others, I came here to school and ended up returning to a place that attracted me for the colorful and easy-going life it offered. We boasted that hippies and clergymen, bikers and bankers, professors and business men could rub shoulders comfortably in a pool hall, a book shop, a church, or a natural-foods store along Dickson Street. You could walk from the campus to Dickson, mail a letter, do your laundry, have lunch, pick up a quart of paint or whisky or motor oil, buy a book, play darts or pool, or go bowling. You could park your Volvo next to a pickup truck or a Cadillac in Jug Wheeler's parking lot. With time, the street has become a little more gentrified and its color a little more the green of greenbacks. More Fayetteville residents have the income to support the new high-end attractions—a grand concert hall, gigantic motorcycles, custom jewelers, and luxury condos, but some of our favorite institutions, from Central Methodist to Collier's to the Dickson Street Book Shop to George's—have stayed in place during these years.

Like Tony, I worked in Special Collections at the University library, where I became familiar with the colorful history of Fayetteville's downtown and with the resources housed in the library that document that story. So I was very happy to help Tony to bring his book to completion. My job has been not so much that of an author but, as Tony has said, of the Terminator.

Ethel C. Simpson

ACKNOWLEDGEMENTS

This book has been a long time coming. Its appearance in print is due to the generosity of people and institutions that helped to finance its preparation and publication. The late Betty Lighton and the Happy Hollow Foundation, a philanthropy of the Lighton family; the Bank of Fayetteville; the Advertising and Promotion Commission of the City of Fayetteville, Frank and Sara Sharp; an anonymous donor; and the Special Collections department of the University of Arkansas Libraries provided important financial support. The authors gratefully acknowledge the skill and patience of Liz Lester, who designed the book, and of Phoenix International Inc., who published it.

EAST DICKSON

EAST DICKSON STREET— AN OVERVIEW

East Dickson Street, in the quiet neighborhood east of College Avenue, is the forgotten part of Dickson. Many people who have written articles about Dickson Street have ignored this part. However, because East Dickson was home to many who played an instrumental role in the development of Fayetteville and West Dickson Street, I chose to include it in this history. East Dickson begins on the western slope of Mt. Sequoyah and runs five blocks west. It crosses Tincup Ravine, now known as Spout Spring, in the 200 block, passes historic Headquarters House in the 100 block, daringly crosses College Avenue in the 10 block and ends at East and Highland Avenues near Central Methodist Church. Until 1908, when the Baptists built their church on the corner of College and Dickson, East Dickson Street was solidly residential. The earliest residents included the McGarrah, Williams, Pittman, Campbell, Ragland, Tebbets, Walker, and Van Hoose families. With the exception of First Baptist Church, East Dickson retained its status as a residential neighborhood until the 1950s. Most residents of this neighborhood were considered well off. Bankers, doctors, druggists, grocers, jewelers, lawyers, politicians, preachers, salesmen, and teachers lived here.

Beginning with the 1950s, many long-term residents began to die or move away. Many houses were converted into apartments or demolished. Since 1951, when the Lion Oil Service Station opened on the southwest corner of College and Dickson, some of the former home sites become commercial or public buildings. In 1962 Herbert Hatfield opened a used-car lot across College from the Lion Service Station and the City of Fayetteville constructed the Fayetteville Public Library in the 200 block. In 1968 SWEPCO constructed its local office on the northeast corner of College and Dickson.

In 1971 there was a serious effort to create a Residential-Office zone along Dickson Street east of College Avenue, but local residents won out

Dickson Street looking east, 2000

in their efforts to preserve the residential neighborhood. Most of the activity that transformed East Dickson into a partly commercial neighborhood has taken place near College Avenue and, for all practical purposes, is a part of the history of the development of College Avenue and Highway 71-Business, rather than the development of Dickson Street.

By the mid 1970s most of the houses in the 100 block were converted into apartments and eventually demolished. In 1980 Jerry Lindsay converted the Lion Service Station into Jerry's Restaurant, and in 1986, the First South Federal Savings & Loan Company constructed a large office building on the site of Hatfield's Used Car Lot. Today it is the Washington County Courthouse. With the exception of this commercial node, East Dickson, compared to West Dickson, remains a fairly tranquil residential neighborhood.

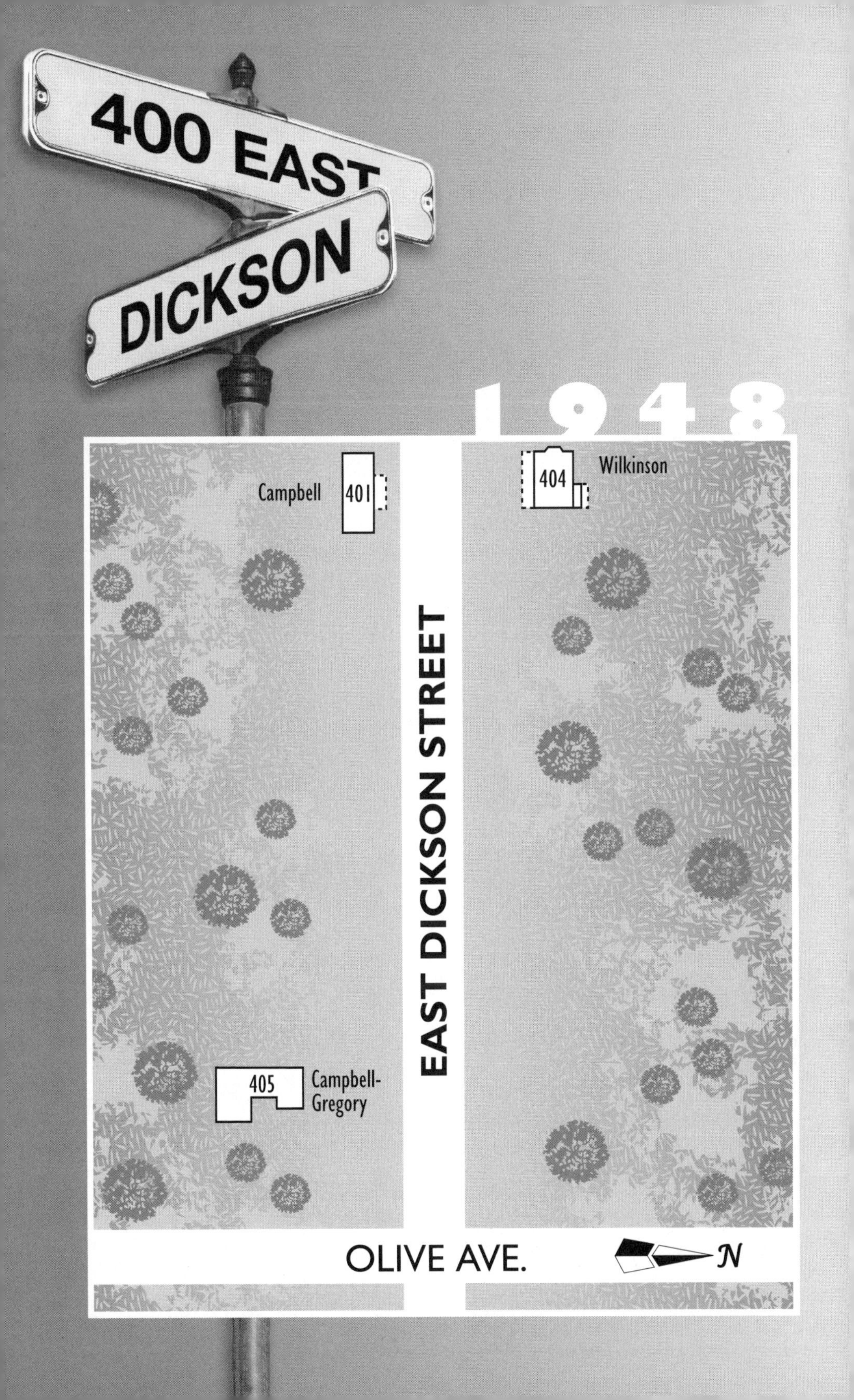
400 EAST
DICKSON
1948
Campbell
401
404
Wilkinson
EAST DICKSON STREET
405
Campbell-
Gregory
OLIVE AVE.
N

Dickson Street begins or, depending on your perspective, ends, in the 400 block of East Dickson. It is on the western slope of Mt. Sequoyah, which was also known as East Mountain.

405 EAST DICKSON

Pittman

One of the first persons to live in the 400 block was Circuit Judge James Pittman. Around 1871 he and his wife constructed a large house at what would become 405 East Dickson, where they lived the rest of their lives. Born in 1838 near Prairie Grove, Pittman fought for the Confederacy during the Civil War. After the war, he moved to Carroll County and married Margaret Peel, a native of Bentonville. In 1867 Pittman returned to Washington County. In 1870 he was elected to the Arkansas General Assembly, representing Benton and Washington County. While there, Pittman helped draft legislation establishing Arkansas Industrial University (University of Arkansas). In 1874 he was elected Circuit Judge. He was re-elected Circuit Judge in 1882 and held the position until his death in 1900. Mrs. Pittman died in 1894.

Judge Pittman

Campbell

In 1905, Frank Campbell purchased Judge Pittman's property. He lived here until his death in 1954. Born in 1857 in Washington County, Campbell obtained a formal education from the Arkansas Industrial University. In 1906 along with other civic leaders, he helped organize the Washington County Fair. Campbell was a leader of the Washington County Republican Party and in 1919 became the first Republican County Judge since Reconstruction. As County Judge, he bought the county's first motorized

405 East Dickson, 1940

equipment and built the first concrete bridge in the county (at Elkins). He also served two non-consecutive terms as Fayetteville postmaster between 1902 and 1932, and was responsible for the construction of the old Fayetteville Post Office on the downtown square. Campbell also served on the Fayetteville Water Board for more than twenty years and was one of the first to recognize the need for a long-term plan for securing an adequate water supply for Fayetteville. Campbell's wife, Effie Williams, was born in Bloomington, Indiana, and the couple were married in 1872. She died in 1932.

Judge Campbell

Gregory

In the 1920s, Frank and Effie Campbell's daughter, Mary, married Jim Gregory. They also lived at 405 East Dickson Street. Born in Kentucky in 1889, Gregory lived in Oklahoma and Missouri before settling in Arkansas in 1928. His first ventures in Fayetteville were the Gregory Finance Company and

Jim Gregory

Central Canners, Inc. He remained in the canning business until the late 1940s. Over the next forty years, he helped develop Drake Field, Walker Park, the Fayetteville Youth Center, and the district on West Avenue formerly housing the Campbell Soup factory and the McBride Distributing Company. However, one of Gregory's proudest accomplishments was his role in obtaining support for Beaver Dam and Lake Fayetteville. Mary Gregory lived at her home until her death in 1977. Jim Gregory lived here until his death in 1987.

Today, the Meldrum family, descendants of the Campbells and Gregorys, owns the Pittman-Campbell-Gregory house.

404 EAST DICKSON

Wilkinson

404 East Dickson, 1970s

Around 1904 Harvey and Jennie Pittman Wilkinson built a house at what would become 404 East Dickson. Born in Polk County in 1863, Wilkinson was a letter carrier and, for several years, postmaster. He delivered mail to Fayetteville residents for more than thirty years. It was said that in Wilkinson's duties as letter carrier, he would have walked more than four times around the world. The Wilkinsons were members of St. Paul's Episcopal Church. Mr. Wilkinson died in 1932. His widow remained at 404 East Dickson until 1957.

Ferrell

Bill Ferrell

Bill Ferrell and his wife, Rita Daugherty, came to Fayetteville in 1950.They purchased the Wilkinson house in 1958. Born in Norfolk, Virginia, in 1910, Ferrell graduated from the College of William and Mary in 1932. Between 1929 and 1938 Ferrell played professional baseball for the Cleveland, Boston, and Washington teams. Before moving to Arkansas, he also coached baseball at William and Mary and at Drexel University. Ferrell was head baseball coach and trainer for the University of Arkansas Razorbacks between 1950 and 1965 and was known as "Ground Hog." Shortly before his death in 1967, Ferrell was inducted into the National Trainers' Hall of Fame. Mrs. Ferrell continued to maintain a home at this address until the mid-1990s.

401 EAST DICKSON

Campbell

In 1923 Joe Campbell, a son of Frank and Effie Campbell, built a house at 401 East Dickson Street. Born in 1884, Campbell was a distributor for the Pierce Oil Company for nearly thirteen years. He was also associated with Central Canners and was at one time the owner of the White River Canning Company. Campbell was also a World War I veteran. Like his father, Joe Campbell was very civic-minded. In 1952 he made an unsuccessful bid for the position of Washington County Clerk. Joe Campbell died in 1958. His first wife, Gray T. Baskin, was a teacher at the Campbell Private School at 354 North Willow, which included kindergarten through the third grade. Campbell's second wife, Virginia, was a bookkeeper at Lewis Brothers Hardware. She lived at 401 East Dickson until 1984. Since that time, many other tenants have rented the Campbell house.

401 East Dickson, 2000

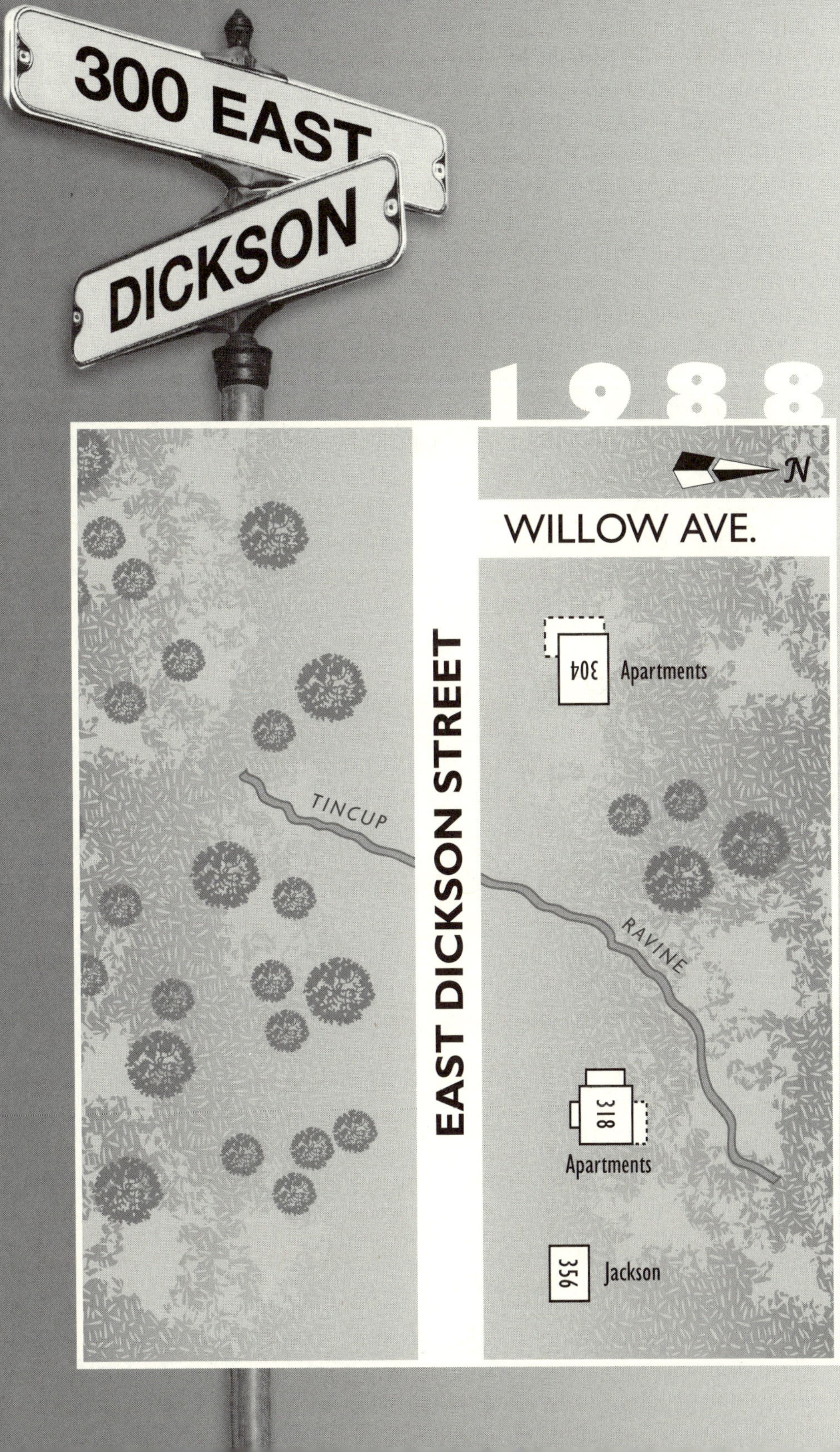
300 EAST
DICKSON
1988
N
WILLOW AVE.
EAST DICKSON STREET
304 Apartments
TINCUP
RAVINE
318
Apartments
356 Jackson

300 BLOCK

Continuing on the western slope of Mt. Sequoyah and eventually bottoming out at Tin Cup Ravine, now known as Spout Spring, is the 300 block of East Dickson. Throughout its history, it has been the least populated block. The only residences in this block are on the north side.

356 EAST DICKSON

Lois Glass

Around 1959, Lois Glass moved into a newly constructed brick house at 356 East Dickson, between the Ferrell home at 404 East Dickson and the home at 318 East Dickson. Glass, an employee of the Ozark Grocer Company, lived here until 1985. She died in Rogers in 1999. Miss Glass's house continues to be a single-family residential dwelling.

356 East Dickson, 2000

318 East Dickson, 2000

318 EAST DICKSON
Bossemeyer

Around 1919, Henry and Nettie Bossemeyer constructed the large house near Spout Spring at what would become 318 East Dickson. The Bossemeyers owned this house until 1944. Born in 1867 at Union, Iowa, Bossemeyer was a salesman for the Henry Von Wallpaper Company. Mr. and Mrs. Bossemeyer were active members of the Baptist Church and for many years he served as deacon.

Several families rented the Bossemeyer house during the 1940s and 1950s. In 1957 Maxine Englehart purchased the house. She was affiliated with Central Presbyterian Church and lived at 318 East Dickson until 1975. During the 1970s, the Bossemeyer-Englehart house was converted into apartments. Since that time, it has been home to many residents.

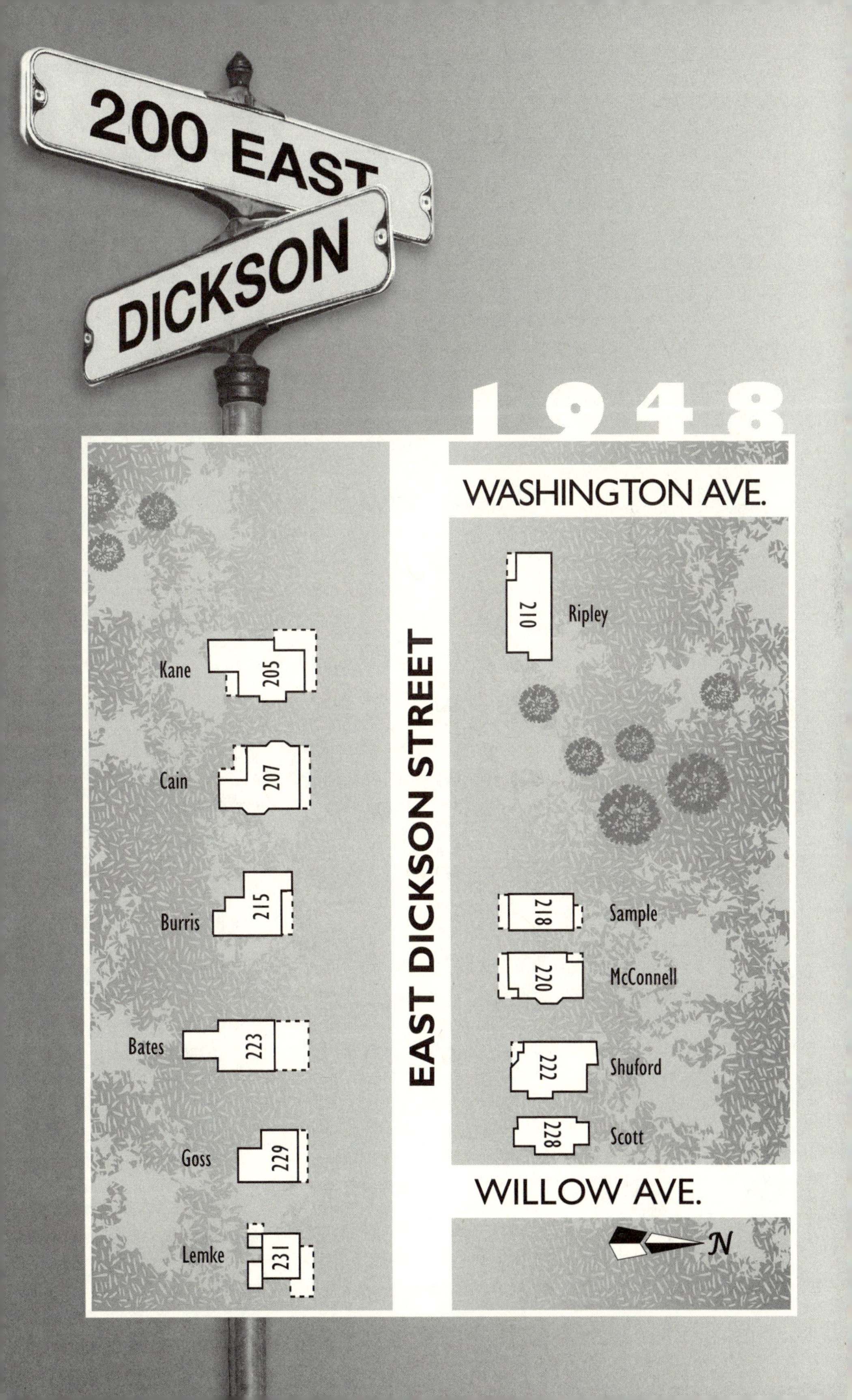
200 EAST
DICKSON
1948
WASHINGTON AVE.
EAST DICKSON STREET
WILLOW AVE.
N
Kane
205
Cain
207
Burris
215
Bates
223
Goss
229
Lemke
231
Ripley
210
Sample
218
McConnell
220
Shuford
222
Scott
228

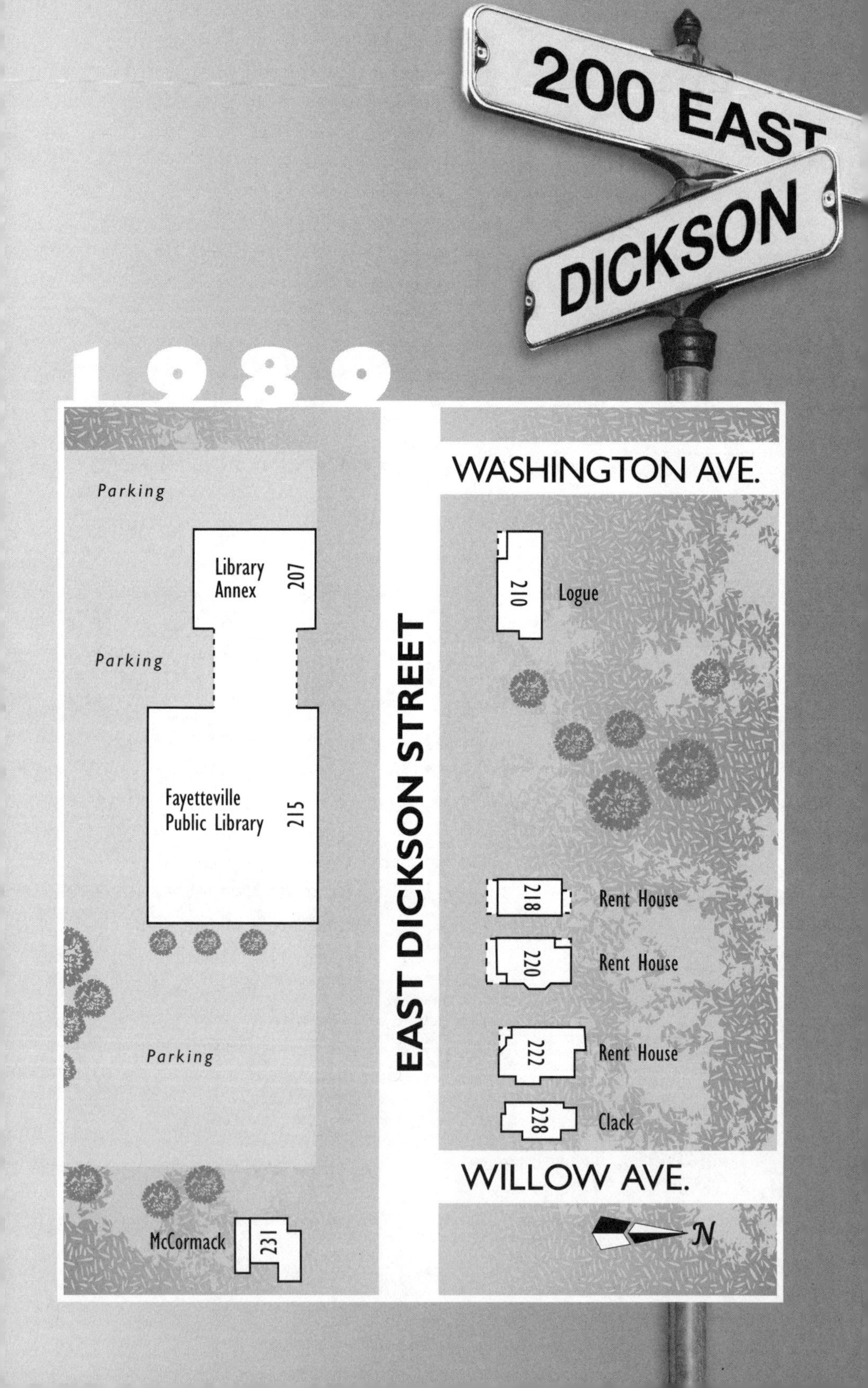

200 EAST
DICKSON
1989
Parking
Library Annex
207
Parking
Fayetteville Public Library
215
Parking
McCormack
231
EAST DICKSON STREET
WASHINGTON AVE.
210
Logue
218
Rent House
220
Rent House
222
Rent House
228
Clack
WILLOW AVE.
N

Traveling uphill, away from Tin Cup Ravine, later renamed Spout Spring, is the 200 block of East Dickson. For most of its history, this block has been the most populated part of East Dickson Street. The McGarrah and Williams families owned most of the undeveloped property in the block until the 1880s, when Reverend Nathaniel Ragland moved there.

McGarrah and Williams

Most of the south side of the 200 block was owned by the McGarrahs, some of Fayetteville's earliest settlers, who arrived here around 1828. William McGarrah (1790–1864) was a son of George McGarrah and became a leading merchant in antebellum Fayetteville. He and his wife Elizabeth, their daughter Sarah, and several other family members lived on the property later occupied by the Fayetteville Public Library. Sarah McGarrah (1836–1910) married Thomas Williams in 1851. Born in Washington County in 1832, Williams traded livestock before and after the Civil War. Williams had a reputation as a good walker. He once walked as far as Pettigrew, a distance of forty miles. Thomas Williams died of malaria in 1886. Sarah Williams lived in the East Dickson neighborhood her entire life and was affiliated with both the Baptist and Presbyterian Churches.

231 EAST DICKSON

Lemke

Professor Lemke

The house at 231 East Dickson was constructed around 1899 and was for a time the home of Reverend C. D. and Josephine Cheatham. In 1938, the Lemkes moved there. Born in 1891 in Wausau, Wisconsin, Walter J. Lemke was educated at the University of Wisconsin, Indiana University, and Northwestern

231 East Dickson, 1970s

University. In 1928 he and his wife, Marie Hamp, came to Fayetteville, where he was head of the University of Arkansas News Bureau and the first professor in the Department of Journalism, which now bears his name. He organized the Arkansas High School Press Association to encourage high school journalism and was one of the founders of the Arkansas Press Women's Association. He was chairman of the department until his retirement in 1959. During World War II, Lemke and his wife sent mimeographed copies of "Uncle Walt's News-

Walter Lemke at home

letter" to former U of A students in military service throughout the world. These world-famous letters communicated information among service men and women about their friends and classmates in foreign theaters of war as well as about events back home and at the university. Lemke received hundreds of replies from air fields, ground battlefields, warships, and submarines. Intensely interested in local history, Lemke was a founder of the Arkansas Genealogical Society and of the Washington County Historical Society. He published its journal *Flashback* until his death in 1968. Mrs. Lemke lived at 231 East Dickson until her death in 1971.

229 EAST DICKSON
Rife

The house at 229 East Dickson was constructed around 1899 and was first owned by William Stoffer, a banker. Add and Clara Rife lived there between 1924 and 1945. Born in 1880 in Fair Dealing, Missouri, Rife moved to Arkansas in 1904. In 1910 he married Clara Baker, a native of Fayetteville. Rife had two professions. Early on, he worked with marble monuments and memorial stones. It is said that while at a picnic at Osage Mills (Benton County), Rife carved a representation of an open Bible in the nearby limestone bluffs. For the major part of his working life, however, Rife worked as a piano tuner for the Guisinger Music House on the southeast side of the Fayetteville square. Rife had a habit of carving his name and date on the pianos he worked on. His name might be seen in a few antique pianos in Northwest Arkansas. Clara Rife was a deputy Circuit Clerk for Washington County during the 1920s. Between 1945 and 1963 229 East Dickson was the home of Mary T. Goss.

223 EAST DICKSON
Shelton

In 1911 Mary Shelton moved to 223 East Dickson Street. Born in 1855 in Russellville, Kentucky, she came to Arkansas with her parents, Thompson Ewing and Delila Shelton, around 1880. In 1886 Major B. R. Davidson, a lawyer for the Frisco Railroad, persuaded Mary Shelton to open a school in the Quarles House, a large family hotel on the corner of East and Meadow Streets. Mary Shelton taught there for a few years and then taught school in Blackburn, Wyman, Baldwin, and Viney Grove. In 1892 Miss Shelton returned to Fayetteville to become the first principal of Jefferson Elementary School. She held this position until 1899. In 1911 several prominent residents of Fayetteville persuaded Shelton to open a private school in her home where their children could have the best education possible. The Mary Shelton Private School could accommodate thirty pupils. Between 1911, when it opened, and 1931, when Miss Shelton retired, approximately six hundred children received their primary education here. They included children of the Futrall, Vincenheller, Miller, Reynolds, Heerwagen, and Putnam families. One of my sources, Lina Hayes Watson, also obtained her early childhood education from Miss Shelton. Graduations were held across the street at the home of Austin Shelton and at the First Christian Church on College Avenue. Miss Shelton lived at 223 East Dickson until her death in 1935.

Mary Shelton

223 East Dickson, 1911

217–215 EAST DICKSON

Ragland

Born in 1848 in Kentucky, Nathaniel B. Ragland was educated at Culver-Stockton College in Missouri. After arriving in Fayetteville in 1885, he served the First Christian Church for 50 years, 22 years as pastor. Ragland was a very popular minister. He christened, married, and buried several hundred Fayetteville residents, regardless of their religious affiliation. Reverend Ragland and his wife, Fannie Sparr, built their home at 215 East Dickson Street, the former site of the McGarrah home, which had burned in 1877. Between the 1880s and early 1900s the Ragland home was the focal point of the 200 block of East Dickson Street. It was the site of many church-related social functions. Fannie Ragland died in 1896. Five years later, in 1901, Reverend Ragland married Beatrice Shelton, one of Mary Shelton's sisters. The Raglands lived at 215 East Dickson until Ragland's death in 1933 and Mrs. Beatrice Ragland's death in 1947. According to

Reverend Ragland

Ladies of First Christian Church, 1912

Ragland's great-granddaughter, Bette Stamps, Ragland's house was full of beautiful antiques and a voluminous library. Not only was Ragland well-educated, he was a kind, soft-spoken and compassionate man.

217–215 EAST DICKSON
Fayetteville Public Library

In 1959 Fayetteville launched a campaign to build an airport and a new library. Voters approved a bond issue of $550,00 and the library became a service of the City of Fayetteville. By that year, the collection had grown to more than 11,500 books. It also included three hundred phonograph records, as well as magazines, maps, and other resources. In 1962 the Fayetteville Public Library replaced the Ragland house at 215 E. Dickson. It is fitting that Fayetteville's library, with its strong commitment to the preservation of Fayetteville's history, was built on the home site of one of the town's first settlers, William McGarrah, and of one of its most beloved ministers, Nathaniel Ragland. Fayetteville Architect Warren D. Segraves designed the library building. It was officially known as the Roberta Fulbright Library, in honor of the mother of Senator J. W. Fulbright and long-time publisher of the *Northwest Arkansas Times.*

Fayetteville Public Library, 2000

MedArk Clinic/Fayetteville Library Expansion

In 1962 the MedArk Clinic, another project of Warren D. Segraves, replaced the homes at 207 and 205 East Dickson. Drs. Wade Burnside and Wilbur G. Lawson were the first physicians to occupy the MedArk Clinic. Other physicians to practice here included William F. Harrison and pediatricians Harold A. Decker, James D. Mashburn, and James E. Haynes. They remained there until the late 1980s.

By that time the library was experiencing additional growing pains and the need for expansion became quite evident. When the MedArk building at 207 East Dickson became available, the city purchased it and renovated the two buildings to create additional space for library materials, patrons, and staff. A glass-enclosed structure joined the two buildings and provided wheelchair access to the lower level of the old library. The addition housed the offices of the Ozarks Regional Library, the Grace Keith Genealogy Collection, and a bookstore run by volunteer Friends of the Library. Grace Keith, Helen Brannen, Mary Jo Godfrey, and Barbara Hale of the library staff provided invaluable assistance with this project.

207 EAST DICKSON

Conner

Around 1900 Caleb C. Conner and his wife, Sarah Trent, built a house one door west of the Raglands, at 207 East Dickson, and lived there until 1915. Born three miles southeast of Fayetteville in 1842, Conner fought for the Confederacy during the Civil War. After the war, he taught school. During the 1890s he was in the wholesale grocery business, operating for a time as the Conner-Boles Mercantile Company. In 1905 Conner organized the Conner Wholesale Grocer, located on the Fayetteville square. In 1907 he sold it to the Fayetteville Grocer Company (later known as the Ozark Grocer Company), which was in the 500 block of West Dickson. Conner also ran a steam mill in Farmington, was active in the Washington County Fair Association, and was a member of the county school board. He died in 1915. Sarah Trent Conner was born near Fayetteville in 1843 and died in 1913.

Williams

Hosea L. Williams and his wife, Edna Curry, lived at 207 East Dickson from 1916 to 1938. Born in 1886 to Alf L. and Josie Williams, Hosea Williams was a great-grandson of William McGarrah and was the last descendant of the McGarrah family known to live on East Dickson Street. Williams was a tie and lumber inspector for the Frisco Railroad. He was also at one time an agent of the Bear State Oil Company, which had a station in the 300 block of West Dickson. During the 1920s he was a deputy tax collector. This house was torn down around 1962 to make way for the Med-Ark Clinic and expanded public library.

205 EAST DICKSON

Conner

In 1898 Jeff Conner and his wife, Clementine Benbrook, built a house at 205 East Dickson. Born in 1861, Conner was the vice-president of Conner Wholesale Grocer Company. He was also long associated with the Disciples of Christ Church and was known as Brother Jeff. Jeff and Clem Conner lived here until 1911, when they moved across the street to 218 East Dickson. They lived there until Jeff Conner's death in 1934 and Clem Conner's death in 1936. Jeff's sister-in-law Jimmie Conner operated a boarding house at 205 East Dickson until 1924, when she moved to Chicago.

Kane

Robert Lee Kane and his wife, Beulah Jenkins, lived at 205 East Dickson between 1924 and 1955. Born in Kentucky in 1865, Kane received his formal education at Clinton Academy in Hickman County, Kentucky. In 1903 Kane moved to Quitman (Cleburne County), Arkansas, where he helped organize the Bank of Quitman. His first job there was cashier. In 1912 he became the president of the bank. In 1921 Kane purchased a controlling interest of the Bank of Cave Springs in Benton County. This house was also torn down to make way for the Med-Ark Clinic and expanded public library.

201 EAST DICKSON

McAdams

A. C. McAdams

In 1899 Albert C. McAdams moved to 201 East Dickson Street. Born in Ohio in 1860, McAdams moved to Arkadelphia, Arkansas, in 1883 and opened a drugstore there in 1886. In Arkadelphia he married Olive Gould, a music teacher from Kentucky. In 1898 Mr. and Mrs. McAdams moved to Fayetteville, where McAdams opened the Live and Let Live Drug Store on the southwest corner of the Fayetteville square. He was told by local inhabitants that he wouldn't succeed as druggist if he did not sell whiskey. Because of his refusal to sell it, McAdams' life was threatened on several occasions. In 1897 he hired T. Fred Shuler, a former A.I.U. student, to assist him.

In 1901 McAdams opened a second Live and Let Live drugstore in Depot Town (the 400–500 blocks of West Dickson Street). Although the Live and Let Live has faded from memory, the store in Depot Town was perhaps one of the best known drug stores in Fayetteville. This was where Fred Shuler did most of his work. Shuler was so popular with University of Arkansas students that the 400 block of Dickson became known as "Shuler Town."

On November 22, 1926, tragedy struck the McAdams Family. According to their neighbor, Cloe Long, who lived in the 100 block of East Dickson, the McAdams home caught fire. Both Mr. and Mrs. McAdams escaped unhurt; however, feeling the chill of the night air, Mrs. McAdams ran back into the house for a wrap, and never returned. It is interesting to note that there has never been a house at this site since this tragic fire.

228–210 EAST DICKSON

Williams

Most of the north side of the two-hundred block was owned by Alf L. Williams and his wife, Josie Maguire. Born in 1852, Alf was the oldest son of Thomas Williams and Sarah McGarrah. Alf Williams was a powerful force in the local timber industry. In 1882 he founded the A. L.

Williams Tie and Timber Company. It is said that he provided all of the cross-ties for the Ozark & Cherokee Railway, which ran from Fayetteville west through Farmington, Prairie Grove, Lincoln, and Summers, to Westville, Tahlequah, and Okmulgee, Oklahoma. Williams also helped organize the Washington County Bank. In 1922 Alf and Josie Williams retired to California, where they lived the rest of their lives.

Alf Williams

228 EAST DICKSON
Scott

Vine Q. Blumenberg was the first inhabitant of the red brick house at 228 East Dickson, which was built around 1929. Roy and Adortha Scott moved there in 1944. Born in 1890 in Winslow, Scott was educated in the public schools of Arkansas. In 1913 he married Adortha Crippin. Scott was active in both business and politics. He owned a barber shop, a bakery, and a transfer company. He was also a member of the Fayetteville City Council from 1926 to 1932. In 1942 he was elected County and Probate Clerk of Washington County, and held this office until 1952. Between 1954 and 1957 he was mayor of Fayetteville. In 1951 he became a charter member of the Washington County Historical Society and served this worthy organization until his death in 1965. Mrs. Scott, who was born in War Eagle in 1902, was a telephone operator. She lived at 228 East Dickson until her death in 1974.

222 EAST DICKSON
Shuford

Born in 1871 in Kentucky, Fannie Shelton married Eugene Shuford in 1891. They built a house at 222 East Dickson in 1903. Eugene Shuford helped organize the Fayetteville National Building and Loan Association in 1896. Fannie Shuford was the first "Frisco Matron." This position, created in 1922, was sponsored by the City Federation of Missionary Societies. Mrs. Shuford and subsequent matrons were responsible for assisting weary passengers arriving at the depot. During her tenure, Fannie Shuford assisted thousands of sick persons, mothers in need of help with babies, and

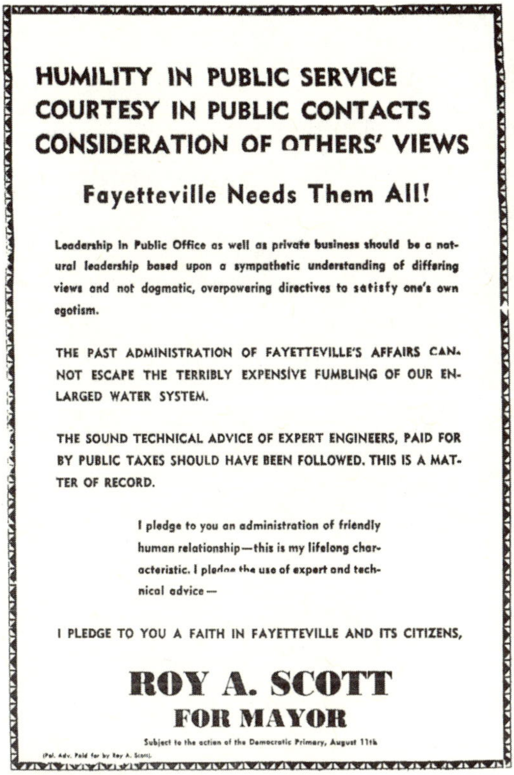

HUMILITY IN PUBLIC SERVICE
COURTESY IN PUBLIC CONTACTS
CONSIDERATION OF OTHERS' VIEWS

Fayetteville Needs Them All!

Leadership in Public Office as well as private business should be a natural leadership based upon a sympathetic understanding of differing views and not dogmatic, overpowering directives to satisfy one's own egotism.

THE PAST ADMINISTRATION OF FAYETTEVILLE'S AFFAIRS CANNOT ESCAPE THE TERRIBLY EXPENSIVE FUMBLING OF OUR ENLARGED WATER SYSTEM.

THE SOUND TECHNICAL ADVICE OF EXPERT ENGINEERS, PAID FOR BY PUBLIC TAXES SHOULD HAVE BEEN FOLLOWED. THIS IS A MATTER OF RECORD.

I pledge to you an administration of friendly human relationship—this is my lifelong characteristic. I pledge the use of expert and technical advice—

I PLEDGE TO YOU A FAITH IN FAYETTEVILLE AND ITS CITIZENS,

ROY A. SCOTT
FOR MAYOR

Subject to the action of the Democratic Primary, August 11th

(Pol. Adv. Paid for by Roy A. Scott)

Mayor Scott

Roy A. Scott for Mayor ad, 1953

228 East Dickson, 1970s

222 East Dickson, 1980s

travelers seeking food, lodging, or local transportation. Mrs. Shuford was authorized by the police to chase away persons of questionable character. The Shufords remained at 222 East Dickson until 1949.

220 EAST DICKSON

Shelton

Austin Shelton and his wife, Eva Reese, also moved to East Dickson in 1903. Born in Kentucky in 1874 Austin and his brother Tom were in the grain, feed, seed, and flower business. They sold their business to the Adams family, who developed it into Adams' Flowers. Austin and Eva Shelton lived at 220 East Dickson until 1920. And, yes, Austin and Tom were brothers of the aforementioned Shelton sisters.

McConnell

In 1923 Ben and Bessie McConnell purchased the Austin Shelton home. Born near West Fork in 1887 McConnell married Bessie Douglas in 1908. He worked for the McIlroy Bank for forty-four years, first as a cashier and later as senior vice-president. Upon retiring from the bank in 1964, McConnell reflected on the changes of consumer habits. "People

220 East Dickson, 1980s

Shelton sisters

used to borrow money only in cases of emergencies. . . . Occasionally they borrowed to purchase a home, but down payments were considerably larger and payment periods considerably shorter." In 1970 Mr. and Mrs. McConnell moved to Bunkie, Louisiana.

218 EAST DICKSON
Conner

In 1904 Clint Conner and his wife Jimmie Hunt constructed their home at 218 East Dickson. Five years later, Clint Conner died in San Diego, California. In 1911 Clint's widow Jimmie swapped houses with her brother-in-law Jeff Conner, making 218 the residence of Jeff and Clementine Conner and 205 the residence of Jimmie Conner. Clementine Conner lived here until 1936.

210 EAST DICKSON
Ripley

Professor Ripley

In 1942 Giles E. and Harriet Ripley constructed the newest house in the block, located at 210 East Dickson. Ripley, a native of Indiana and an alumnus of Purdue University, taught physics at the University of Arkansas from 1908 until his death in 1943. He was also Dean of Men between 1923 and 1937. Mrs. Ripley continued to live at 210 East Dickson until 1956. After that, Rolla and Mabel Clinehens called 210 East Dickson home between 1957 and 1971.

210 East Dickson, 2000

210 East Dickson
Re-Zoning Effort of 1971

In 1971 Fayetteville dentist Jacob Agee petitioned the Fayetteville Planning Commission to re-zone the Ripley-Clinehens property at the corner of Washington and Dickson from low-density residential to residential-office. Agee wanted to use the building for his dental practice. Local residents believed that if this house were re-zoned, all of East Dickson, as well as the historic Washington and Willow Avenues, would succumb to commercialization. After all, the Fayetteville Library and Medark Clinic had already moved to East Dickson. The residents of tree-lined Washington Avenue insisted that bulldozers should not invade their homes. The Fayetteville Planning Commission denied Dr. Agee's request and residents won the battle to save one of Fayetteville's most historic neighborhoods from what they called "creeping concrete." Today 210 East Dickson remains residential.

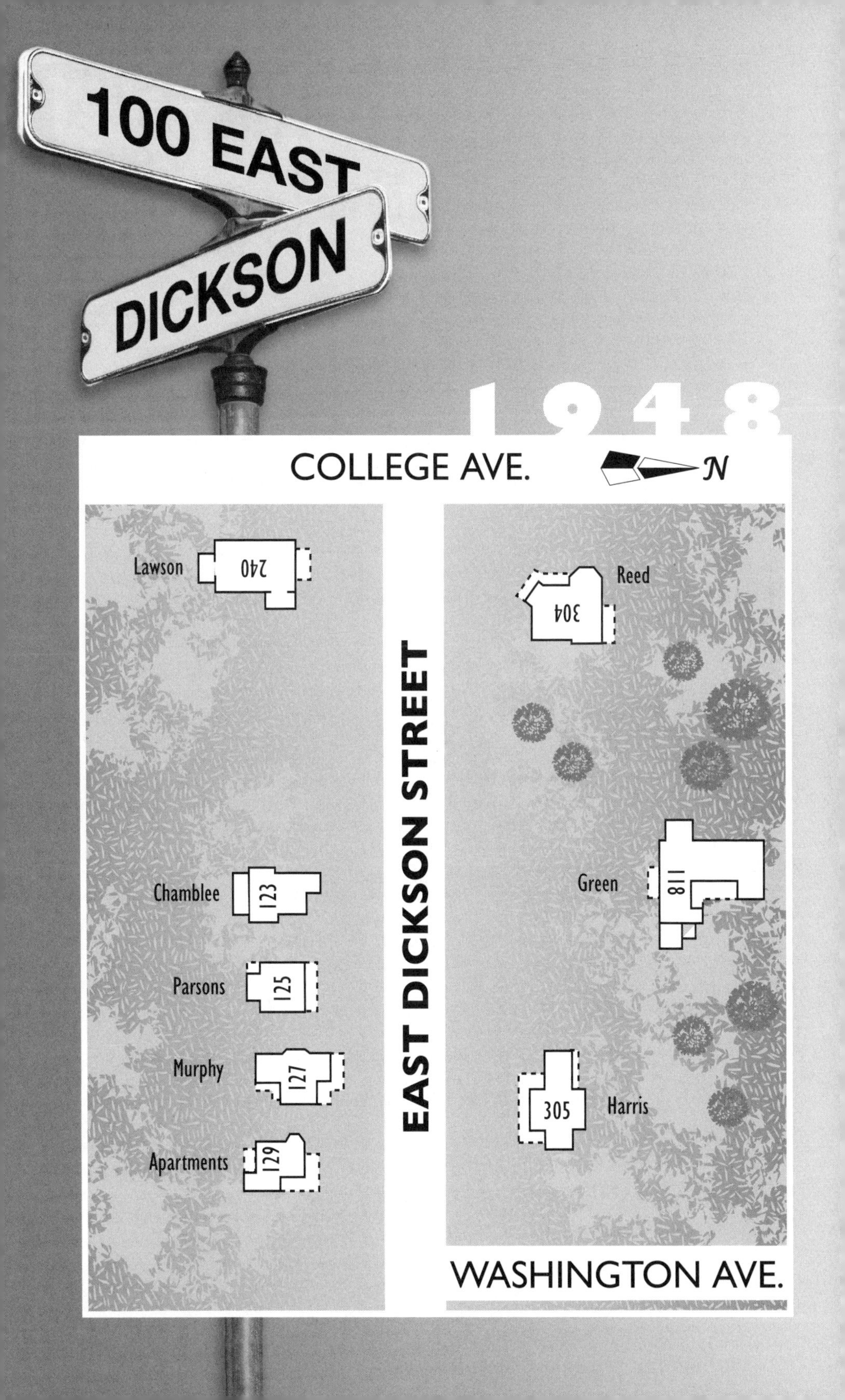
100 EAST
DICKSON
1948
COLLEGE AVE.
N
Lawson
240
Reed
304
EAST DICKSON STREET
Chamblee
123
Green
118
Parsons
125
Murphy
127
Harris
305
Apartments
129
WASHINGTON AVE.

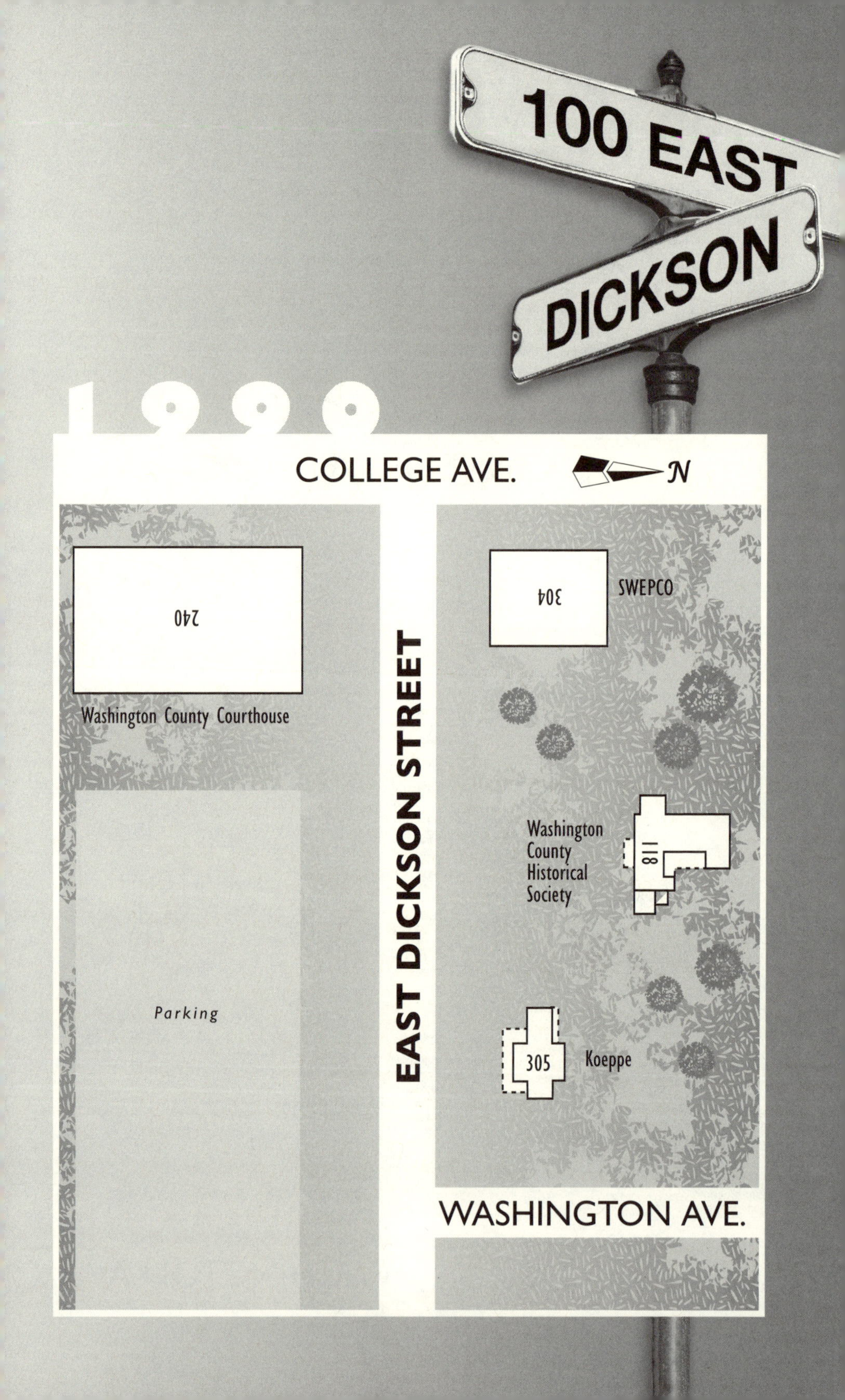

100 EAST
DICKSON
COLLEGE AVE.
N
240
Washington County Courthouse
Parking
EAST DICKSON STREET
304
SWEPCO
Washington County Historical Society
118
305
Koeppe
WASHINGTON AVE.

100 BLOCK

Dickson Street becomes relatively flat in the 100 block of East Dickson and remains so until the 200 block of West Dickson. The 100 block contains one of Fayetteville's most famous structures, Headquarters House, at 118 East Dickson Street. Built in 1853 by Jonas Tebbetts, this house served as headquarters during the Civil War for whichever force, Confederate or Union, happened to be occupying Fayetteville at the time. Until the 1880s,when it was owned by the Charles Walker family, it was the only residence in the block. In 1888 residences were constructed on both sides of Headquarters House. The first was on the northwest corner of Dickson and Washington and the second was on the northeast corner of Dickson and College.

Across the street on the southeast corner of College and Dickson was "Bloody Corner" in reference to the Battle of Fayetteville, which took place near this location on April 17, 1863. Arkansas College and First Christian Church owned this corner during the 1860s. Between the 1870s and 1890s, this corner was owned by James H. and Martha Van Hoose. Around 1896 local realtor R. S. Mitchell purchased and developed much of the property.

Headquarters House at 118 East Dickson, 1990s

118 EAST DICKSON

Walker

C. W. Walker

Born in Fayetteville in 1835 to Arkansas Supreme Court Chief Justice David Walker, Charles Walker graduated from Princeton University and studied law at the University of Tennessee until the Civil War interrupted his studies. After the war, he practiced law in Fayetteville with Thomas M. Gunter. In 1867 he married Serena Jernigan. For more than fifty years Walker was a deacon in the Baptist Church. Walker was also a city councilman, mayor, representative, and a delegate to the Arkansas constitutional convention of 1868. He purchased the house at 118 East Dickson in 1873 from the Joseph and Rebecca Davis estate and lived there until 1920.

Appleby

Charles Appleby

In 1920 Charles and Mary Appleby moved here. Born in Washington County in 1865, Appleby received his education in the public schools of the county. In 1900 he moved to Fayetteville. Appleby and his brother George had approximately two hundred acres of apple orchards and nearly one hundred fifty acres in strawberries. In addition, the Applebys had evaporating and canning businesses in Fayetteville, Hiwasse, and West Fork. Their labors helped to make Benton and Washington Counties a fruit-growing center of the southwest. In 1933 Appleby was killed in a car-train accident near Westville, Oklahoma. Appleby's wife was Mary Lorie Hughey, a native of Ohio. She lived here until 1936.

Green

Paris R. Green and his wife, Gladys Johnson, moved to 118 East Dickson in 1940. Born in Cincinnati, Arkansas, in 1894, Green owned and operated Green Chevrolet for several years. He founded the Southwest Casualty Insurance Company, was a major contributor to Fayetteville City Hospital, and was a charter member of the Washington County Historical Society. Born in 1896, Mrs. Green was a member of Central Methodist Church and the Shamrock Club. She died in 1961. Mr. Green remained at 118 East Dickson until 1966.

P. R. and Gladys Green

Washington County Historical Society

The Washington County Historical Society acquired 118 East Dickson in 1967 and moved into the building in 1968. Founded by "Uncle Walt" Lemke in 1950, the society held its first meeting in 1951 in the student lounge of University Lutheran Church. Charter members included Walter Lemke, Roy Scott, Paris Green, and Fount Richardson. It was officially incorporated as a nonprofit institution in 1960. The society's

Washingtn County Historical Society, 1968

first location was at 12½ East Center Street, across from the Historic Washington County Court House. For the first eight years, all the printing for the society was done at the University of Arkansas Department of Journalism. Its quarterly publication, *Flashback,* is published by volunteers. The society has published a series of local history bulletins and supported the publication of historical materials, such as the diary of Marian Tebbetts Bains. It has held occasional pilgrimages to historic sites in the county and has supported the placing of markers at locations including Headquarters House, Cane Hill, Bloody Corner, the site of the William F. Quesenbury House, and the Trail of Tears site on Sixth Street near the University of Arkansas.

NORTHWEST CORNER OF WASHINGTON & DICKSON
Harris

John R. Harris

In 1888, Fayetteville architect and builder A. M. Byrnes built a residence east of Headquarters House, on the northwest corner of Dickson and Washington. Its postal address is 305 North Washington Avenue. The first known resident was Judge B. J. Brown, who lived there in 1889. Clifton and Fannie Gray also lived there during the 1890s. The Harris and Hodson family owned the property the longest. Born in Missouri in 1847 and reared in Springdale, John Harris was in the hardware and lumber business in Springdale before coming to Fayetteville around 1900. John and Mary Harris purchased the house around 1904. While in Fayetteville, Harris served as president of the Bank of Fayetteville. In 1908 he helped finance Citizens Laundry in the 100 block of West Dickson. Harris died in 1929. Born in 1866, Mrs. Harris was a native of Ashboro, North Carolina and lived at 305 North Washington until her death in 1965. Their daughter, Hadley Harris, was the wife of Edgar A. Hodson. She was born in 1895 and lived in the Harris home until 1976. She won third place in the Fayetteville Democrat's 1916 "Who's Who" contest, in which contestants were given various clues with which to guess the names and addresses of sixty-five businesses in the city.

Northwest corner of Washington & Dickson, 2000

NORTHEAST CORNER OF COLLEGE & DICKSON

Reed

John A. Reed and his wife, Lena Bates, also built their home in 1888. Their house was west of Headquarters House on the northeast corner of Dickson and College, later site of the SWEPCO building. Their postal address was 304 North College Avenue. Born in 1860, Reed was a son of George W. and Mary J. Reed, who lived in the 600 block of West Dickson. John Reed was a graduate of Arkansas Industrial University and was associated with his father's merchandising business, Reed & Ferguson. The Reeds married in 1883. John Reed died at home in 1921. Lena Reed lived here until her death in 1950.

Lena Bates Reed

Northeast corner of College & Dickson, 1903

SWEPCO

In 1968 the Southwestern Electric Power Company purchased and demolished the Reed home on the northeast corner of College and Dickson and constructed a new office building, also designed by Warren Segraves, for its Fayetteville office. SWEPCO, a unit of American Electric Power, has its home office in Shreveport, Louisiana, and provides electric service to more than one hundred sixty cities and towns in Arkansas, Louisiana, and Texas.

129–119 EAST DICKSON

Van Hoose

Around 1877, James H. Van Hoose purchased most of the property on the south side of the block from LaRue Harrison. Born in 1830 in Kentucky, Van Hoose moved to Washington County in 1839. In 1855 he married Melinda Ann McIlroy. She died in 1864. Five years later Van Hoose married

SWEPCO, 1995

Martha W. Skelton, who died in 1933. Van Hoose was known as a charitable man; having no children of his own, he and his wife reared a girl named Mary W. Eaton, who was orphaned during the Civil War. Van Hoose was in the merchandising business and was at one time affiliated with William McIlroy. By 1880 Van Hoose settled in the insurance business. He served as

James H. and Martha Van Hoose

Mayor of Fayetteville in 1880–1881 and again in 1888–1890. In 1896 he was elected to the Arkansas General Assembly. In 1899 Van Hoose was accidentally shot and killed during a squirrel-hunting expedition near Wyman.

129 EAST DICKSON
Long

In 1897 the Gregg family built a boarding house at 129 East Dickson. Around 1920 Thomas G. and Elizabeth Long and their daughter Cloe Long moved here. Born in Tennessee in 1867, Elizah "Dove" Hayes and Thomas G. Long were married in 1890 and lived in California for the first year of their marriage. They then lived in Huntsville, Arkansas, until 1916, when they moved to Fayetteville. Mr. Long was the proprietor of Long's Meat Market and the Manhattan Cafe. He died in 1923. Mrs. Long died in 1934. Cloe Long was a bookkeeper for Washington County National Bank and lived at 129 East Dickson until 1947. This house was demolished around 1982.

127 EAST DICKSON
Murphy

Eugene Murphy lived at 127 East Dickson between 1931 and 1972. Born in 1896 in Mineral Wells, Texas, Murphy moved to Springdale in 1900. He started a printing career with the *Springdale News.* In 1913 he began working for the *Fayetteville Daily Democrat* as a mechanical superintendent. He worked there until retiring in 1955. Eugene Murphy was a member of Central Presbyterian Church.

Eugene Murphy

"Cat Greeting George Parsons"

125 EAST DICKSON

Parsons

Around 1916 George and Metta Parsons purchased a house at 125 East Dickson. It was located near the present site of the Washington County Tax Collector's drive-up window. Born in 1870 in Waterbury, Connecticut, Parsons lived in Michigan, Oklahoma, Texas, and Missouri before settling in Fayetteville in 1904. Parsons was in the jewelry business. More important, he was clock regulator for the Frisco Railroad and the City of Fayetteville, a very important position in the days of timely train service. Parsons regularly traveled to other Frisco stations in northwest Arkansas to inspect watches and clocks. He was a member of Washington Chapter No. 1 of the Masonic Lodge and of Central Presbyterian Church. Parsons was also a well-known lover of animals. Neighbors were impressed at the devotion he and his cat had for one another. On many an afternoon, Mr. Parsons' cat walked to the corner of College and Dickson to await his master's return from either the depot on Dickson

Tax collector's drive-up near 125 East Dickson, 2000

Street or the jewelry store on the Fayetteville square. Parsons died in 1935. Mrs. Parsons lived here until her death in 1962.

123 EAST DICKSON

Hight

Around 1919 Mrs. Cener S. Hight purchased a house at 123 East Dickson. She was the second wife of County Judge Jefferson T. Hight, whom she married in 1897, and the stepmother of neighbor Beulah Lawson. Cener Hight was a member of First Presbyterian Church. She also served on the boards of the Southern Memorial Association and the Evergreen Cemetery. Mrs. Hight lived at 123 East Dickson until 1941, one year before her death.

Chamblee

Wilson G. and Jessie Chamblee lived at 123 East Dickson between 1941 and 1965. Born in 1892 in Pleasant Glade, Texas, Chamblee was an operator of Motor Services Company. He was a member of Central United Methodist Church.

SOUTHEAST CORNER COLLEGE & DICKSON

Lawson

Charles Lawson

Around 1917 Charles Lawson built a house on the corner of College and Dickson (the site of the present Washington County Courthouse). Born in Wesley (Madison County), Lawson was the president of Ely-Walker Dry Goods Company of St. Louis. He also had interests in stores in Muskogee, Oklahoma, Monette, Missouri, and Harrison, Arkansas and was once president of Campbell & Bell in Fayetteville. Lawson died in 1930 while on a business trip in St. Louis. His wife, Beulah Hight Lawson, was the daughter of Washington County Judge Jefferson Hight and Mary Shannon. Born in 1870, she married Lawson in 1891. During the 1920s Mrs. Lawson maintained a small park for neighborhood children on the north side of her home. She lived here until her death in 1955.

Southeast corner of College & Dickson, 1940s

Southeast corner of College & Dickson, 1940s

Hatfield

Around 1962 the Lawson home, which, for the most part, had been rented after Mrs. Lawson's death in 1955, was torn down. Herbert Hatfield replaced it with a used-car lot that he called the Cadillac Ranch. It remained at this location until 1984.

Hatfield Pontiac-Cadillac ad, 1968

Washington County Courthouse, 1995

Washington County Courthouse

An important development in the history of the 100 block of East Dickson Street occurred in 1986. The First South Federal Savings and Loan Company constructed a four-story brick office building (First South Centre) on the lot formerly occupied by the Lawson house and Hatfield's Cadillac Ranch. In 1988, First South went bankrupt. The Resolution Trust Company, a federal government agency set up to deal with assets of defunct savings and loans, offered the building to Washington County. In December 1989, Washington County residents approved the issuance of bonds for the purchase and renovation of the First South Centre for use as a new courthouse. County offices began moving into the building in 1992.

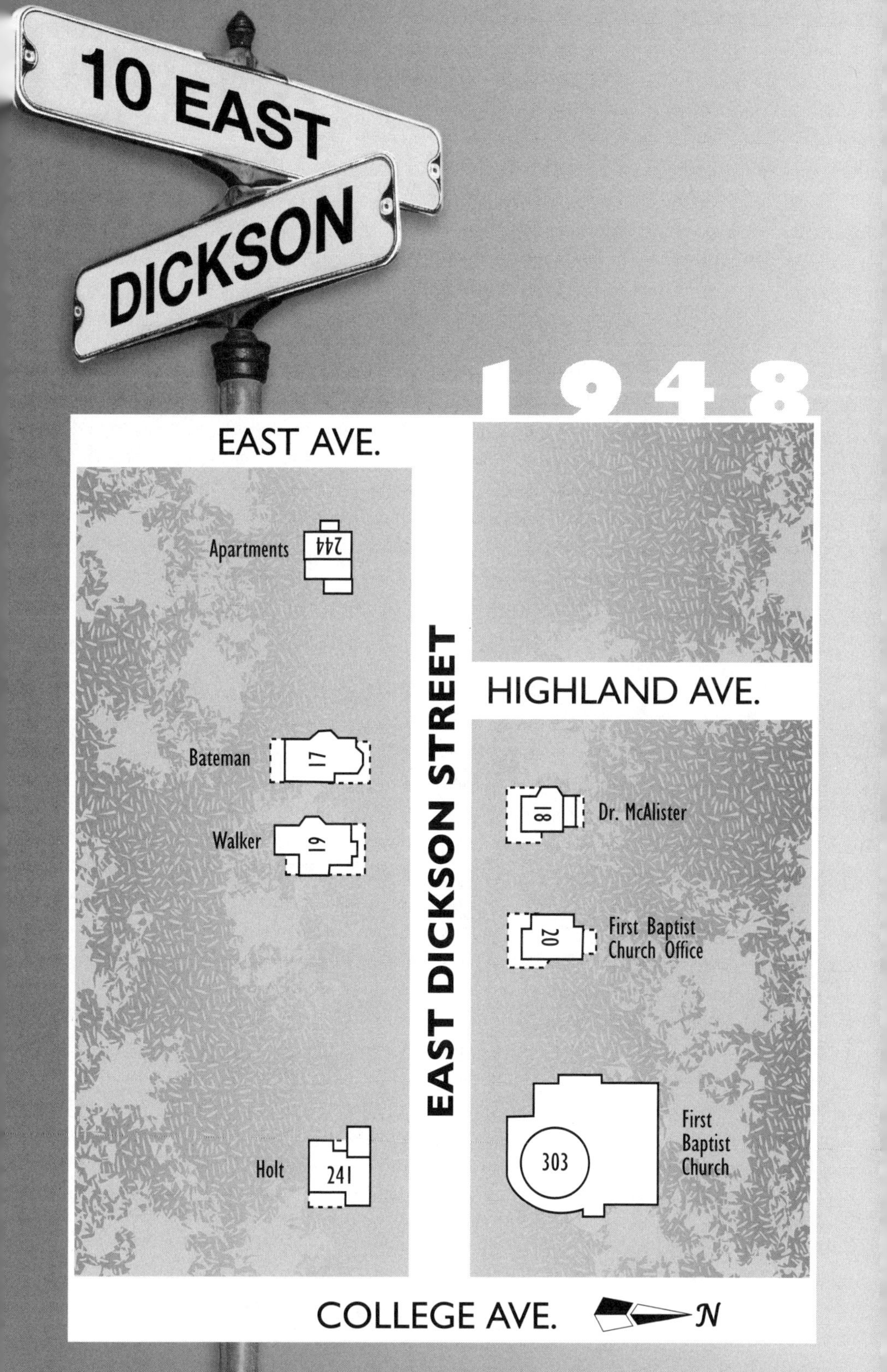

10 EAST
DICKSON
1948
EAST AVE.
Apartments
244
EAST DICKSON STREET
HIGHLAND AVE.
Bateman
17
Walker
19
Dr. McAlister
18
First Baptist Church Office
20
Holt
241
First Baptist Church
303
COLLEGE AVE.
N

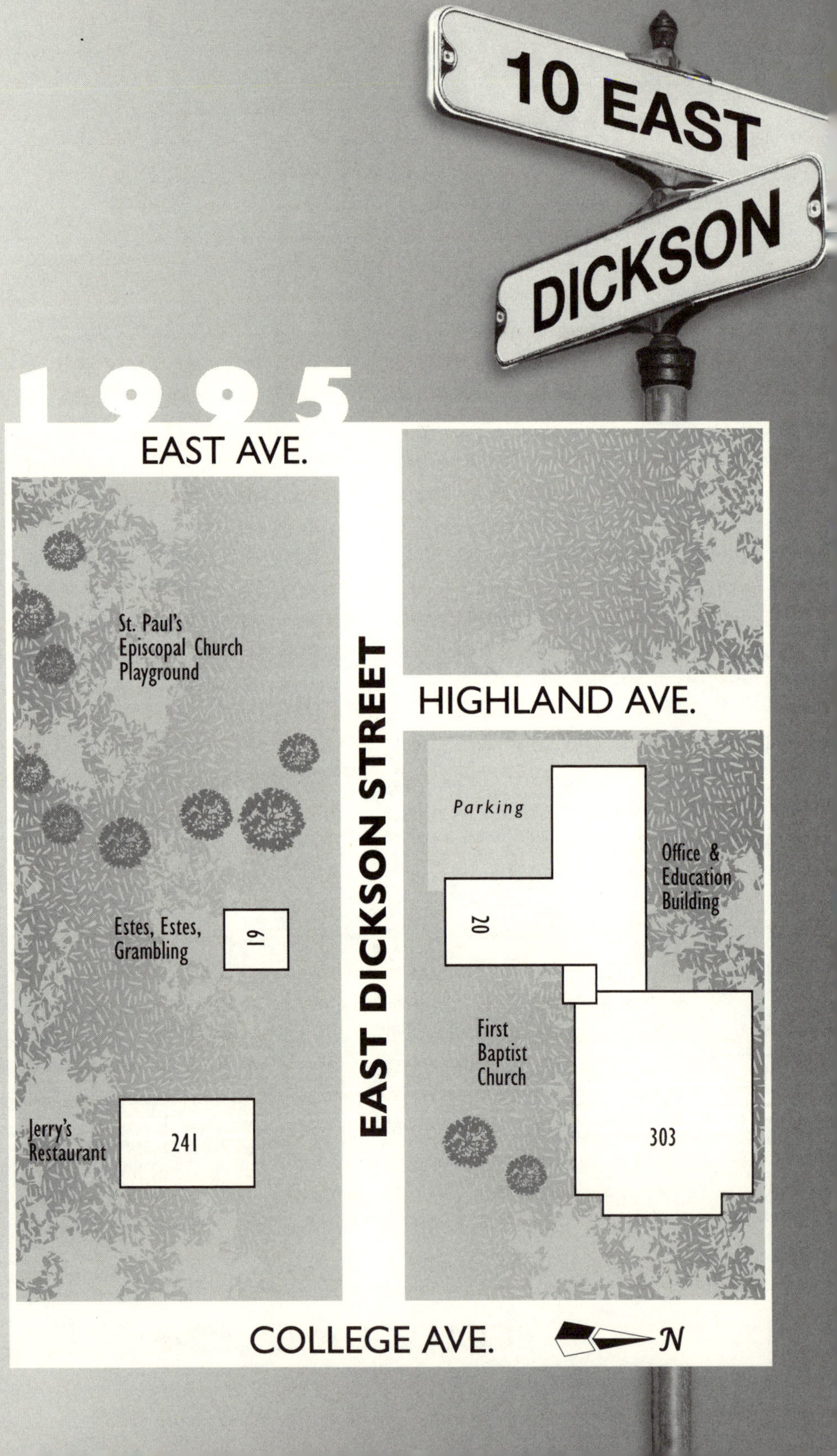
10 EAST
DICKSON
1995
EAST AVE.
St. Paul's
Episcopal Church
Playground
Estes, Estes,
Grambling
19
Jerry's
Restaurant
241
EAST DICKSON STREET
HIGHLAND AVE.
Parking
Office &
Education
Building
20
First
Baptist
Church
303
COLLEGE AVE.
N

Although it no longer seems a part of the residential neighborhood, East Dickson continues for one more block west of College Avenue. For several decades College Avenue and the 10 block of East Dickson were residential streets, and crossing College was not as life-threatening as it later became. Until the 1890s, the 10 block of East Dickson was the home of the Dukes and Riverscombs. In the late 1890s and early 1900s the Hight and Williams families purchased property on the north side of the block and in 1908 First Baptist Church completed construction of their church.

SOUTHWEST CORNER COLLEGE AND DICKSON

Duke

Julius Linn Duke and his wife, Helen Gaines, lived on the southwest corner of North College Avenue and East Dickson Street, more recently the site of Jerry's Restaurant. Their postal address was 241 North College Avenue. They built their home in the 1860s and lived there until about 1895, when they purchased the Stirman house across the street at 226 North College Avenue. Born in 1843 in Pike County, Missouri, Duke moved to Fayetteville with his family in 1854. During the Civil War, he served in the Confederate Army. After the war, he returned home to Fayetteville and opened the J. L. Duke Jewelry Company on the square. Duke married Helen Gaines of Greenwood in 1868, served on the school board, and was a Mason and a Knight of Pythias. Born in Livingston, Alabama, in 1851 Mrs. Duke

J.L. and Helen Duke

THE DEMOCRAT'S PLAN FOR A STREET RAILWAY.

Since the excitement of last year, we have not heard this subject discussed. At that time it was proposed to construct a street railroad from the Public Square via College Ave. and Dickson St. to the entrance of the University. This plan fell through for some reason. The agent who presented the scheme said that the proposed road would cost about $12,000.00. Believing this to be largely over estimated, we have had an engineer friend prepare the DEMOCRAT's plan for a street railroad.

Our scheme is represented in the following sketch.

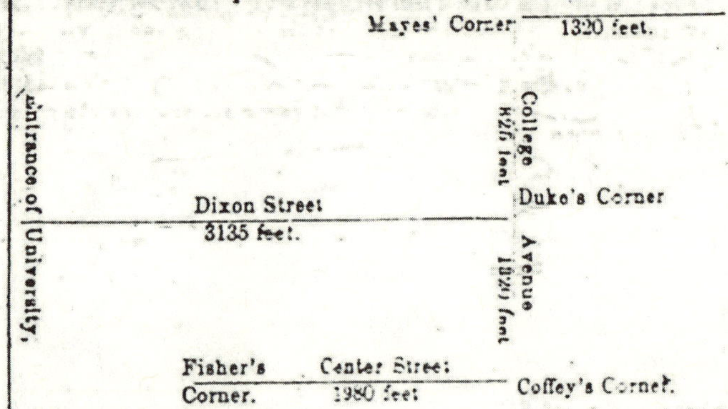

The line would start near Fisher's corner on Center street, and, passing the Public Square, turn onto College Avenue at Coffey's corner. Passing up College Avenue, one branch turns at Duke's corner onto Dixon street, and passes the Depot, stopping at the entrance to the University. The other branch extends from Duke's corner along College Avenue to Mayes' corner, and thence passes due east one-fourth mile.

We propose two cars for this road at the start. The cars always meet at Duke's corner. Each car will make a trip over its line once in half an hour. The car passing from Fisher's corner to the University entrance should be hauled by two mules, while one will suffice for the other. They will begin running at 6 a. m. and stop after the night train has gone south. In this way there will be seventy-two trips made by both cars in one day over the line.

The following estimate is in excess of the actual cost of the materials and construction, the road, including stable turnout, being 8750 feet long. The road will consist of cross-ties spaced 6 feet a part and buried in the ground about 9 inches. Stringers of oak will be spiked to the cross-ties. These will be about 2 inches under the ground, and run lengthwise of the track. The rails will be spiked to these stringers, and will be flush with the surface of the ground. Knees of angle-iron will be bolted into the cross-ties and stringers, and will prevent the track from spreading.

Proposed street car line, 1889

moved to Arkansas in 1857. She was a graduate of Miss Sophia Sawyer's School in Fayetteville. She was widely known as the "pincushion lady," for she had made, entirely by hand, nearly one thousand velvet pincushions, which she sold to benefit the First Christian Church, of which she was a devoted member. J. L. and Helen Duke's daughter, Helen, married John C. Futrall, long-time president of the University of Arkansas. Futrall was a familiar figure on Dickson Street as he made his way back and forth between his home and the campus.

Wilson

Professor Wilson

In 1909, Birton and Hallie Wilson purchased the Duke house. A native of New York, Wilson was born in 1874. He obtained his formal education in the public schools of New York and Georgia. In 1896 Wilson obtained a Bachelor of Science and master's degree in engineering from the Georgia School of Technology. In the fall of 1896 he began his career as a professor of mechanical engineering at the University of Arkansas. For several years Wilson was also superintendent of the University of Arkansas Buildings and Grounds Department. In 1898 he married Hallie Barlow, a native of Kentucky. She died in 1943. Professor Wilson remained here until 1945.

Lion Service Station

In 1951 the Duke-Wilson house was torn down to make way for Charles and Clarke McClinton's Lion Oil Company service station. Originally managed, and later owned, by Bob Maeder, the Lion Service Station was a full-service gas station, selling Lion Brand petroleum products, Kelly-Springfield Tires, and Globe Batteries. Bob Maeder's Lion Station also lubricated engines, washed and polished cars, balanced wheels and provided road service. The Lion Service Station remained at 271 North College Avenue until 1977.

Lion Oil grand-opening ad, 1951

Jerry's Restaurant

In 1980 Jerry Lindsay converted Bob Maeder's Lion Service Station into Jerry's Restaurant, which remained at this location until 2004. Known simply as Jerry's, this restaurant was a favorite spot for old-fashioned breakfast and lunch. Their specialties were country ham, pork chops, biscuits and gravy, and omelettes.

19–17 EAST DICKSON

Riverscomb

Around 1871 George and Jane M. Riverscomb purchased property on the southeast corner of East Avenue and Dickson, around the corner from St. Paul's Episcopal Church. Born in Virginia in 1824, Riverscomb fought in the Mexican-American War. He lived in Mississippi, New Mexico, and California before settling in Arkansas in 1871. Riverscomb was not considered a successful businessman, but he was active in local politics and civic affairs. He was a deputy under Washington County Sheriff Pettigrew in 1872 and was acting sheriff during Pettigrew's suspension. Riverscomb was also a deputy assessor and a member of the

Jerry's Restaurant, 1995

Fayetteville City Council. He was an active member of the Mexican War Veterans Association, which petitioned Congress to grant pensions to Mexican War veterans. Riverscomb married Jane M. Blakemore, of Mt. Solon, Virginia, in 1870. The Riverscombs owned this property until the early 1920s. Known as "River" to friends and neighbors, upon his sudden death in 1879 he was praised as a very trustworthy public servant and neighbor.

19 EAST DICKSON
Walker

Born in Huntsville in 1896 Henry Walker was Washington County Sheriff between 1927 and 1932 and Circuit Clerk between 1933 and 1936. In 1934, he and his wife, Fannie Day, moved to a house at 19 East Dickson, which was built around 1928. They were there until 1949. Walker's house was torn down about 1950.

Henry Bryan Walker I and Henry Bryan Walker III in front of 19 East Dickson, 1940s

Southeast corner East & Dickson (note St. Paul's in upper left and Central Methodist in right), 1910s

Paul Young Jr. Architect

In 1962 a new commercial building was constructed at 17 East Dickson, on the site formerly occupied by Henry Walker's house. The first occupant was Paul Young Jr., a well-known architect. A graduate of Washington University, Young's first assignment as an architect was helping to design five Arkansas state parks, including Devil's Den near Winslow. In 1937 he formed the architectural firm of Paul Young and Associates. They designed several buildings still existing on Dickson Street, including Central United Methodist Church, First Baptist Church, the Coca-Cola Bottling Plant (which subsequently went through several retail incarnations), the UARK Theatre Building, Collier Drugstore, and the Palace Drugstore (Wallace's Campus Bookstore). Young had his offices here until retiring in 1983.

Estes, Estes, and Grambling

In 1987 Peter Estes, Peter Estes, Jr., and Douglas Grambling located their general law practice at 19 East Dickson. The senior Estes began practicing law in 1946 with Price Dickson. Shortly thereafter, he started his own practice. A 1942 graduate of the University of Arkansas Law School, the elder Estes was Deputy Prosecuting Attorney for Washington County between 1946 and 1954. Estes was admitted to practice law before the U. S. Supreme Court in 1952. He was active in the American, Arkansas, and Washington County Bar Associations and served as the Washington County Bar Association president in 1971–1972. Estes retired from full-time practice in 1976. Pete Estes, Jr. continues the honorable tradition of his father and, like his father, is a well -liked and respected member of the legal community of Northwest Arkansas.

Estes, Estes and Grambling, 1995

17 EAST DICKSON
Bateman

17 East Dickson Street was built around 1928 and originally housed Mrs. Hayden McIlroy's Nymph Dance Studio. Around 1931, it was divided into rental apartments. Mary C. Bateman was one of the longest tenants. Born in Forrest City in 1876, she married Robert P. Bateman in 1896. He died in 1897 and Mrs. Bateman never remarried. She moved to Fayetteville in 1905 and was an instructor of voice culture in the Department of Music at the University of Arkansas. Mrs. Bateman held this position until 1923. Afterward, Mrs. Bateman was manager of the ladies' ready-to-wear department of the Boston Store until 1951.She was also choir director at St. Paul's Episcopal Church until 1944. Mrs. Bateman lived at 17 East Dickson until her death in 1967.

St. Paul's Episcopal Church Grounds

In the 1980s St. Paul's Episcopal Church, which had established their church on neighboring East Street in 1872, purchased the apartment

Southeast corner of East and Dickson, 1995

house in which Mrs. Bateman resided and briefly operated the locally famous Episcopal Thrift Shop. The building was demolished around 1984. The property was a beautifully landscaped playground until late 2000, when St. Paul's undertook a major expansion project.

22–18 EAST DICKSON
Hight

Around 1895 Dr. John P. Hight, a brother of County Judge Jefferson T. Hight, purchased a rent house at 22 East Dickson. The house had been built in the 1870s on the site of the Fayetteville Female Seminary, which was burned during the Civil War. It was the birthplace of Toll Ladd, a well-known barber who had a shop in the 400 block of West Dickson during the early 1900s. Dr. Hight sold this house to the First Baptist Church in 1906. He built a second house next door at 20 East Dickson, and sold it to the church in 1924. Hight was an ardent supporter of women's suffrage and was a charter member of the Washington County Equal Suffrage Association. It was said that, when women were granted the right to vote, he offered to pay the poll tax for any woman who would register.

18 East Dickson, 1911

18 EAST DICKSON
Williams

One door west of Dr. Hight's rent houses, at 18 East Dickson, lived Jeff and Nannie Williams. They also built their home around 1895. Born in 1862, Jeff Williams was an employee of the Shawnee Milling Company of Shawnee, Oklahoma, and also worked for Armour Meat Company in Fayetteville. Williams was a member of the First Christian Church and the Knights of Pythias Lodge. Mrs. Williams rented rooms, mostly to traveling salesmen. During the 1920–1921 school year the Sigma Phi Epsilon Fraternity rented rooms in the house. Mr. Williams died in 1926. Mrs. Williams lived at 18 East Dickson until her death in 1939.Their property has more recently been occupied by the First Baptist Church parking lot.

Dr. Max F. McAllister

Dr. Max F. McAllister, one of my sources on this project, was born in the 200 block of West Dickson Street in 1904. McAllister received his education at the University of Arkansas at Fayetteville and the University of Arkansas Medical School in Little Rock. He also received a doctoral degree in public health from Vanderbilt University in Nashville, Tennessee. During World War II, McAllister served as a medic in North Africa. After the war, he moved to St. Louis, Missouri. In 1947 McAllister returned to Fayetteville and bought the Williams house at 18 E. Dickson. He divided it into an apartment and office space for his medical practice as an ear, nose, and throat specialist. He maintained his office at this place until 1978.

NORTHWEST CORNER COLLEGE AND DICKSON

First Baptist Church

In 1906, during the pastorate of Dr. W. A. Whittle, the First Baptist Church commenced construction of a new church on the northwest corner of Dickson and College, the site of Dr. Hight's first rent house. The new church was completed in 1908 at a cost of $38,000 and was dedicated by the Reverend George W. Truett of Dallas, Texas. The Baptists worshiped in this church until 1959. In 1924 the membership purchased Dr. Hight's rental house at 20 East Dickson and used it as a residence for its pastor until 1948.

First Baptist Church, 1908

First Baptist Church and Education Building, 1948

First Baptist Church, 1959

First Baptist Church Education Buildings, 1995

Around 1948, during the pastorate of Dr. Walter L. Johnson, First Baptist Church demolished the parsonage at 20 East Dickson and replaced it with an education building. In 1958–1959, under the leadership of Dr. Andrew M. Hall, the church constructed a larger sanctuary at a cost of $300,000. Designed by Fayetteville architect Paul Young, the building was completed in 1959. Since its founding, First Baptist Church has sponsored many missions, including a significant ministry to the University of Arkansas through the Baptist Student Union.

In 1985 First Baptist Church purchased the Williams house at 18 East Dickson and used it as a day care center until 1991, when it was moved to Rebecca Street in the Washington-Willow Historic District. Between 1992 and 1995, the church expanded and renovated its education building, which now occupies the Jeff and Nannie Williams homesite.

Chester Goss Shooting

Around 9:30 A.M. on Sunday, December 4, 1955, several worshipers, on their way to morning services at First Baptist Church, witnessed what they thought was an older man having a heart attack as he headed east across College Avenue, and ran to his assistance. Police clarified the incident in the following morning's newspaper. According to their reports, Charles Friddle shot Chester Goss in the back as he reached the far side of College Avenue (near the courthouse). The 54-year-old Goss, a veteran of World Wars I and II, was a night dispatcher for the Yellow Cab Company and was walking to his home at 229 East Dickson, where he lived with his mother, Mary T. Goss. The 66-year-old Friddle, whom Goss did not know, shot Goss from the parking lot of the Lion Service Station (later Jerry's). Although at first Goss made signs of recovery, he died at the Veteran's Administration Hospital a couple of weeks later. According to police, Friddle was convinced that Goss was a leader of a gang who were shooting holes through his house with television rays. He pleaded innocent by reason of insanity but was convicted of first degree murder.

WEST DICKSON

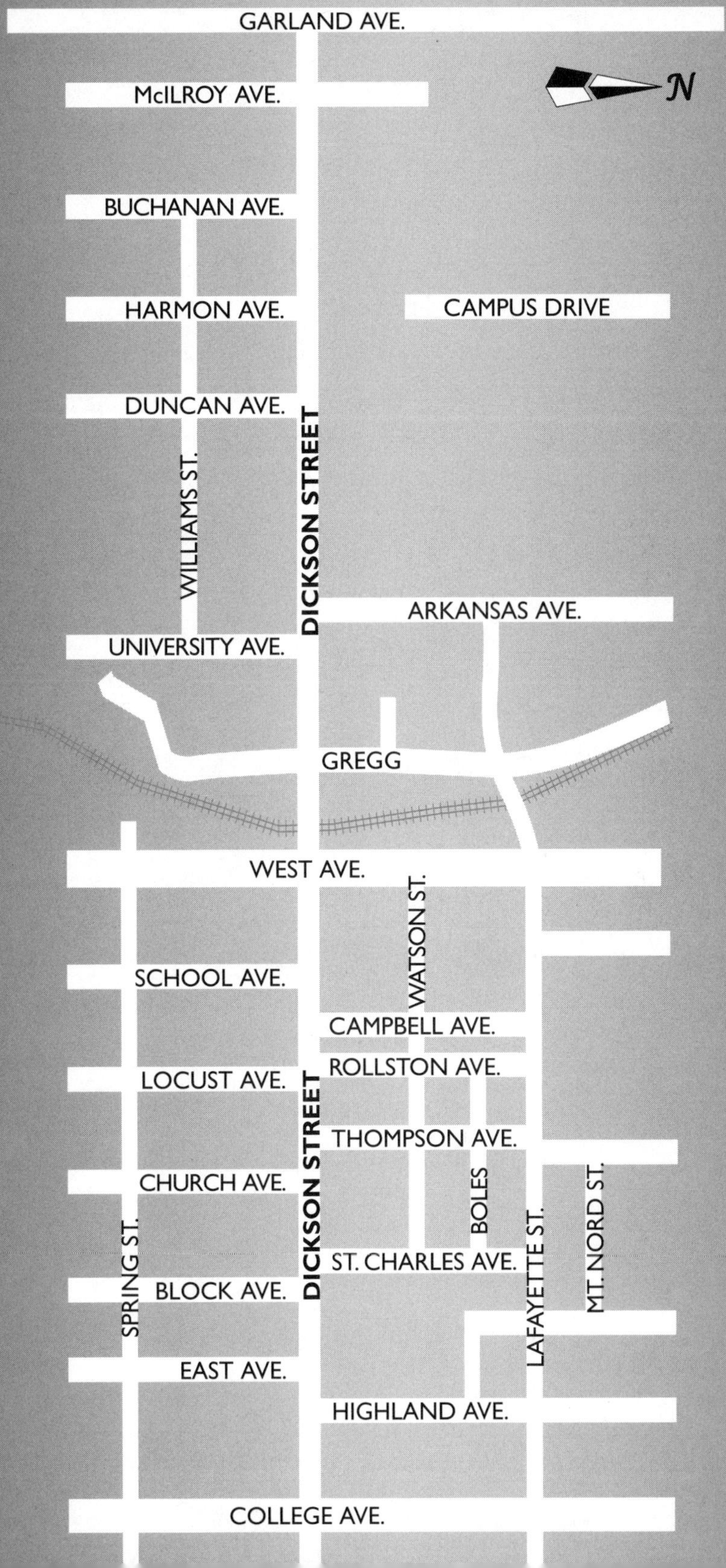

WEST DICKSON STREET—AN OVERVIEW

West Dickson Street is ten blocks long. Beginning where East Dickson ends—at Highland and East Avenues—West Dickson slopes toward the west in the 100, 200, and 300 blocks, empties into Town Creek in the 400 and 500 blocks, carelessly crosses the Frisco tracks in the 500 block, begins its trek toward the University of Arkansas in the 600 and 700 blocks, makes one more dip in the 800 block, resumes its uphill climb in the 900 block, and ends on level ground on the University of Arkansas campus in the 1000 block. For many years, Arkansas Highway 16 ran along parts of Dickson Street from College Avenue to Arkansas Avenue on the west. The highway then went around the University, first north on Arkansas Avenue, then west on Maple, north on Garland, and finally west out of town on Wedington Road.

Like the 10 block of East Dickson Street, the 10 block of West Dickson has been a fairly tranquil neighborhood. Until 1892, it was the home of the Dicksons. Four additional residences were a part of this block until the 1950s. Since 1899, the 10 block has been home to Central Methodist Church. Central Presbyterian Church appeared in 1906 and left only in 1961. Since 1962, the Fayetteville Post Office has shared the 10 block with a much larger Central Methodist Church. The rest of West Dickson Street is another story . . .

For most of its early history, the remainder of West Dickson Street consisted of undeveloped pasture and a handful of residences, including those of the Campbells, Suttons, Boleses, Watsons, Fergusons, Williams, Reeds, and McIlroys. In 1871, the State of Arkansas established the Arkansas Industrial University on a large portion of the McIlroy farm, on what became the north side of the 700 through 1000 blocks of West Dickson. Around 1875, "Uncle Gus" Lewis established the first known Dickson Street business. His mercantile catered to the university community and was located near the present- day location of George's. Six years later, in 1881, the Frisco Railroad came to town and Dickson Street changed forever.

As most histories of Fayetteville and Dickson Street show, West Dickson Street began to develop into a commercial neighborhood after the arrival of the railroad. In the 1880s and 1890s a number of businesses opened in the 300 through 500 blocks. These earliest establishments included Cazort Brothers Lumber and Northwest Arkansas Lumber Company, Ozark Grocer, and two railroad hotels, the Southern and the Frisco. In the 1900s and 1910s numerous secondary businesses, including Citizen's Bank, Frisco Drugstore, Palace Drugstore, U of A Barber Shop, Bates Brothers Market, Citizens Laundry, Vickers' Laundry, Wright's Shoe Store, and Champion's Variety Store, came to Dickson. At the same time, a number of boarding houses opened up in the 200 through 400 blocks, including the Gilbert House, O.K. Hotel, and Scott Hotel, to accommodate people who worked on Dickson Street. Many households in the upper blocks of Dickson also rented rooms. Most of those who lived in the lower-numbered blocks were employees of Dickson Street businesses, while those living in the higher-numbered blocks worked at the University of Arkansas. Students appear to have lived in both places.

Steady growth continued throughout the 1920s and 1930s with the opening of Kelley Brothers Lumber, Fashion Shop Cleaners, Fayetteville Business College, Simpson-Mintum Wholesalers, Shipley Baking Company, and the Coca-Cola Bottling Company. Complementing the arrival of these core businesses were the Majestic Cafe, the Deluxe Restaurant, and the Hob Nob Liquor Store. Another arrival was crime. The first known nightly police patrol began in 1920 after a series of petty thefts in the commercial district. During the Depression, many Dickson Street businesses supported President Roosevelt's National Recovery efforts by proudly displaying the NRA logo in their windows.

In 1940, Bill Sonneman undertook fuller commercial development in the 600 block when he opened the UARK Theatre. Its white-brick, modestly Art-Deco style set the tone for the expansion of Sonneman's enterprises when, in 1947 he constructed apartments and additional shops next door to the UARK and a bowling alley and dance hall across the street. In the 1940s and 1950s Holland Brothers Locker Plant, Stump Furniture, Collier Drug Store, Jug Wheeler's Drive-In, and Roger's Recreation Hall opened for business on Dickson Street.

Shuler Town ad, 1920s

During the 1950s and 1960s, Texaco, Fayetteville Linen Supply, Polk's Furniture, and First National Bank came to Dickson Street and the Bates Brothers Market, one of Dickson Street's oldest businesses, said goodbye. The 600 block became even more commercial with the opening of a "shopping center" containing the Palace Drug Store and a Piggly Wiggly

First Known Dickson Street Improvement District

During the early 1900s, Fayetteville was known to have some of the muddiest and dirtiest streets in Arkansas, and Dickson Street was no exception. On June 20, 1906, the first known Dickson Street Improvement District was formed. Its mission was to enhance Dickson Street by paving it from the University of Arkansas to East Avenue, and thereby to answer some of the complaints often made by University faculty and students. The first known Dickson Street Improvement District Commissioners included John P. Scott, J. L. Mitchell, A. B. (Uncle Gus) Lewis, B. F. McAllister, James McCormick, J. S. Bates, and C. J. Leverett, all of them Dickson Street merchants.

supermarket. Across the street, Underwood's Jewelry shared space with the architecture firm of Fay Jones and Maurice Jennings. Commercialization of the 600 block also meant the loss of two well-known residences—the Reed and Williams houses. Two non-commercial enterprises that remain in the 600 block are the UARK Apartments and the former University Lutheran Church, which graces the corner of Arkansas Avenue and West Dickson Street. During the 1960s the few remaining turn-of-the-century boarding houses in the 700 through 900 blocks also began to disappear.

Dickson Street began to decline between the late 1960s and mid-1970s. Many of the street's larger wholesale and retail businesses, including Kelley Brothers, Fayetteville Business College, and Woodruff's Cleaners, had either closed or moved away to new commercial developments on the outskirts of Fayetteville. Dickson Street was almost dead. However, by the mid 1970s, with the doubling of enrollment at the

?

What does this mean:

"MEMBER N.R.A.

WE DO OUR PART!"

IT MEANS that the firm or store which displays it is cooperating with the President in his drive to increase employment.

It means that this employer has agreed to accept a shorter working week in order that new jobs may be created.

It means that he is paying a "decent living wage" for this shorter week.

It means that his employees have accepted shorter hours so that others, now unemployed, may be enabled to share in their work.

It means that all those who display it are worthy of your patronage and your whole-hearted cooperation because they are doing their part."

Finally, it means a concerted drive by all industry to wipe out unemployment and end the depression!

Look for it! Talk about it!

Already business has started on the up-grade. Let's all speed it up. The President has united all the forces of recovery in this one concerted drive. You can do your part by becoming a **"MEMBER NRA"**

This advertisement sponsored by the following:

SANDFORD & SON

BERNARD F. SILVERMAN, Jeweler

RAZORBACK TOGGERY

MAJESTIC CAFE

U. OF A. CAFE

PALACE DRUG STORE

CARDINAL DRUG STORE

CITIZENS BANK

OZARK BARBER SHOP

J. W. GRAY, Jeweler

U. OF A. BARBER SHOP

O. K. TAXI

Dickson Street NRA ad, 1930s

Dickson Street Business District, 1940s

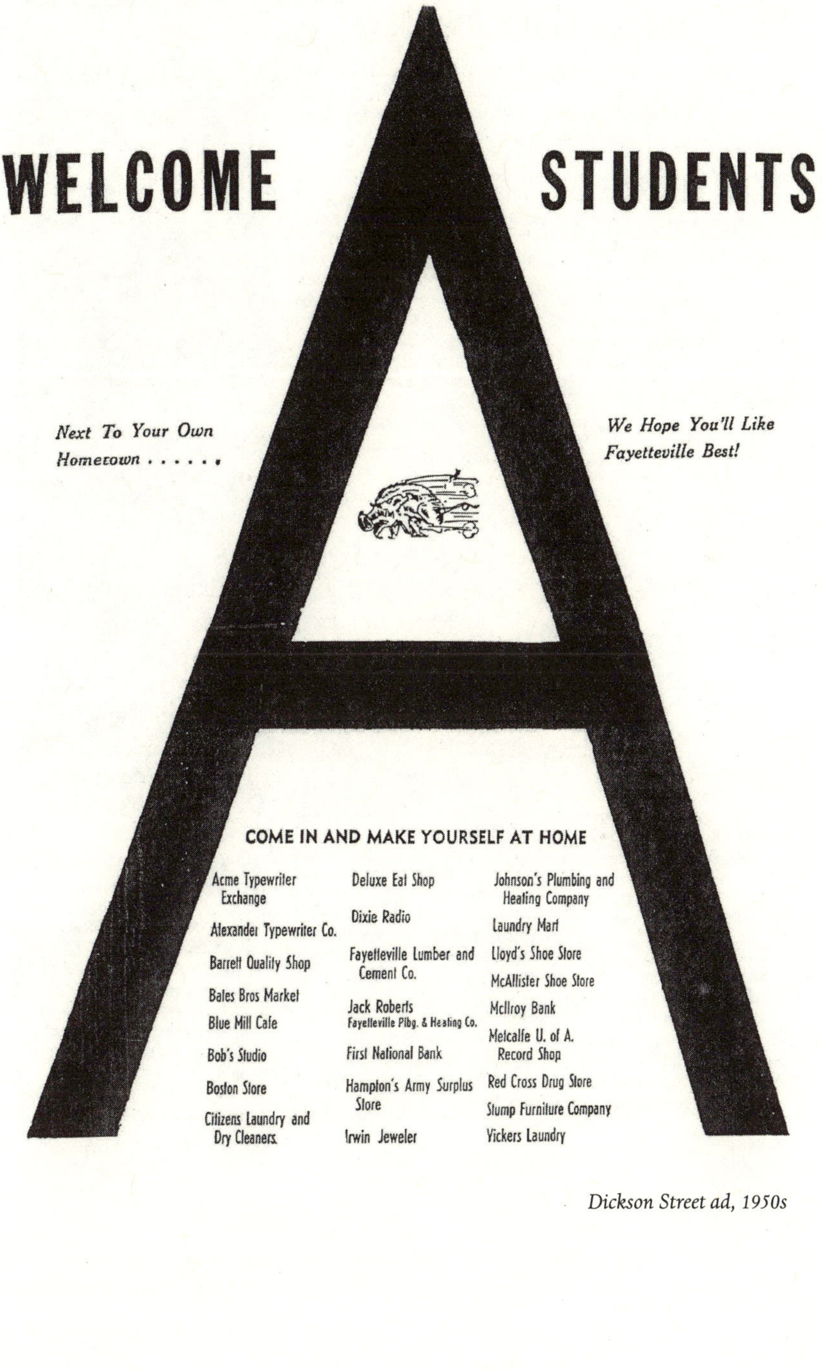

Dickson Street ad, 1950s

Luke the Duke

"Don't Forget the Common People"

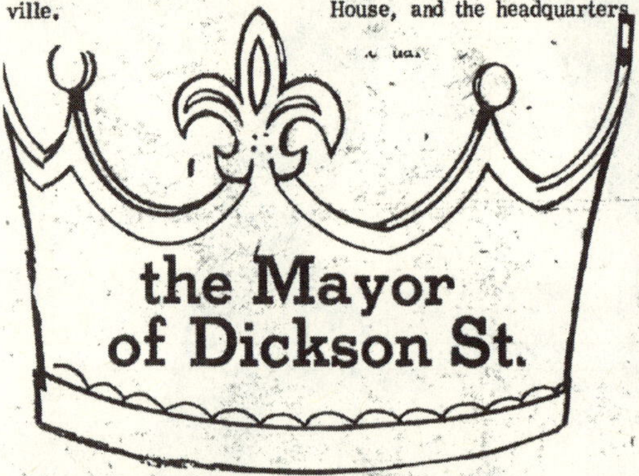

Luke the Duke, the Mayor of Dickson Street, has something to say to GRAPEVINE readers. Since our article on Luke (November 30, 1977), channel 5 television has done a story on Dickson Street. According to Luke the story seemed to focus on only the area of Dickson Street from the Post Office toward the campus, what might be called "the strip." He believes channel 5 might have missed some of the real Dickson Street, · the heart of the old traditional part of Fayetteville.

If you take all of Dickson Street you must begin high on campus hill in the west, and go way east to where the street ends on a hill full of fine homes. In between there is a lot more.

Beginning in the east, Luke points out the Kappa Sigma House. In his college days the Mayor was a Kappa Sig. He says the fraternity is the oldest and largest on the campus. Down the street he notes Polk's Furniture, the oldest such business in town. Further down is Shipley Bakery, the oldest and largest in Northwest Arkansas. East of the Bakery is the U.S. Post Office. Next to the Post Office are three of the largest churches in the whole of Washington County!—Then comes the large, new Southwestern Electric Power Company building, the Cadillac agency, the Roberta Fulbright Public Library, the Ozarks Regional Library (in the basement), the famous civil war era Tebbets House, and the headquarters of the Washington County Historical Society.

The point in all this, says Luke, is that some people are busy spreading the notion that Dickson Street is strictly a place where "everybody wears blue jeans". The Mayor doesn't deny blue jeans, "but you can also rent a tuxedo on Dickson Street. Mr. Tux does a good business, and that's on Dickson Street, too."

He'd like to see local government take a more active interest in the street by using tax money to make improvements. "Seems like when Mr. H.U.D. gets done with the white folks on the Square he could come down here with the common folks and plant a few pecan trees--for shade--something like that--just don't forget the common people--".

Joe Neal, for the Mayor

Mayor of Dickson Street, 1978

"It's the only place you can go cruisin' without a car and do it right." *Bill Hippe*

Dickson Street at night, 1970s

Dickson Street looking west, 1970s

University of Arkansas, a slight re-birth occurred. West Dickson Street began to evolve from an industrial and service district catering to all of Fayetteville into a neighborhood catering mostly to students. However, this re-birth was short-lived. By the late 1970s, the influence of the automobile was felt in Fayetteville as everywhere else in the country. The student population abandoned Dickson Street for Highways 62 and 71, where larger parking lots accommodated their cars. Dickson Street became a strip of virtually nothing but restaurants, bars, and nightclubs catering to college students and other Fayetteville youth. The change in Dickson Street bothered many long-time Fayetteville residents, while visitors thought of it as a seedy and disreputable, even dangerous, place. Three murders in 1980–1981 did not help Dickson Street's deteriorated image.

PRIDE IN DICKSON STREET

Dickson Street Merchants Association

Several Dickson Street merchants were not convinced that Dickson Street was dead. In 1983, Pat and Helen Martin, owners of the DeLuxe

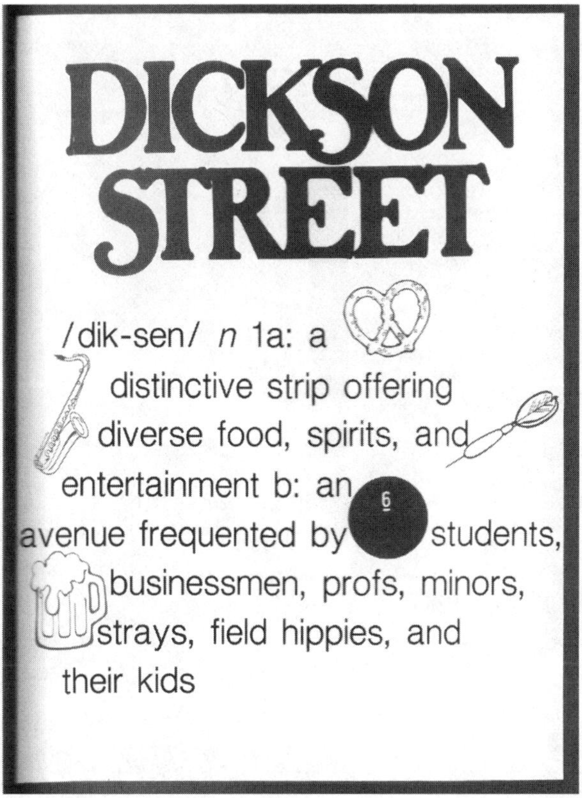

Dickson Street defined, 1980

Restaurant and Butch Coger, owner of the Camera Shop, organized the Pride in Dickson Street Association. Their goal was to recreate Dickson Street as the thriving thoroughfare it had once been. They inspired businesses to spruce up their properties and in 1984 they sponsored the first Springfest. This annual celebration included a parade, arts, crafts, games, and bands, and celebrated merchants' attempts to renew the street.

Although Pride in Dickson Street had some success in the early 1980s, the negative image persisted. In 1986, the year I moved to Fayetteville, both merchants and residents believed that Dickson Street was at its lowest point ever and that the only way to go was up. It was rumored to be unsafe to go there after dark or to drive through without locking your car doors and rolling up your windows. There may have been some truth to this, but being new to the area I was too ignorant to know the difference. Indeed, there were many vacant storefronts, perhaps a dozen or more,

Dickson at night, 1980s

Dickson Street looking west toward Gregson Lodge, 1980s

and at times West Dickson Street looked frightening. But a number of very popular small businesses helped keep Dickson Street alive. The Grill, the Restaurant on the Corner, Dickson Street Book Shop, Jose's, Lily's, the Dream Merchant, the Rock Bottom Bookstore, Library Club, Camera Shop, Bull's Eye Pub, Flying Possum Leather, Polly's, Borealis, the Boardwalk Cafe, Editype, Kinko's, and others lined Dickson Street, replacing a previous generation that had faded away. Although some of these were replaced in their turn, some of them remain, and contributed to the gradual stabilization and renewal of Dickson Street.

These new businesses, along with the Pride in Dickson organization, persevered and continued to revitalize Dickson Street by enticing a large anchor to the street. Such an anchor would have to attract people to the street as the Frisco, Kelley Brothers Lumber Company, and the Ozark Grocer had done between the 1920s and 1960s. Dickson Street finally began to shed its reputation as a dangerous and unsavory place in the late 1980s, when Fayetteville and the University of Arkansas agreed to build

above: *Map ad, 1980s* right: *Dickson Street ad, 1990s*

an arts center on West Dickson. Today, West Dickson Street is dominated not by the Frisco, lumber yards, cleaners, hotels, and wholesale groceries, but rather by the Walton Arts Center, the Bank of Fayetteville, and many nightclubs and restaurants attempting to capitalize on the recent arrival and continued success of the arts center, the steady growth of the University of Arkansas, and the ever-increasing number of Fayetteville visitors and transplants.

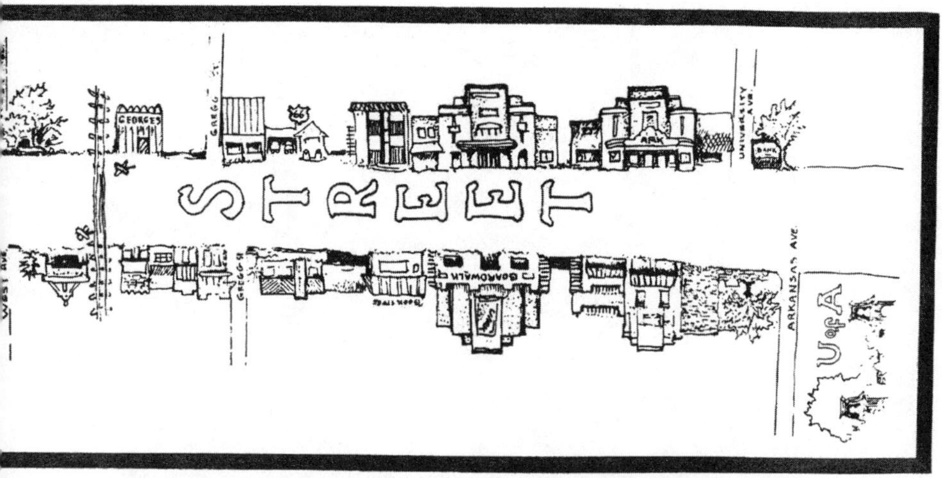
GEORGES
GREGG ST.
UNIVERSITY AVE.
ARK
BANK
STREET
WEST AVE.
GREGG ST.
BOARDWALK
ARKANSAS AVE.
U of A

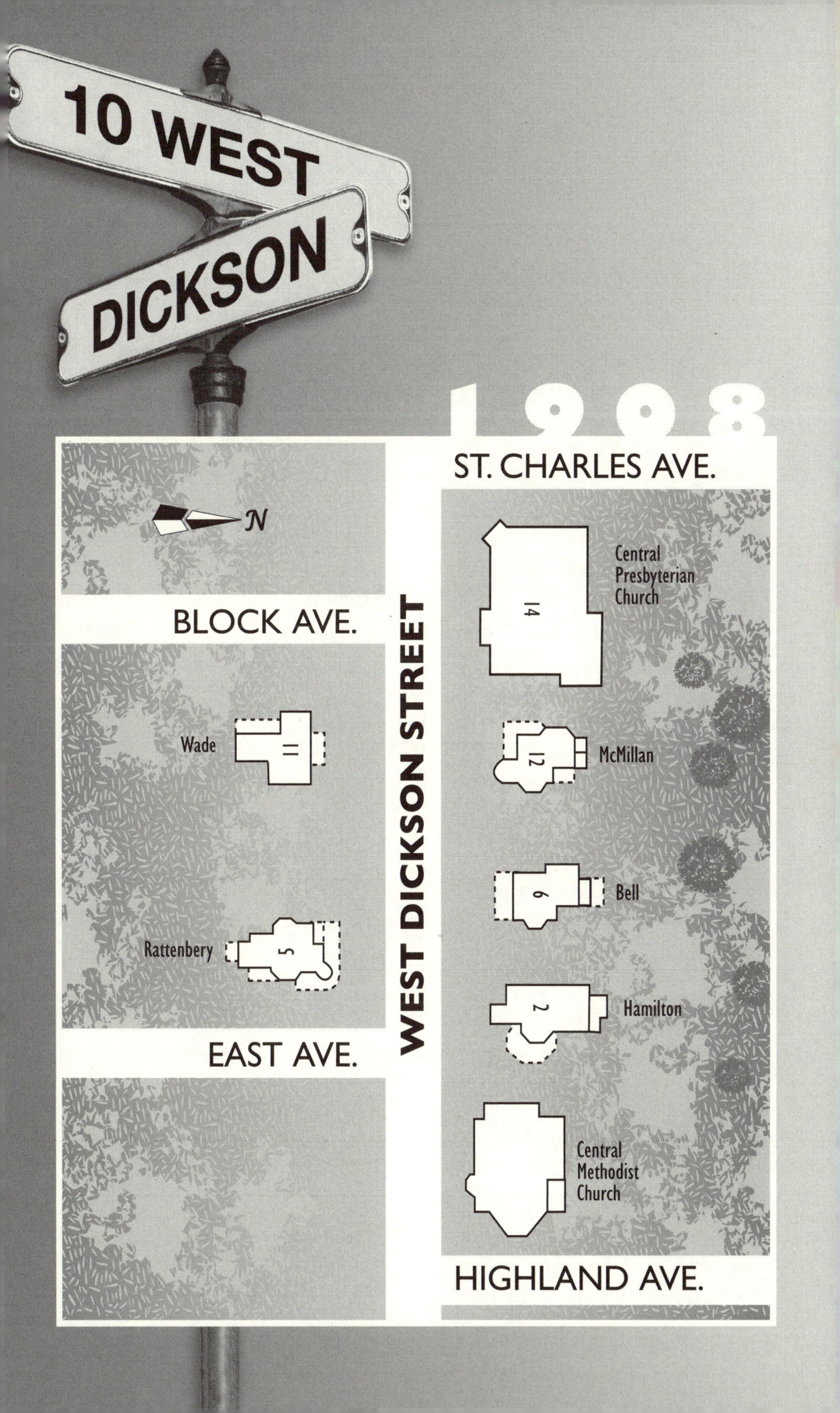
10 WEST
DICKSON
N
ST. CHARLES AVE.
BLOCK AVE.
WEST DICKSON STREET
Central
Presbyterian
Church
14
Wade
11
McMillan
12
Bell
9
Rattenbery
5
Hamilton
2
EAST AVE.
Central
Methodist
Church
HIGHLAND AVE.

10 WEST
DICKSON

1995

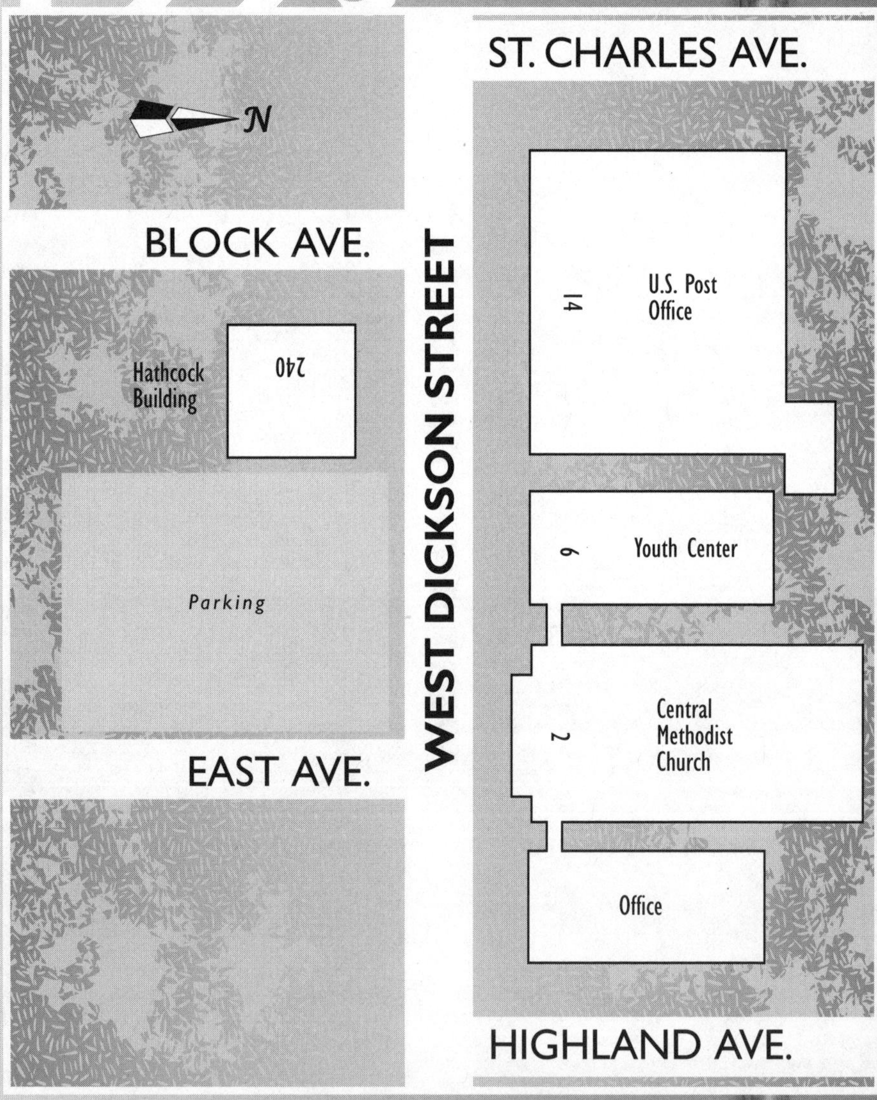
N
ST. CHARLES AVE.
BLOCK AVE.
Hathcock Building
240
Parking
EAST AVE.
WEST DICKSON STREET
14
U.S. Post Office
6
Youth Center
2
Central Methodist Church
Office
HIGHLAND AVE.

10 BLOCK

Dickson Street is flat in the first block of the western part of the street. The home of the Dickson family, the 10 block of West Dickson is the one that gave Dickson Street its name.

2 WEST DICKSON

Dickson

The eponymous Joseph L. Dickson came to Fayetteville in the early 1840s, after his father Ephraim Dickson was appointed U.S. land registrar by President James K. Polk. Dickson and James Stirman operated an antebellum mercantile store on the north side of the square. Dickson and his wife, Sarah McKissick, were married in 1847. Shortly afterward, they built their home on a twenty-acre plot on what was then the north edge of Fayetteville, on the site presently occupied by the Central United Methodist Church. During the Civil War the Dicksons, like many others, fled to Texas, and during the Battle of Fayetteville, their house was used as a hospital. After the war they returned, but Joseph Dickson did not long survive. He died in 1868 of consumption. In the 1870s Mrs. Dickson operated a private school there, charging tuition of $1.50 per month. Between Mrs. Dickson's death in 1892 and 1900, the Dickson house was the home of Arkansas Industrial University President John L. Buchanan. He was president in 1899 when its name was changed to the University of Arkansas.

Hamilton

A. C. Hamilton

In 1900 Andrew C. and Mary Kate Hamilton purchased Sarah Dickson's house. Because of its tranquil setting, Mrs. Hamilton named the property Locust Shade. Born in County Down, Ireland, in 1852, Hamilton was educated in Belfast. He came to America in 1871. In 1880 he married Mary Kate Downs, a native of Virginia. They resided in Waco, Temple, and Galveston, Texas, where Hamilton was in the wholesale grocery business. En route to St. Louis in 1896, Hamilton stopped in Fayetteville to investigate the possibility of buying apples. He was so impressed with the apple industry here that he returned to Galveston and immediately brought his family to Fayetteville. Until his death in 1913 Hamilton was known as a successful marketer of green and dried apples.

Mary Kate Hamilton and her son, Scott, continued to live in the Dickson house until 1931. Mrs. Hamilton was the chairwoman of the City Beautiful Club and was instrumental in making Fayetteville the "cleanest and prettiest town of its size in Arkansas" by the time of the University of Arkansas's semi-centennial celebration of 1922. Scott Hamilton was a well-known student at the University of Arkansas and a veteran of World War I. After the war, Hamilton returned to the University of Arkansas, where he obtained a degree in economics. Between 1925 and 1930 Scott Hamilton was secretary of the Fayetteville Chamber of Commerce. In later years he was a booster for the cities of Hot Springs, Fort Smith, and Little Rock. Scott Hamilton Drive in Little Rock is named in his honor.

Milsap

In 1939 Mrs. Virgie Milsap moved to 2 West Dickson. Born in Prairie Grove in 1880, she was a nurse at Fayetteville City Hospital and had formerly lived in the Williams boarding house at 611 West Dickson. Shortly after moving to 2 West Dickson, she converted the house into Fayetteville's first known nursing home. Mrs. Milsap was also associated with the Washington County Home near the corner of Gregg and Township. She left 2 West Dickson in 1950, shortly before the Methodists began their expansion.

6 WEST DICKSON

Bell

Next door to the Hamiltons at 6 West Dickson was the home of Charles and Ella Bell. They built it around 1903. Born in 1852 in Sebastian County, Bell was a preparatory student at the Arkansas Industrial University during the 1873–1874 school year. He was engaged in the timber businesses in Texas, Oklahoma, and Arkansas. Married in 1877,

6 West Dickson, 1910s

Charles and Ella Bell first lived near Waldron. In 1897 they moved to Fayetteville, originally living in the 700 block of West Dickson. Bell's lumber business provided timber for the construction of the Lewis Brothers building (Bank of Fayetteville) on the Fayetteville square and for the Ozark Grocer building in the 500 block of West Dickson Street. The Bells were members of Central Presbyterian Church. Charles Bell died in 1923. Ella Bell lived at 6 West Dickson until her death in 1936.

2–6 WEST DICKSON

Central Methodist Church

In 1898, the Dickson family sold a portion of their lot to the Methodist Church so that they could build a roomier meeting house than the church they were using on West Center Street. During the pastorate of Reverend Henry Hanesworth, Central Methodist Church constructed their new place of worship next door to the old Dickson house on the northwest corner of Dickson and Highland. The cost of the new sanctuary was $7,500. The Methodists began worshiping here in 1899.

In 1950 Central Methodist Church was experiencing even more

Central Methodist Church, ca. 1900

growing pains than it had in 1898. Church officials hoped to remodel the older church, but costs for such extensive work were prohibitive. To meet the demands of a growing congregation, they purchased the old Dickson house, demolished it, and began construction of a new church. Designed by Fayetteville architect Paul Young, the church, completed in 1953, could seat about twelve hundred people. In 1953 they demolished the old church and constructed in its place a new Methodist Youth Center. In 1957

left: *Central Methodist Church pulpit and pipe organ, ca. 1900*

below: *Central Methodist Church, 1953*

the church purchased the Bell house immediately west of the new sanctuary so that they could expand their school services. They constructed the existing building shortly thereafter.

On December 15, 1969, an early morning blaze gutted the sanctuary of the church. Loss from the eight-hour blaze was estimated at $600,000. However, the members of the church, under the pastorate of Dr. Joel A. Cooper, restored the sanctuary to its original 1953 design. In 1971 fire burned the church altar, causing approximately $75,000 in damage.

12 WEST DICKSON
McMillan

In 1899 Davis F. and Luella McMillan purchased the Nesbitt house at 12 West Dickson Street, which was built around 1892. Born in Marietta, Georgia, in 1848, McMillan first lived in Greenwood, Arkansas, where he married Luella Robertson in 1875. A few years later, Mr. and Mrs. McMillan moved to Prairie Grove, where they were in the mercantile business for fifteen years. In 1896 they moved to Fayetteville. McMillan was president of the Nesbitt-McMillan Furniture Company and the Bean-McMillan Mercantile Company. He was also a director of First National Bank and of the Ozark Grocer Company. In 1922 the original Gates-McMillan home burned, but the McMillans constructed a new house. Davis F. McMillan died in 1931. Luella McMillan lived here until her death in 1944.

14 WEST DICKSON
Gates

In 1877 Noah Putnam and Lucy Jane Gates moved to a house where later would stand the west end of the U. S. Post Office. They lived there until 1888. Born in Kentucky in 1832, Gates was superintendent of Little Rock public schools between 1869 and 1872. In 1872 he came to Fayetteville to serve as the first president of Arkansas Industrial

Professor Gates

Agri-Day parade on 10 block of West Dickson, 1917

University. The following year, however, he became principal of the Normal Department. He served in this capacity until 1875, when he was again called to the presidency. In 1877 Gates returned to his former position as principal of the Normal department. In 1884 Gates became superintendent of public schools in Fort Smith. Five years later he became superintendent of schools in Fayetteville. Gates held this position until retiring in 1900. In addition to helping popularize public schools in Little Rock, Fort Smith, and Fayetteville, Gates organized the Arkansas State Teachers Association. In commercial affairs, Gates was a major force in attracting the Frisco Railroad to Fayetteville. It is said that he incurred most of the expenses of surveying the route of the Frisco railway through Fayetteville.

Central Presbyterian Church

In 1903, during the pastorate of Denmark native Reverend Rasmus Thomsen, the congregation of Cumberland Presbyterian Church, located on North Block Street, elected a building committee to oversee the erection of a larger church. The committee, which included neighbor Charles Bell, purchased a site on the northeast corner of Dickson and St. Charles. Construction of the new sanctuary was completed in 1906 and the first services were held on March 18. That year, by virtue of the union of the Cumberland Presbyterian Churches with the Presbyterian Church U.S.A., the Fayetteville Cumberland Presbyterian Church changed its name to Central Presbyterian Church. In 1953 the First Presbyterian Church on South College Avenue united with Central Presbyterian Church. In 1961, both churches sold their properties and built a church on Calvin Street in northeast Fayetteville. Central Presbyterian Church on Dickson Street was demolished to make way for the Fayetteville Post Office.

Fayetteville Post Office

In 1961 the U. S. Post Office purchased the lots formerly occupied by the McMillan house and Central Presbyterian Church and began construction of a new post office for Fayetteville. The present building has more than 14,000 square feet of floor space and occupies a one-third acre lot. When it opened on January 2, 1963, the Fayetteville Post Office had fifty-three employees, eight rural routes, and sixty city routes, including parcel

Central Presbyterian Church, 1930

U.S. Post Office, 1995

post. According to my former letter carrier, Sandy Young, in 1995 there were 294 employees, sixty-one rural routes, and forty-seven city routes. This illustrates how much Fayetteville grew in only thirty-five years!

5 WEST DICKSON

Whitlow

W. H. Whitlow and his wife, Annie Birnie, a native of Fort Smith, built their home around 1880 at 5 West Dickson Street, the current site of a nicely landscaped parking lot. The Whitlows lived across the street from Charles Bell and Professor Gates. Born in Missouri in 1851, Whitlow graduated from the Ozark Institute in 1869. He then became a clerk in the drugstore of P. M. Cox. In 1875 Whitlow and George Lake opened the Whitlow & Lake Drugstore where he was the senior druggist until moving to Ft. Smith in 1905.

Rattenbury

George and Minerva Rattenbury purchased 5 West Dickson from the Whitlows in 1906. Born in Detroit, Michigan, in 1851, Rattenbury moved to Chattanooga, Tennessee, when he was eighteen. In 1873 Rattenbury married Miss Minerva Hunt, a native of Tennessee. In 1888 the Rattenburys

5 West Dickson, 1910s

5 West Dickson, 1970s

came to Fayetteville, where he was an agent of a St. Louis grocery company and for several years manager of Ozark Grocer Company. Rattenbury also served as a director of First National Bank of Fayetteville and of the O.K. Truck Manufacturing Company of Muskogee, Oklahoma. He was also a director of the Washington County Fair Association. Mr. Rattenbury died in 1920. Mrs. Rattenbury lived at 5 West Dickson until 1925.

Eason

In 1925 Alcuin P. Eason and his wife, Emma Rowe, a native of Greenwood, Arkansas, purchased the Rattenbury house. Born in 1881 in Coldwater, Mississippi, Eason was the son of John T. Eason and Elizabeth Bourdon, who moved to Fayetteville in 1888. In 1907 father and son opened an insurance company on the northwest side of the square. In 1914 the Eason Insurance Company became a representative of the United States Fidelity and Guaranty Company (U.S.F. & G.) of Baltimore. Eason had a controlling interest in the business until the 1960s. Mrs. Eason died in 1970. When Mr. Eason died three years later, the house was demolished and replaced with a parking lot.

11 WEST DICKSON
Wade

H. King Wade

11 West Dickson was the home of H. King Wade and his wife, Kate Bibb. The Wades built this house around 1885 on the site later occupied by the Hathcock Building. Born in Kentucky in 1856, Wade was educated in the public schools of that state and at Vanderbilt University in Nashville, Tennessee. In 1884, five years after their marriage, the Wades moved to Fayetteville. Wade's first job here was as agent for the Adams Express Company, which shipped strawberries and other small fruits. In 1895 he became a cashier at the McIlroy Bank & Trust Company. He worked there until retiring in 1929, by which time he was also on the bank's board of directors. He was also a director of the Ozark White Lime

Wade House, 1890s

Company. Only his closest business associates and friends knew of Wade's quiet generosity. Just two weeks before his death in 1929, he discovered a young deaf and dumb boy living in Fayetteville, provided for him financially, and arranged for his education at the Deaf Institute in Little Rock. The Wade family occupied the house from 1885 until Mrs. Wade's death in 1944.

SOUTHEAST CORNER BLOCK AND DICKSON

Hathcock Building

Dr. P.L. Hathcock

In 1949, five years after Mrs. Wade's death, Dr. P. L. Hathcock purchased the Wade house, demolished it, and constructed a new office building on the site. Dr. Hathcock, a 1901 graduate of Vanderbilt University, was on the staff of the Fayetteville City Hospital and a member of the Washington County Medical Society. Originally housing Hathcock's medical practice and other professional offices, the Hathcock Building currently houses many small professional offices. It is believed the fence and wall surrounding the Hathcock Building also surrounded the previous structure.

Hathcock building, 1995

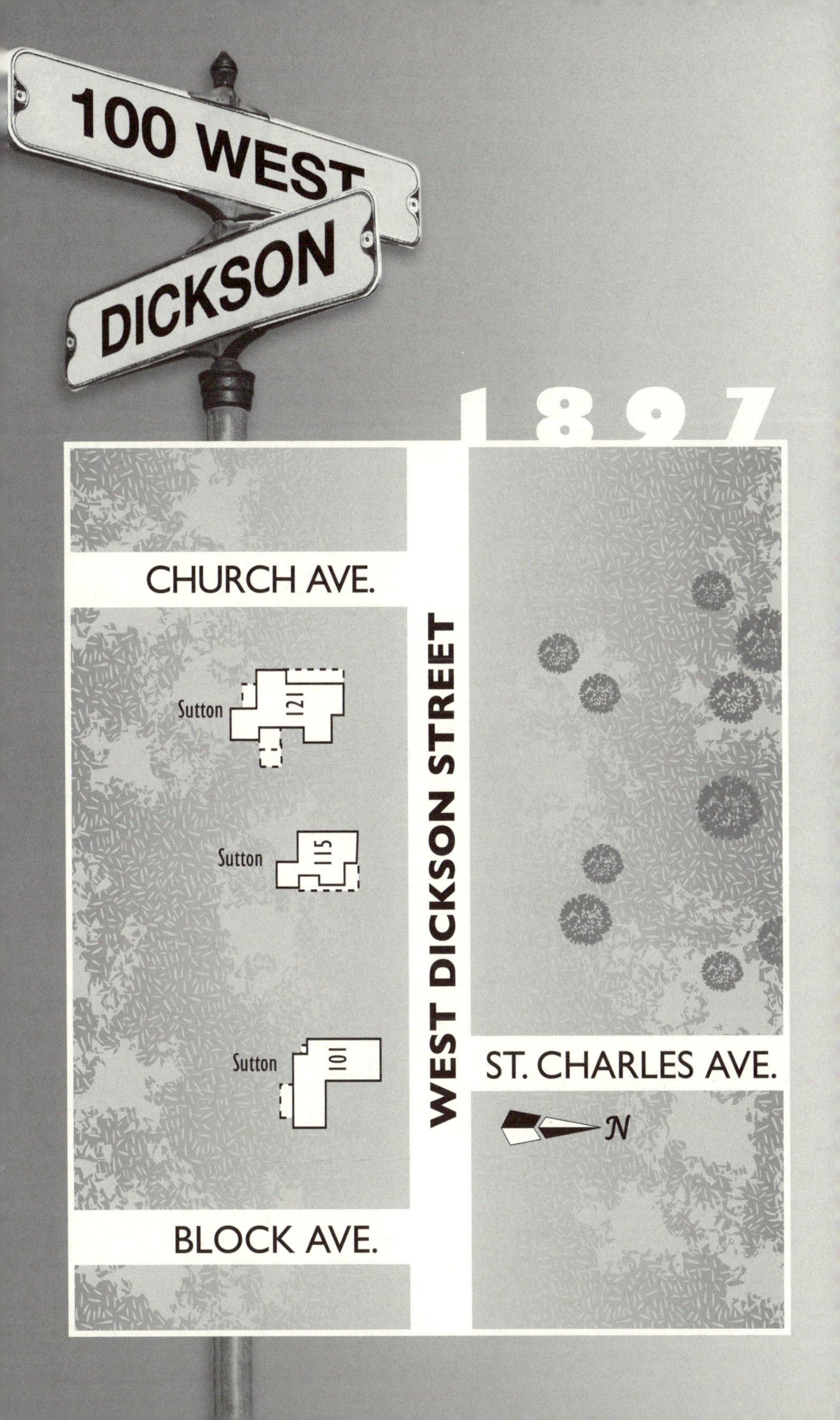
100 WEST
DICKSON
1897
CHURCH AVE.
WEST DICKSON STREET
Sutton
121
Sutton
115
Sutton
101
ST. CHARLES AVE.
N
BLOCK AVE.

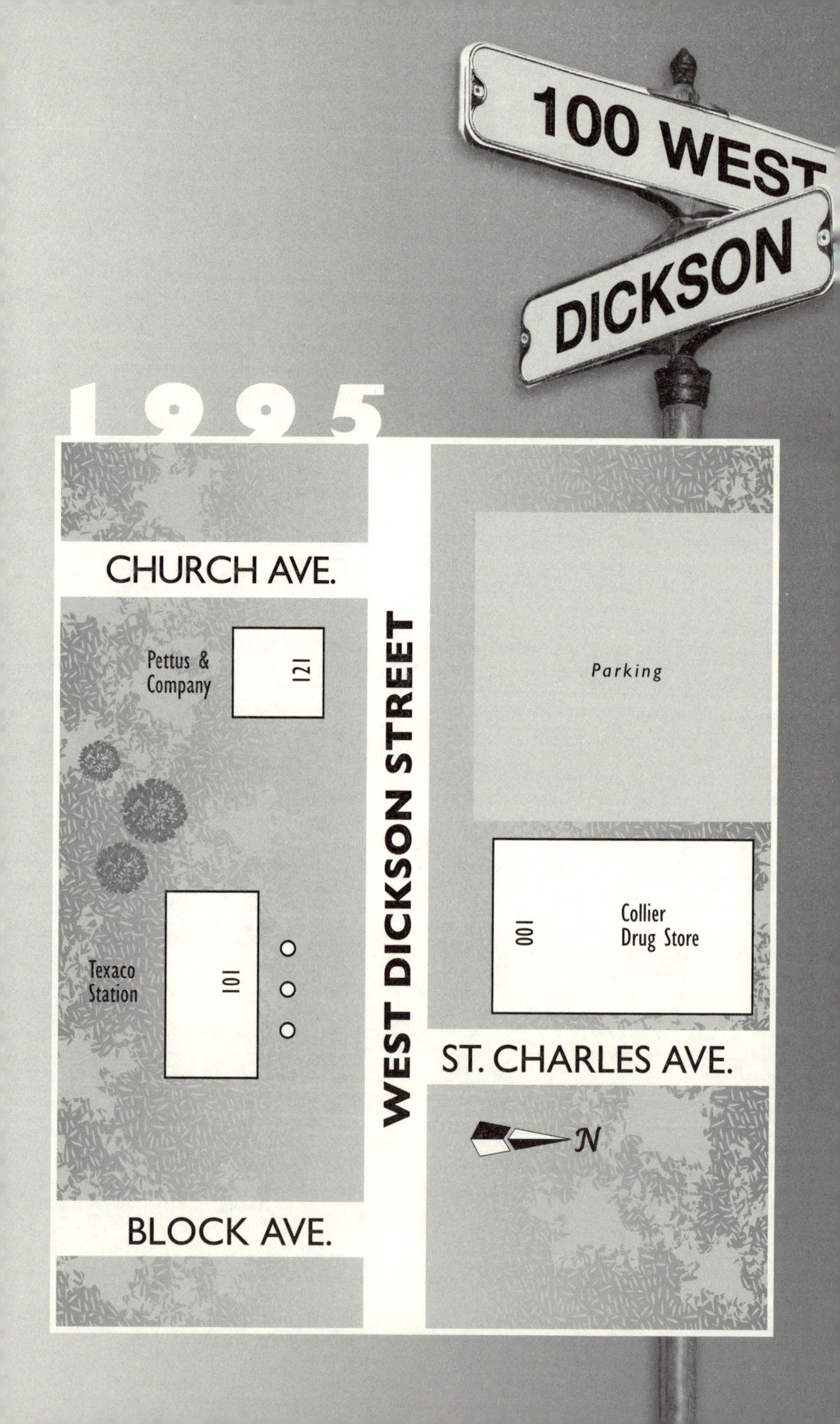
100 WEST
DICKSON
1995
CHURCH AVE.
Pettus & Company
121
Parking
WEST DICKSON STREET
Collier Drug Store
100
Texaco Station
101
ST. CHARLES AVE.
N
BLOCK AVE.

West Dickson begins its downhill roll in the 100 block. Until the early 1900s it was the home of the Sutton and Boles families.

101–151 WEST DICKSON

Sutton

Seneca Sutton

In 1836 Charles W. Deane built one of the first houses in Fayetteville at the corner of Block and Dickson, at that time the northern edge of the town. Around 1840 Seneca Sutton and his wife, Isabella Houston, natives of Kentucky and Missouri, respectively, came to Fayetteville and purchased it. According to newspaper accounts, the Sutton home was a center of attraction and represented the ideal of wealth and luxury. The Suttons had many interests in Ft. Smith and in Osage Mills (Benton County).They kept a train of six mule teams on the road hauling produce from Ft. Smith to Fayetteville, and beyond to Osage Mills. Their home was a stopping-off point for U.S. Army officers traveling between those towns. Seneca Sutton died in 1857. Isabella Sutton died in 1880.

Mary and Belle Sutton, affectionately known as the "Sutton Sisters," were daughters of Seneca and Isabella Sutton. They lived in the Sutton home until the 1890s, when they built a home next door, at 115 West Dickson, the present site of a parking lot. Mary and Belle Sutton never married. Both ladies were active members of First Presbyterian Church. They lived at 115 West Dickson until Mary Sutton's death in 1918 and Belle Sutton's death in 1922.

George Sutton, born in 1848, was one of Seneca and Isabella Sutton's two sons. He and his wife, Margaret Cooper, built their home on the southeast corner of Church and Dickson in the 1890s. It was known as 121 West Dickson, near the current site of Pettus & Company. George Sutton learned the harness-maker's trade and was prominently identified

Tree Protest #1

For many years, at the intersection of West Dickson Street and St. Charles Avenue stood Fayetteville's oldest and largest oak tree. This oak tree was one of the original landmarks in Fayetteville. J. H. Van Hoose, of the 100 block of East Dickson Street, recalled that quite a ruckus occurred in 1888, when the City of Fayetteville widened Dickson Street from twenty-eight feet to fifty-six feet. Apparently, and perhaps prophetically, the city ignored the sentiments of the residents of upper West Dickson Street (who would have included Mrs. Dickson, the Gateses, the Wades, and the Suttons), and cut down the trees that had lined the block for several decades. However, the residents were most upset about the removal of a large oak tree near the present U. S. Post Office. It grew on what the Native American population and the first European settlers called Prairie Hill. According to Van Hoose, before Fayetteville settlers began planting them, many areas in town boasted very few trees. The large oak there provided a shady spot in which early settlers could congregate.

with that industry in Washington County. Mr. Sutton was also a stockholder in the Washington County Fair Association. He died in 1907. Mrs. Sutton was born in Tennessee in 1855. She was a member of the Woman's Missionary Society, the Woman's Christian Temperance Union, and the United Daughters of the Confederacy. She lived at 121 West Dickson until her death in 1925.

George and Margaret Lee moved into the Sutton Sisters house at 115 West Dickson in 1933. Margaret Lee was the Sutton sisters' niece. Lee, a native of Missouri, moved here in 1928. He was a real estate agent. George Lee died in 1944. Margaret Lee continued living here until 1968. Shortly after her departure, the Mary and Belle Sutton house was demolished. Since 1968 a parking lot has occupied the site.

101 WEST DICKSON

Texaco Station

In 1957 Doyle E. Brooks built a Texaco Service Station on the site of the original Sutton homesite. He owned it until 1969. Before being badly damaged by fire in 1995, it was known as the Old Tyme Texaco Station, since by that time only a few gas stations still offered full automotive service to their customers. Besides selling gasoline and automotive products, the Texaco Service Station attendants provided regular repair and tune-up services.

Following the closing of the Texaco station, the canopy was removed and the building converted into a shop for women's apparel.

Texaco station, 1995

Texaco Grand-Opening ad, 1957

121 West Dickson, 1928

121 WEST DICKSON
Watson Mortuary

Shortly after Margaret Sutton died in 1925, the George Sutton house at 121 West Dickson was converted into apartments and became known as the Sutton Apartments. Among the many tenants were members of the Phi Mu Sorority. In 1945 Edmond P. Watson, Jr. and his wife, Lina Hayes Watson, purchased the property and moved their mortuary, the Watson Burial Association, from Block Street to 121 West Dickson. In 1968, Watson's Mortuary moved to College Avenue. Their building

Watson Mortuary ad, 1946

had a clock and blue neon sign on it, an important landmark in Fayetteville. Watson's also had a small fountain on the property. It is a very sad irony that in 1946 Edmund P. Watson, Sr. was hit by a car and killed in front of the mortuary. As with the Mary and Belle Sutton house, the George Sutton house was demolished in 1968. Since that time, the site has been a parking lot.

100 WEST DICKSON

Boles

Clementine Watson Boles

Clementine Watson Boles lived across the street from the Suttons, in a house that faced what is now Watson Street, until her death in 1921. Born in 1839 in Virginia, Clem Watson moved to Van Buren in 1847 with her parents, William A. Watson and Christina Crews. Shortly before the Civil War, the Watsons moved to Fayetteville and settled on property now bordered by Lafayette Street, Dickson Street, St. Charles Avenue, and Rollston Avenue. (St. Charles Avenue was named after one of the Boles's sons, who died at an early age.) In 1877 Clem Watson married Thomas D. Boles, who died in 1883. Clem Boles, a true patriot, was a member of both the Daughters of the American Revolution and the Mildred Lee Chapter of the Daughters of the Confederacy, a director of the Jefferson Davis Monument in Arkansas, and the state director of the Arlington Memorial Association of Washington, D. C. Clementine Boles was also a major financier of late-nineteenth- and early twentieth-century Fayetteville real estate. For several years, Mrs. Boles owned a popular roller skating rink on the rear portion of her lot. It was on the site now occupied by Collier Drug Store. The adjoining lot was used by small traveling shows. In the fall of 1906 the Rabbit's Foot Company came to Fayetteville. During their show a juvenile delinquent shot a fire cracker, which burned the company's tent. No one was hurt, but Mrs. Boles just narrowly escaped the burning tent.

Citizen's Laundry, 1910s

Citizens Laundry

In 1908 Mrs. Boles leased her skating rink site to H. S. and Sterling Price, Jack Walker, I. W. Guisinger, W. F. Bell, and John R. Harris. They were the original financiers and proprietors of Citizens Laundry. Located at 100 West Dickson Street between 1908 and 1924, Citizens Laundry had more than ten thousand square feet of space and nearly thirty-five employees. Citizens Laundry's sales pitch implied that other laundries did not return all of the customers' clothing; the slogan for the new laundry was "We Return Everything But the Dirt." In 1918 J. F. Rieff bought Citizens Laundry and relocated the business to West Avenue around 1925.

Dyke Lumber Company ad, 1957

100 WEST DICKSON
Dyke Lumber Company
"Early City Planning Gone Awry"

There was much controversy over the 1924 arrival on Dickson Street of the Dyke Lumber Company. At a mass meeting at Central Presbyterian Church, several local residents petitioned the City of Fayetteville to enact a zoning ordinance to protect churches, houses, hospitals, and schools from invading commercial enterprises. Mayor Allan M. Wilson promised the group that no building permit would be issued until a new zoning ordinance was passed. The City of Fayetteville then passed a new zoning ordinance forbidding the erection of any canning factory, poultry house, livery barn, lumber yard, planing mill, machine shop, blacksmith shop, public garage, filling station, or any other noisy or objectionable structure within three hundred feet of any church building or public school of the city. Regardless of the new zoning law, economics ruled the day, a situation that has often repeated itself in Fayetteville. The Dyke Lumber Company paid E. P. Watson (Clem Boles' brother) $10,500 for the Citizen's Laundry site. They moved across the street from Central Presbyterian Church and remained at the corner of Dickson and St. Charles Avenue until 1961. Founded by Martin T. Dyke of Fort Smith, and his sons Nathaniel, Frank, and Martin, the Dyke Lumber Company sold lumber, roofing supplies, and paint.

White Way Celebration
The Lighting of West Dickson Street

In 1922 the City of Fayetteville, as well as a number of residents and businesses, helped to honor the University of Arkansas's semi-centennial by presenting the city and the university with a lighted way on the most popular route from the Fayetteville square to the University of Arkansas, first north on Block and then west on Dickson. Dean William Nathan Gladson of the School of Engineering was an expert in municipal lighting systems and helped select the most modern lighting of the day. The Fayetteville Gas and Electric Company provided the lights and the manpower to install them. The White Way Celebration took place on June 10, 1922, attended by approximately three thousand people. It began with the firing of a small cannon down the street toward the university. Dean Gladson and other dignitaries then turned on the lights. After the initial awe, there was some disappointment among the crowd. Apparently there was a short in the wiring, as the lights west of the tracks flickered and then blew out. Regardless of the incomplete success, the crowd enjoyed the remainder of the late spring evening. The White Way Celebration concluded with a parade, led by the ROTC down Block and Dickson Streets to the University campus. This route from the square to the campus has been the standard parade route in Fayetteville since that time.

Collier Drug Store Grand-Opening ad, 1950

Collier Drug Store

In 1949 Morris Collier, the owner of the Red Cross Drug Store on Center Street, decided to move to a less congested part of town with plenty of customer parking. He thereupon initiated construction in October of that year of a modern Art Deco building at 100 West Dickson to house the new Collier Rexall Drug Store. Built by the Tune Construction Company,

Collier Drug Store, 1950s

Collier Drug Store fountain, 1950s

Dickson Street looking east from 100 block, 1950s

Collier Drug opened in March 1950. In 1966 Collier expanded into the vacated Dyke Lumber Company building to the north. The drug store's trademark was a twenty-eight foot high stucco tower in front of the building with the store's name written in metal at the top. Collier's was the first store in Fayetteville to have a "magic door," operated by a photoelectric cell. As soon as you walked up to it, the door would open by itself! When it opened, Collier's Dickson Street store was one of the first self-service drugstores. It had a classic soda-fountain with chrome and leatherette seats. Over the years Collier Drug, in addition to its prescription delivery service, has offered a complete stock of sick room supplies, cosmetics, perfumes, and greeting cards. The store also houses a comprehensive camera shop and photo-developing lab. When the store was remodeled near the end of the century, the distinctive sign was preserved, one of Dickson Street's landmarks. Collier Drug, Fayetteville's last family-owned drugstore, now has many stores throughout Fayetteville and other towns in the area. It has a reputation of treating its employees like family. In 2007, Collier Drug closed its store one day to honor the life of its longtime deliveryman Louis Bryant, who delivered prescriptions for nearly 60 years.

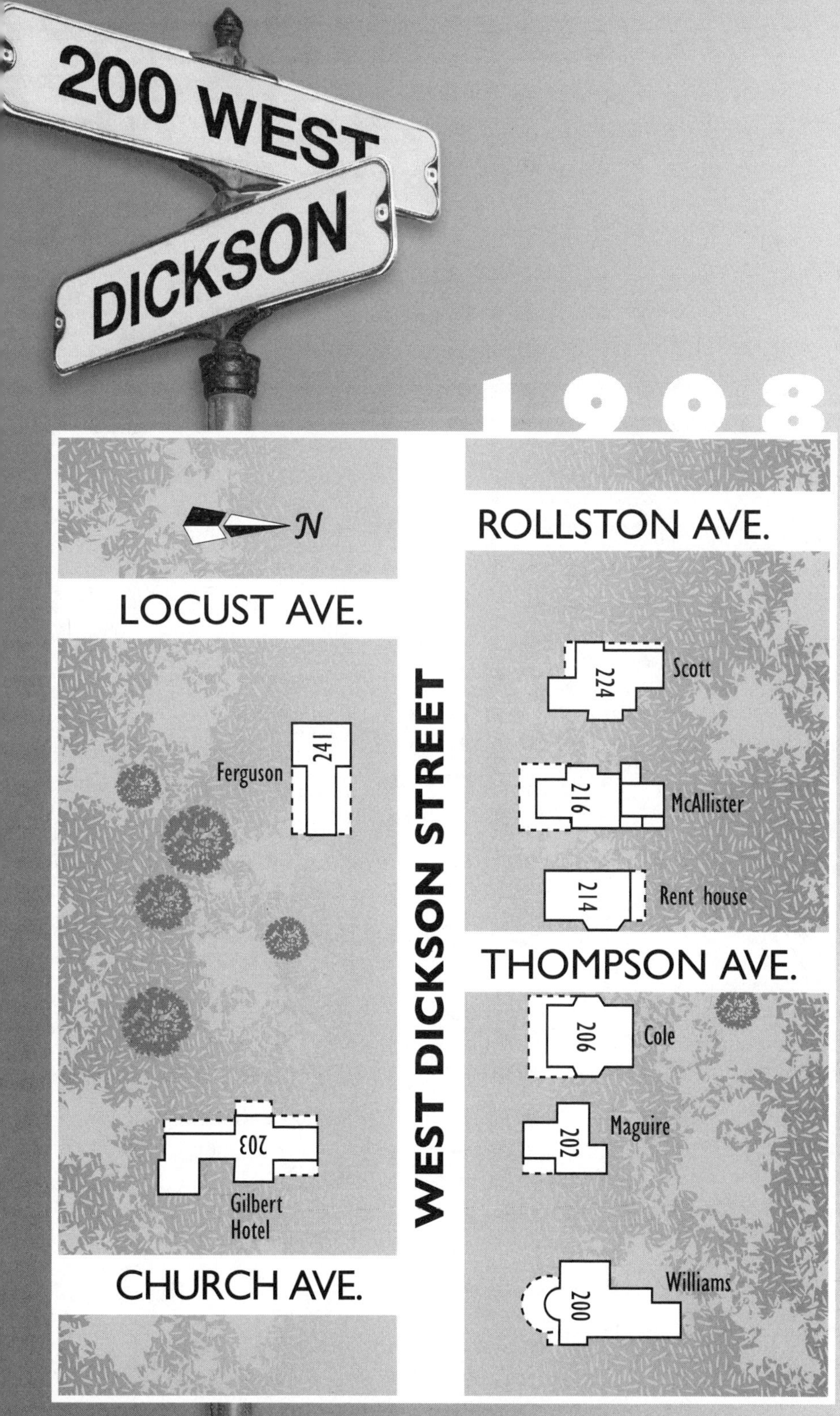
200 WEST
DICKSON
1908
N
ROLLSTON AVE.
LOCUST AVE.
WEST DICKSON STREET
224
Scott
241
Ferguson
216
McAllister
214
Rent house
THOMPSON AVE.
206
Cole
202
Maguire
203
Gilbert Hotel
CHURCH AVE.
200
Williams

200 WEST
DICKSON

1995

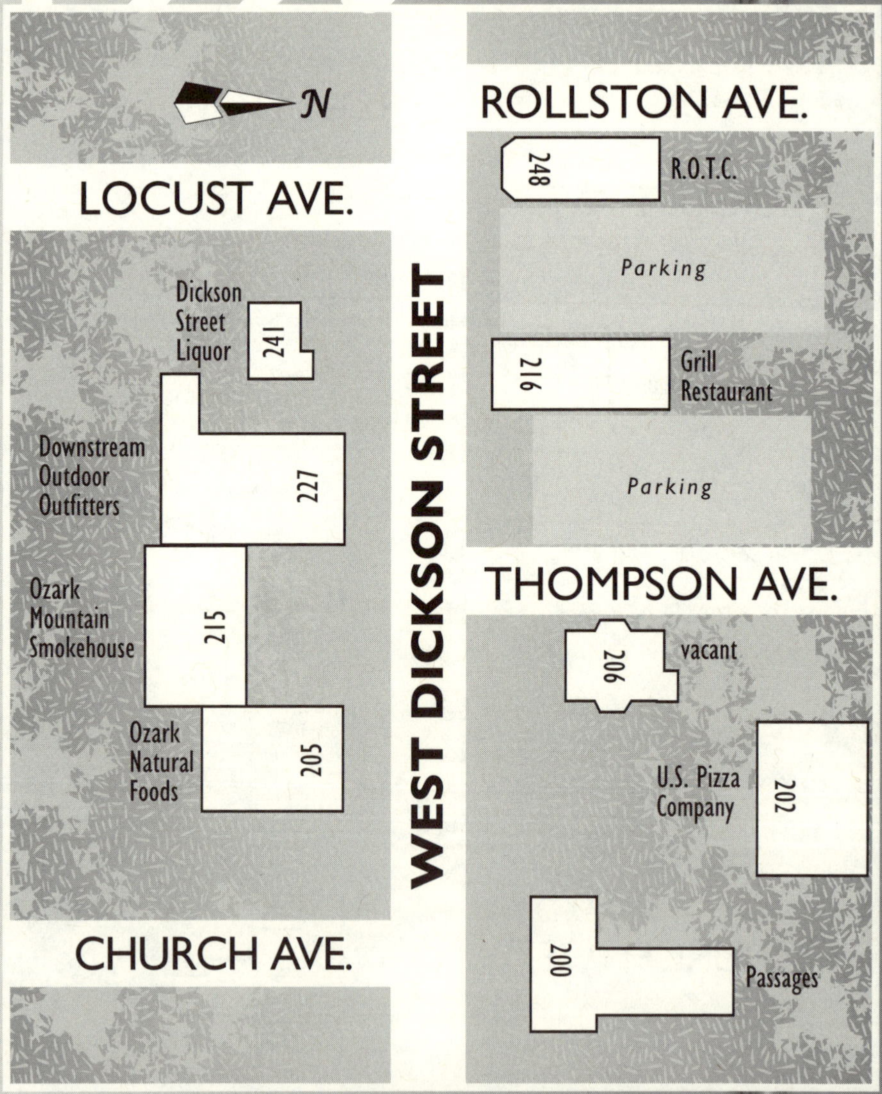

N
LOCUST AVE.
ROLLSTON AVE.
248
R.O.T.C.
Parking
Dickson Street Liquor
241
216
Grill Restaurant
Downstream Outdoor Outfitters
227
Parking
WEST DICKSON STREET
THOMPSON AVE.
Ozark Mountain Smokehouse
215
206
vacant
Ozark Natural Foods
205
U.S. Pizza Company
202
CHURCH AVE.
200
Passages

200 BLOCK

West Dickson Street continues its descent toward Town Creek in the 200 block. Until the 1870s and 1880s, the undeveloped property on the north side of the block was owned by the Campbells, who lived in the 300 block, and by the Boles family, who lived in the 100 block. The H. W. Wallace family owned the property on the south side of the block until the 1870s, when the Gilberts and Fergusons purchased it.

203 WEST DICKSON

Gilbert

In 1882 John and Martha Gilbert bought the old Wallace house from local realtor and developer James A. Ferguson. Built by the Wallace family sometime after the Civil War, the front of this very large house faced west, rather than north. In time, the Gilbert house would be known as 203 West Dickson Street, the current site of the Ozark Mountain Smokehouse. Born in Phillips County, Arkansas, in 1823 "Uncle" John Gilbert was a veteran of the Mexican-American War. In 1865 the Gilberts moved to Walnut Grove (near Prairie Grove) and in 1875 moved to Fayetteville. Shortly after John Gilbert's death in 1887, Mrs. Gilbert, who was known by neighbors as a very compassionate lady, opened her home to boarders and it became known as the Gilbert Hotel. Martha Gilbert died in 1906.

Meals 40c, Good Service — Rates $1.50 per Day

GILBERT HOTEL

CHAS. GOFF, Prop.

Well Ventilated Rooms, Nice Lawn and Shade

Good Water, Baths, Etc.

3 BLOCKS EAST OF DEPOT

203 W. Dixon — Phone 125-J

Gilbert Hotel ad, 1920

Midway Hotel, 1939

Gilbert Hotel/Midway Hotel

During the early 1900s boarders could rent a room at the Gilbert Hotel for $1.50 per day. Meals cost an additional forty cents. The Gilbert Hotel advertised that it had well- ventilated rooms, a nice lawn and shade, good water and baths. By the mid 1910s, when the Gilbert Hotel was owned by Lizzie Cox, the Gilberts' granddaughter, it had become known as an "assignation" or brothel. Fayetteville Police Chief Stirman stated that it had become common knowledge that the Gilbert House had become disorderly and that a woman of Mrs. Cox's experience must have known about it. Furthermore, the police were simply tired of the situation. The hotel was closed and Cox was fined $25.00. In 1923 Edna Brashears of Eureka Springs took over the hotel, cleaned it up, renamed it the Midway Hotel, and tried to attract a better class of patronage. In 1932 H. H. "Scotty" Taylor purchased it and renamed it the New Midway Hotel. In 1938–1939, the house was rented by the Future Farmers of America Club of the University of Arkansas. In 1940–1941 the Gilbert house was known as the Midway Cooperative House. It was demolished shortly thereafter.

205 WEST DICKSON

Holland Brothers Locker Plant

In 1946 Alsey L. and Urban D. Holland purchased the former Gilbert property and constructed a large cold-storage plant on the site. Until they

Forget Your Old Ideas About Buying Meat!

Buy It Wholesale—And Save Money!

You can select the kind of meat you want in wholesale quantity . . . we'll expertly process it for you just as you wish for your locker or home freezer. You're bound to save money (up to 20%) by purchasing meat in this modern way. Get wise . . . start buying wholesale now!

You Take No Chances When We Process And Freeze Your Meats!

DON'T GAMBLE with your valuable foods and the health of your family by trying to process and freeze large amounts of meats yourself. Bring them to our plant for proper processing and handling.

Holland Bros. Locker

203 W. DICKSON FAYETTEVILLE, ARK.

Holland Brothers ad, 1952

closed the Dickson Street plant in 1973, Holland Brothers provided quality meats by the side or the quarter for home freezers. In addition, Holland Brothers processed and cured meats, and sold cheese, butter, eggs, fruit juices, and ice cream. They also sold packaging material and home freezers.

The very popular King Pizza, part of a regional chain, operated at

Flooded street, 1970 (notice Holland Brothers in background)

205 West Dickson between 1976 and 1986. This store received a lot of publicity in 1984 when a Razorback basketball player, in Japan for some exhibition games, said he was hungry for King Pizza, which had delivery service. The owner flew to Hong Kong to meet the team and brought pizzas with him.

215 WEST DICKSON
Pettigrew Milk Company

W. B. Pettigrew opened the Pettigrew Milk Company at 207 (now 215) West Dickson in 1937. Like most milk companies of that day, Pettigrew offered daily delivery service of their Pasteurized Grade "A" Milk. In 1940 Fount P. Earle purchased the dairy and renamed it the Pasteurized Milk Company. He owned it until 1951. In 1952, when Roscoe B. Kuhn took over operations, it became the College Club Dairy. All of their milk came from producers in Benton, Madison, and Washington counties. Under these various names, the dairy processed and delivered pasteurized and homogenized milk, cream, chocolate milk, buttermilk, cottage cheese, and butter. College Club Dairy also introduced single-service bottles and containers for their milk products. College Club moved off Dickson Street in 1964.

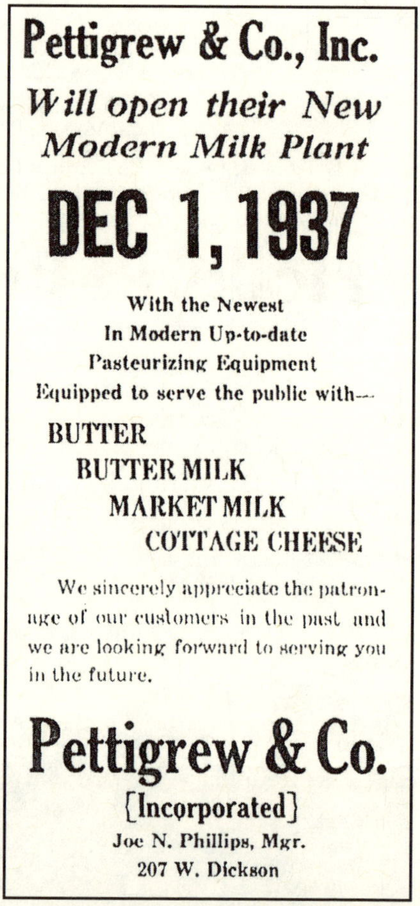

Pettigrew Milk Company Grand-Opening ad, 1937

College Club Dairy ad, 1962

Ozark Mountain Smoke House

In 1974 Frank Sharp opened a Fayetteville branch of the Ozark Mountain Smokehouse at 151 West Dickson, most recently occupied by the Pettus Law Firm. In 1982 he constructed the present Ozark Mountain Smokehouse building at 215 West Dickson. The Smokehouse also occupies a portion of the building next door. The Ozark Mountain Smokehouse sells smoked meats and cheeses, as well as a line of preserves and

Ozark Natural Foods, 1995

Ozark Mountain Smokehouse, 1995

Ozark Mountain Smokehouse interior, 1980s

condiments. The building, a popular location for meetings and parties, contains several distinctive features, including walls paneled with a variety of Arkansas woods, a hugely spreading Wisteria vine, and an elaborate ironwork fence next to the front sidewalk. Frank and Sara Sharp, who developed their smoke house products into a business with customers nation-wide, have been active promoters of Dickson Street and many Fayetteville cultural, social, and political causes.

227–241 WEST DICKSON

Ferguson

J.A. Ferguson

Born in 1840 in Washington County, James Ferguson served the Confederacy during the Civil War. After his marriage to Nancy Tuttle in 1868, he and his bride settled in Fayetteville. Around 1876 they purchased the Wallace estate on the south side of the street and built a large brick house on the western half of the property. Eventually, the Ferguson home would be known as 241 West Dickson Street, the current site of Dickson Street Liquor. Ferguson owned Ferguson Lumber Company, which had operations in

241 West Dickson, 1890s

all of northwest Arkansas, including Hill City Lumber Company and the Red Star Spoke Factory of Fayetteville. Ferguson also dealt in real estate and at one time owned a considerable amount of property on and around Dickson Street. He died in 1918. Nancy Ferguson was a member of St. Paul's Episcopal Church and of the Southern Memorial Association. She lived at 241 West Dickson until about 1919. Their house was demolished in the 1930s.

227 WEST DICKSON

Sines Body Shop

In November 1946 Glenn A. Sines established Sines Body Shop on the eastern half of the former Ferguson lot near the Pettigrew Milk Company. In addition to body and fender work, Sines Body Shop produced tops for convertibles, seats, and seat covers. They also specialized in cutting and installing safety and plain car glass. Sines also did welding and made awnings for the home. The shop was at 227 West Dickson Street until 1969, when Sines relocated at the corner of Old Farmington Road and

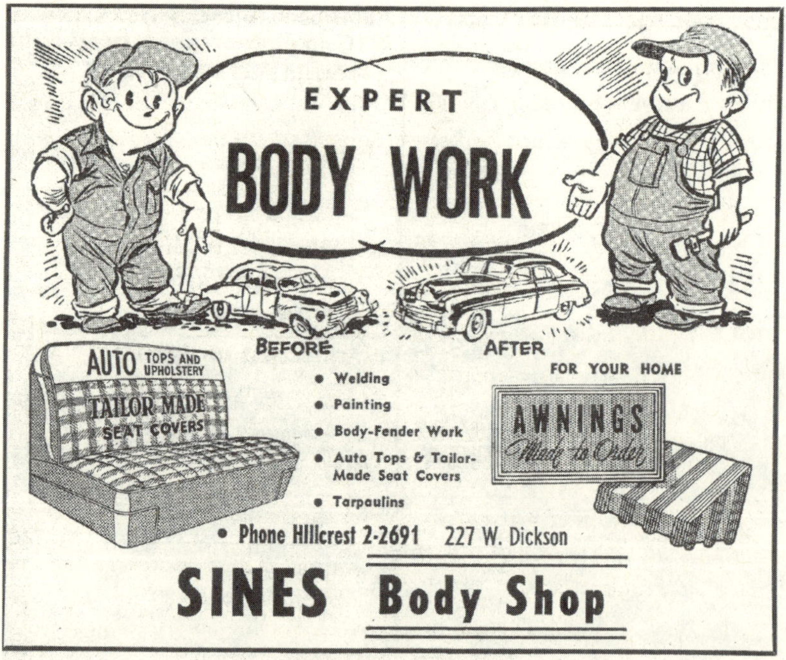

Sines Body Shop ad, 1954

227–241 West Dickson, 1920s

the Highway 71 Bypass. One of the most popular employees was Sarge West, who, for several years after leaving Sines, worked for Shelter Insurance Claims Office in Springdale.

Nightclubs

Since the 1970s the building formerly housing Sines Body Shop has been occupied by many short-lived bars and nightclubs, including Poor Richard's, Notchy's, and Omar's. One of the last clubs to occupy the site was the notorious Landing Strip. The City of Fayetteville closed it in 1982 after two patrons were stabbed outside of the club. Until 2000

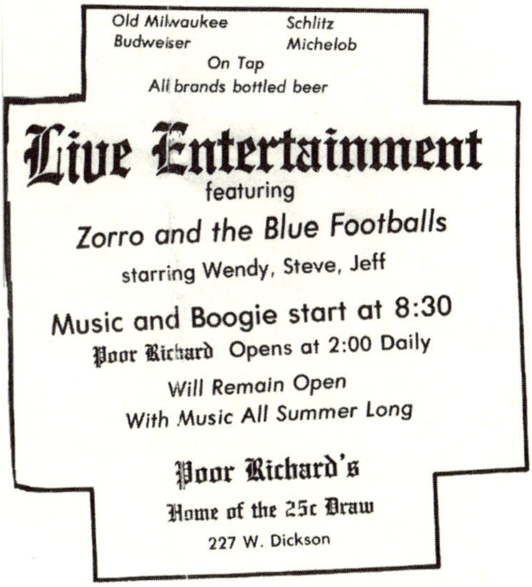

Poor Richard's ad, 1975

the building housed Downstream Outdoor Outfitters, but it subsequently returned to its earlier use as a club, this time the Dickson Theater, featuring movies and live entertainment.

241 WEST DICKSON
Conoco Service Station

In 1937 John M. Hilton, the local representative of Conoco (Continental Oil Company), constructed a filling station on the western half of the former Ferguson lot, now known as 241 West Dickson. The station was an English-style building of glazed brick. According to its advertisements, the station had two modern restrooms. The garage had a washing and greasing stall equipped with an automatic lift. John M. and Lydle L. Hilton ran the Conoco until the early 1940s, when William Keeton took charge. J. R. Stout and Dee King owned it until it closed in 1964.

Conoco Grand-Opening ad, 1937

Dickson Street Liquor, 1995

Dickson Street Liquor

In 1964 Bill House purchased the old Conoco Service Station at 241 West Dickson and converted it into Dickson Street Liquor, which has been there since that time. The front of the building is relatively unchanged except for enclosing the service bay, and there is a drive-up window on the west side of the building.

200 WEST DICKSON

Rex House

In 1882 B. F. "Frank" and Angeline Smith, Tennessee natives, purchased the property at 200 West Dickson and constructed a new house in 1889. Smith was a druggist and was one time owner of the City Drug Store on the Fayetteville square. He died in the 1890s. Angeline Smith died in 1897. Their daughter, Gertrude Smith, lived in the family home until 1904. Between the early 1900s and 1938, when the Fulbright family constructed the Coca-Cola Bottling Plant on the site, this house was owned by the Add Cole family and was known as the Rex House boarding house.

Rex House, 1916

Fayetteville Coca-Cola Bottling Company

In 1938 the Fulbright family purchased the Rex House at 200 West Dickson, demolished it, and constructed a Coca-Cola bottling plant on the site. Designed by Fayetteville architect Paul Young, the Coca-Cola Bottling Company had its grand opening in 1939. Hal Douglas, a son-in-law of the Fulbrights, managed the bottling company until 1951, when Allen B. Reynolds assumed management. The bottling plant was unique for Fayetteville. Passers-by could see through front windows bottles being filled with Coca-Cola and then capped as they proceeded down a series of conveyor belts. The Coca-Cola Bottling Company remained at 200 West Dickson until 1962, when the plant was moved to

Coca-Cola Bottling Plant ad, 1944

Proposed Coca-Cola Bottling Plant, 1938

Passages, 1995

U.S. Pizza Company, 1995

North Gregg Street. Later the building was converted for use by various retail and service establishments.

206 WEST DICKSON

Cole

Around 1908 Add N. Cole and his wife, Addie Land, purchased the Jack L. Maguire houses at 204 and 206 West Dickson. The Coles took up residence at 206 West Dickson Street. A native of Arkansas, Cole was on the board of directors of the Ozark White Lime Company and had other business interests in Chester, Arkansas. Mrs. Cole was born in Tennessee in 1872, moved to Winslow with her parents in 1882, and married Add Cole in 1890. In 1920 their daughter Faye and her husband Clarence Roller, separated. On the afternoon of March 15, 1920, while Mr. Cole was in Chester, Roller came to the Cole residence with a .32-caliber Colt automatic revolver, shot and killed Mrs. Cole, and critically wounded his wife before killing himself. Newspaper accounts claimed that Roller was on drugs at the time. Shortly after this gruesome incident, Mr. Cole moved to Chester, where he died in 1942.

Maria Dressmaking Shop

In 1922 Mrs. Art Winn, of St. Louis, and Mrs. O. T. Woods and Miss Pearl Harp, both of Fayetteville, opened the Maria Dressmaking Shop in the "little brick house" at 306 West Dickson. In 1934 it was owned by Mrs. Mollie Graham, who moved the shop to the Cole house at 206 West Dickson, where it remained until 1945. In addition to making dresses, these seamstresses steam-pleated, hemstitched, and performed any alterations customers requested.

Maria Dress Making Shop ad, 1928

Vacant Boarding House

Gerald and Estelle Baker started a boarding house for male students at 326 Rollston in 1943. They expanded to 206 W. Dickson in 1948. After 1970 a few businesses occupied the former home of Add N. Cole, including the New Music Store and Abaft Jewelers. It fell into major disrepair and its future existence as one of only two residential dwellings on West Dickson Street looked uncertain. However, in recent years there has been a valiant effort to save it.

206 West Dickson, 1992

214 West Dickson, 1931

214–216 WEST DICKSON
Wade Rent Houses

Although not always apparent, beside 206 West Dickson is an alley, North Thompson Avenue. The present parking lot west of the alley was the site of 214 West Dickson. Around 1892 William and Elizabeth Wade constructed two houses originally used as boarding houses, at 214 and 216 West Dickson. They owned both houses until 1905. The houses were ultimately converted into apartments. The house at 214 West Dickson was demolished in 1971; the lot on which it stood has been a parking lot since then. The house at 216 West Dickson was demolished in 1945.

216 WEST DICKSON
The Grill

Since 1946 216 West Dickson has been home to many popular businesses, including King's Market, Waggoner's Bakery and the Grill Restaurant. T. L. Nelms opened this restaurant in early 1980. It was originally known as the Bar & Grill, but the name was changed to conform with Fayetteville liquor laws. In 1998 the Grill joined forces with ROTC and moved to Highway 112. The property became part of the Three Sisters complex.

Clock affixed to Grill Restaurant, 1980s

Grill Restaurant, 1998

BAR-B-QUE

Pork Plate	3.60
Beef Plate	3.75
Ham Plate	3.75
Rib Plate	3.90
Rack of Ribs	11.00

above orders served with cole slaw and corn on the cobb, bread

SIDE ORDERS

Cup of Chili	.90
Sauteed Veggies	.90
Salad	.90
French Fries	.75
BBQ Beans	.75
Baked Potato	.75
Pepper Tray	.75
Cole Slaw	.60
Corn on the Cobb	.60
Hash Browns	.60
Gravy	.30
BBQ Sauce	.30

DESSERT

Cobbler of the Day	.60
w/ice cream	.80

STEAKS

T-Bone 12 oz.	7.50
Beef Kebab	4.75
Chopped Sirloin	3.95
Chicken Fry	3.75

steaks served with salad, corn on the cobb, potato, and bread

DRINKS

Soft Drinks	.45
Iced/Hot Tea	.45
Tomato Juice	.60
Lemonade	.60
Cider	.60
Milk	.60
Coffee	.40
Beer draft/bottled domestic	
Imported Beer	
Wine glass—½ liter/liter	

THE Bar & Grill

DICKSON STREET FAYETTEVILLE

SANDWICHES

BBQ Pork w/wo slaw	1.60
BBQ Beef w/wo slaw	1.75
BBQ Ham w/wo slaw	1.75
Filet of Fish w/wo slaw	1.75
Salami & Cheese	1.75
Cheeseburger ¼ lb.	1.75
Smoked Ham & Cheese	1.75
Clubhouse ham, egg, tomato and lettuce specify dressing.	1.75
Stewball smoked beef, swiss on french loaf with onion, pickles, lettuce.	1.75
Furlong salami, ham, cheese with onion, pickle tomato and lettuce on french loaf.	1.95
Jabo Special polish sausage and kraut on french loaf.	1.95
Loafer w/BBQ sauce or gravy, potato	2.50
Chili Burger w/potato, open faced with cheese.	2.75

15¢ Substitution Charge

OPEN SUNDAY 4 - 9

(next to THE Corner)

Grill Menu, 1981

224 WEST DICKSON

O. K. Hotel

Between the Grill Restaurant and Restaurant on the Corner was a large parking lot. This was the site of the O. K. Hotel, demolished in 1961. A large frame house was constructed at 224 West Dickson around 1892. The owner, John P. Scott, was born in Missouri in 1855 and raised in Washington County. Scott owned the Fayetteville Roller Mills behind the Frisco Depot on West Avenue and once owned a grocery store on the south side of the Fayetteville square. He also served as Circuit Clerk for Washington County between 1890 and 1892. Scott lived here until 1918.

After J. P. Scott moved, John D. and Ella Otto acquired the house. A few years later they converted it into a boarding house and named it the O. K. Hotel. The Ottos ran it until the 1920s. During the 1930s and 1940s it was run by Charles E. and Grace Crawford. At the time, Crawford had retired as president of the Citizen's Bank of Pettigrew. After Charles Crawford's death in 1943 and Grace Crawford's death in 1946, the O. K. Hotel was converted into apartments. When it was torn down in 1961, it was known as the Hat Box Apartments.

top: *O.K. Hotel, 1940*
bottom: *Laundry-Mart ad, 1954*

248 WEST DICKSON

Laundry-Mart

In 1947 Grover Thomas built a small laundry next door to the O. K. Hotel on the corner of Dickson and Rollston. At the Laundry-Mart, customers could do their own laundry or let the staff do the wash to be picked up later. The Laundry-Mart featured Bendix dryers, which reportedly dried clothes in thirty minutes. Laundry-Mart stayed in business at 248 West Dickson until 1973.

ROTC

In 1973 Anita Leflett converted Grover Thomas's laundry into a restaurant. She could not think of a name for the new restaurant, so she called it Restaurant on the Corner or simply ROTC. The name stuck. In addition to its good selection of sandwiches, salads, and pizzas, ROTC was known for its hash brunch, a filling dish combining hash-browned potatoes and pizza ingredients. More important, ROTC was an extremely comfortable hangout for all types of people. Businessmen, attorneys, professors, and students, as well as old hippies, punkers, skaters, and other alternatives were

ROTC, 1992

Welcome
to
The RESTAURANT
ON THE CORNER

~ SINCE 1973 ~
DICKSON STREET
FAYETTEVILLE, ARKANSAS

ROTC

SANDWICHES (comes with chips)

CORNER MELT swiss & american, burger patty, grilled on rye	$3.95
CORNER BURGER lettuce, tomato & pickle, secret sauce	3.75
(with choice of cheese)	3.95
CORNER SPECIAL roast beef & swiss, lettuce, tomato, secret sauce, on rye	4.25
TURKEY SPECIAL with swiss, lettuce, tomato, secret sauce, on wheat	4.25
FRENCH DIP roast beef & swiss, on french loaf with spiced bouillon dip	4.25
CORNER PORKER ham & cheddar, onion, jalepenos, tomato, lettuce, pickle, mustard, grilled on wheat	4.25
SUBMARINE pepperoni, salami, canadian bacon, lettuce, tomato, mozzarella and our own creamy italian dressing on french loaf	4.25
HOT CORNER burger patty, american cheese, onion, jalepenos, lettuce, tomato, secret sauce, grilled on wheat	4.25
VEGETABLE SPECIAL ripe olives, mushrooms, choice of cheese, lettuce, tomato & secret sauce, grilled on rye	4.25
REUBEN corned beef, swiss & sauerkraut, on rye	4.60
TUNA MELT w/cheddar on wheat, lettuce & tomato	4.60
GRILLED CHEESE choice w/tomato, lettuce and mayo	3.25

(more sandwiches–still with chips)

BIG CHEESE swiss, mozzarella, cheddar, secret sauce, tomato and lettuce on french loaf	$3.95
GRILLED HAM & CHEESE choice of cheese, lettuce, tomato, secret sauce, on sourdough	3.95
CLUB turkey, choice of cheese, bacon, lettuce & tomato, mayo on sourdough	4.60

SALADS

(served with sprouts on request–just ask!)

DINNER SALAD	$1.75
CHEF'S SALAD with cheese, egg, bacon, canadian bacon	4.50
VEGETABLE CHEF'S with cheese, egg, mushrooms & ripe olives	4.50
SHRIMP SALAD bacon, mushroom, black olive, egg and cheese	4.95
TUNA SALAD bed of lettuce, tomatoes & pickles	4.95

BEVERAGES

SOFT DRINKS	$ .90
TEA (iced/hot) or COFFEE	.90
MILK or BUTTERMILK	.75 & .95
TOMATO or ORANGE J.	.75 & .95
MOCHA or HOT CHOCOLATE	1.25
ICED COFFEE	1.25
HERB TEA (varies- ask!)	1.25
SPARKLING WATER (bottled)	1.25

HOUSE SPECIALTIES

SPAGHETTI w/meat sauce served with salad & roll	$4.95
HOT BEEF w/fries sliced beef with brown gravy, open-face	5.95
MUSHROOM BURGER w/fries open-face, american cheese with gravy	5.95
HOT TURKEY w/fries open-face with gravy	5.95
CHICKEN & VEGGIES deep fried with sauteed mixed vegetables, served with wild rice blend and roll	6.50
CHEESE OMELET choice, with hash browns & English muffin	3.95
CORNER OMELET choice of cheese and any 3 pizza ingredients, served with hash browns & English muffin	4.95
FRENCH TOAST	3.25
(with bacon)	4.50
STUFFED BAKED POTATO with choice of cheese and any 2 pizza ingredients, sour cream or salad dressing	3.95
HASH BRUNCH hash browns with cheddar and choice of 2 pizza ingredients	4.95

SIDE ORDERS

SOUP OF THE DAY	$1.75
NACHOS	3.95
CORNER NACHOS jalepenos, cheddar and sour cream, plus tomato, guacamole and black olives	4.95
CHICKEN FINGERS	3.95
CHIPS & SALSA	2.45
SAUTEED VEGGIES	1.95
BAKED POTATO	1.95
FRIED MUSHROOMS	1.95
WILD RICE BLEND	1.60
HASH BROWNS	1.60
FRENCH FRIES	1.25
ONION RINGS	1.25

DESSERTS

PIE	$1.25	ICE CREAM	.90
PIE ALA or GOURMET PIE			2.00

additions

cheeses	$.75	extra meat	$1.50
extra veggie	.75	dressing	.40
sprouts	.40	egg	.75

PIZZA

	8"	13"
CHEESE (plain)	$3.50	$7.5
SINGLE TOPPING	3.95	7.9
VEGIE COMBO mushrooms, gr. pepper, onion & ripe olives	5.25	9.9
COMBINATION pepperoni, beef, sausage, mushroom, green pepper & onion	5.25	9.9
SHRIMP SPECIAL with mushroom & pineapple	5.75	10.6
DICKSON SPECIAL jalepeno, mushroom, onion & can. bacon	5.75	10.6
PORKER COMBO sausage, canadian bacon, pepperoni and extra cheese - jalepenos on request!	5.75	10.6
SALSA SUPREME beef and nacho stuff	5.95	10.9
FETA SPECIAL topped with feta cheese, chopped garlic and fresh mushrooms	5.95	10.9
Extra Ingredients (each)	.60	.9

choose from: beef, sausage, onion, mushroom, green pepper, pepperoni, black olive, jalapeno, spanish olive, canadian bacon, pineapple and shrim

BEER & WINE

PREMIUM BRANDS	$1.7
IMPORT, Corona & Heineken	2.2
DRAUGHT, Michelob & Classic Dark	
glass $1.00	pitcher 5.5
NAPA RIDGE, red, white zin, white	
glass $2.00	½ litre 7.2

ROTC menu, 1992

ROTC staff, 1995

Dickson Street looking west toward Gregson Lodge, 1980

all welcome at ROTC. Even Professor, Governor, and President Clinton visited ROTC occasionally. All were welcome as long as they ate something and behaved themselves. ROTC was also known as one of Dickson Street's unofficial art galleries. Long before the Walton Arts Center came to Dickson, people could go to ROTC to see some of Fayetteville's best artwork. With the rush to re-develop Dickson Street, ROTC and the neighboring Grill closed their restaurants, joined forces as The Corner Grill, and moved to Highway 112 in November 1998. The Grill and ROTC buildings were incorporated into the new Three Sisters complex.

Dickson Street looking west toward Gregson Lodge from 200 block, 1955

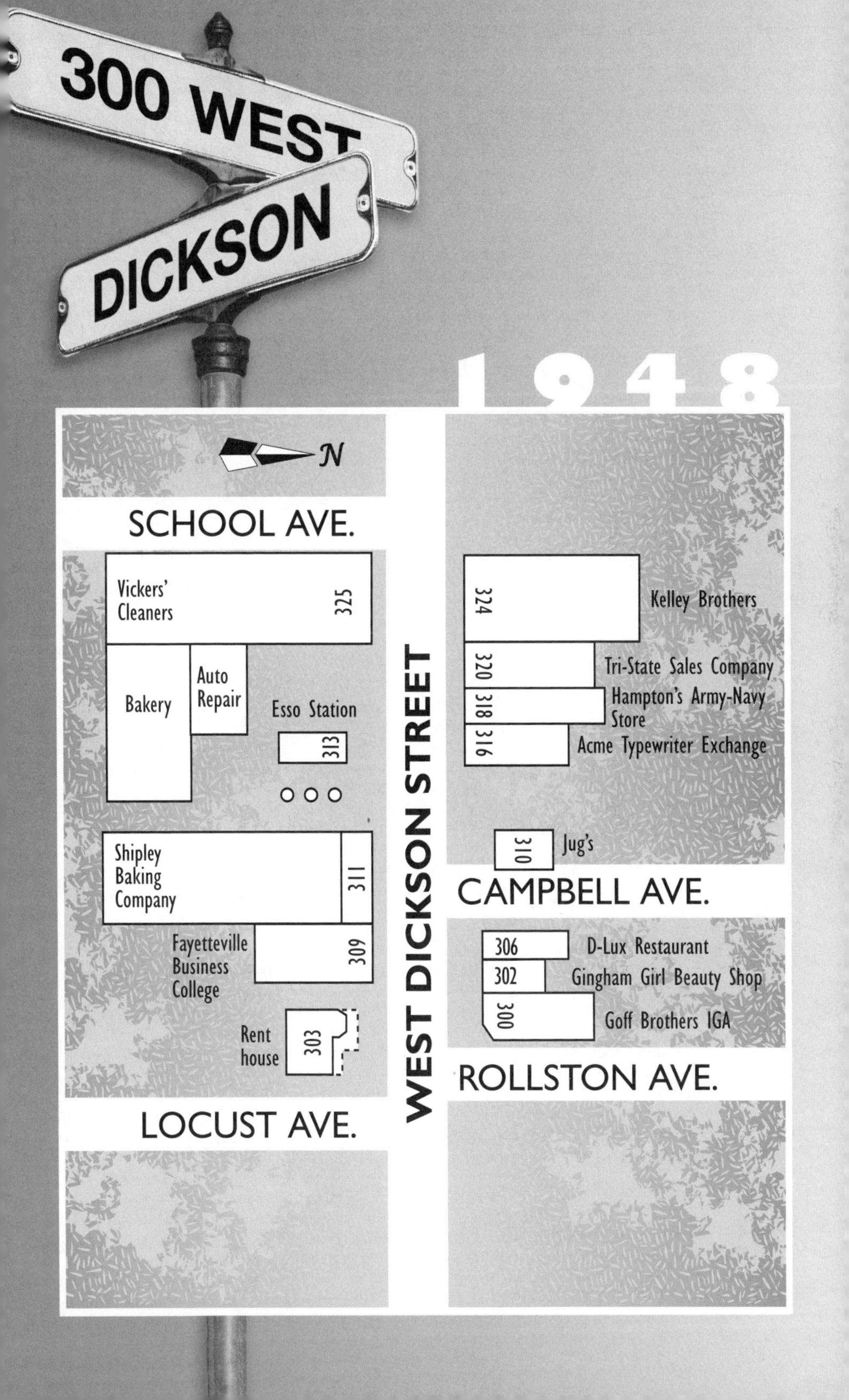

300 WEST
DICKSON
1948
N
SCHOOL AVE.
Vickers' Cleaners
325
Bakery
Auto Repair
Esso Station
313
Shipley Baking Company
311
Fayetteville Business College
309
Rent house
303
LOCUST AVE.
WEST DICKSON STREET
324
Kelley Brothers
320
Tri-State Sales Company
318
Hampton's Army-Navy Store
316
Acme Typewriter Exchange
310
Jug's
CAMPBELL AVE.
306
D-Lux Restaurant
302
Gingham Girl Beauty Shop
300
Goff Brothers IGA
ROLLSTON AVE.

300 WEST
DICKSON

1995

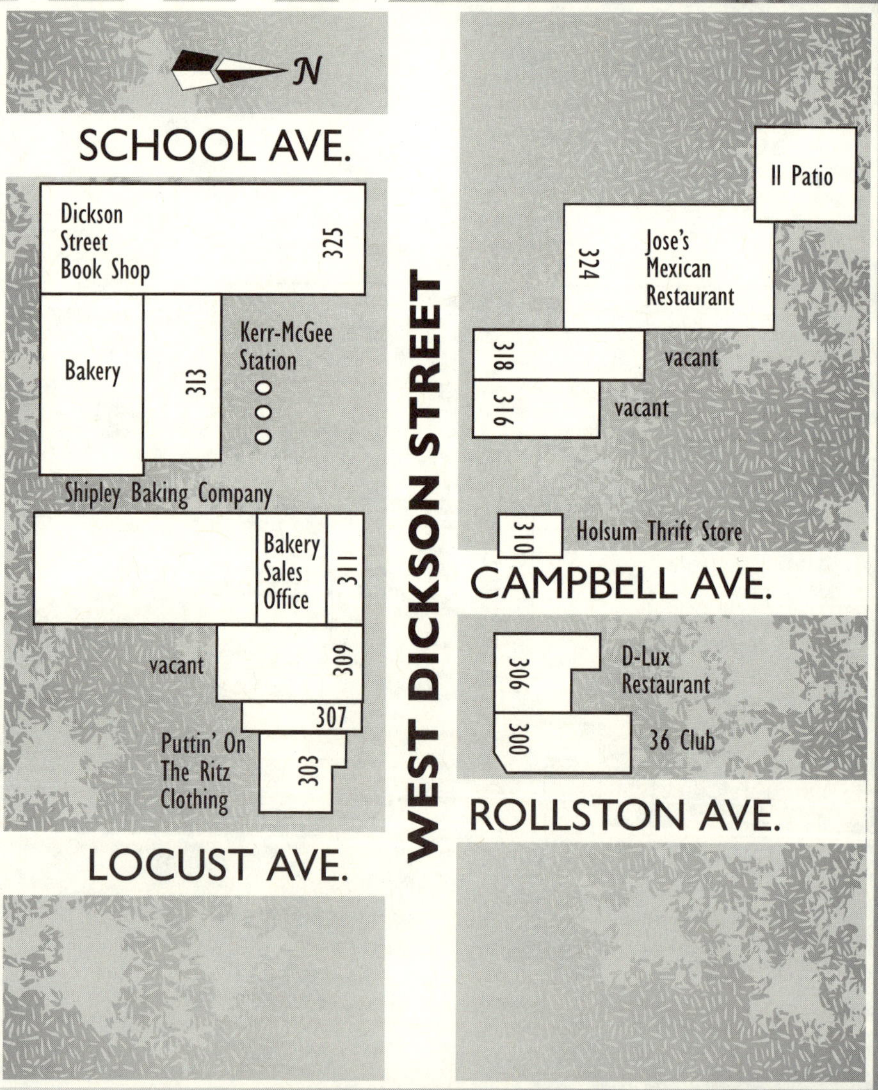
N
SCHOOL AVE.
Dickson Street Book Shop
325
Bakery
313
Kerr-McGee Station
Shipley Baking Company
Bakery Sales Office
311
vacant
309
307
Puttin' On The Ritz Clothing
303
LOCUST AVE.
WEST DICKSON STREET
Il Patio
324
Jose's Mexican Restaurant
318
vacant
316
vacant
310
Holsum Thrift Store
CAMPBELL AVE.
306
D-Lux Restaurant
300
36 Club
ROLLSTON AVE.

The 300 block of Dickson Street continues downhill toward Town Creek. Until the 1880s and 1890s, the Blakemore and Campbell families owned the undeveloped land here. The Blakemores, early Fayetteville settlers, owned most of the property on the south side of the street until 1885. The T. Murray Campbell family owned most of the north side of the street.

301–325 WEST DICKSON

Cazort Brothers

The first known development in the block took place around 1885, when the Cazort Brothers purchased the Blakemore property and constructed a large lumber yard there. J. R., W. A., and G. T. Cazort had their main offices in their home town, Cabin Creek, near Lamar (Johnson County), Arkansas. Nix & Company were their Fayetteville operators and Mr. Peeples was their agent. Around the turn of the century, the Cazort Brothers entered into a partnership with the Northwest Arkansas Lumber Company of Springdale and Fayetteville. Around 1921 this company abandoned the old Cazort Brothers lumber yard and consolidated its operations across the street at 324 West Dickson, which had been open since the late 1890s.

303 WEST DICKSON

John C. Mitchell

In 1894 John C. Mitchell purchased a portion of the Cazort Brothers property. He and his wife, Mary West, built the house on the southeast corner of Locust and Dickson, now 303 West Dickson. Born in Cane Hill in 1849, Mitchell was a school-teacher. From 1892 until 1896 he was principal of Washington Elementary School. In1896 he was elected Washington County Treasurer and held this position until 1900. Between 1900 and 1905 he

John C. Mitchell

303 West Dickson, 1995

was superintendent of the Fayetteville Public Schools and between 1899 and 1905 he was on the University of Arkansas Board of Trustees. As a trustee, Mitchell was instrumental in funding the construction of Carnall Hall, the girls' dormitory, built in 1904. In 1905 he opened the J. C. Mitchell Realty Company in the Arkansas National Bank building on the square. Prior to and during his career as realtor, Mitchell constructed several rent houses in the Dickson neighborhood, three on the north side of this block. Mrs. Mitchell, a native of Cincinnati, Arkansas, died in 1909. Mitchell lived at 303 West Dickson until 1911. After that, this property was a boarding house for some time. Since the 1970s, it has been occupied by several small businesses, including Puttin' on the Ritz clothing store.

309 WEST DICKSON
Fayetteville Business College

The Fayetteville Business College, founded in 1905 by Franz Newcombe, was purchased by H. O. Davis in 1919. It moved to what was known as the Fulbright Building at 309 West Dickson Street in 1937 and remained at that location until 1972. In later years, his son, Frank W. Davis, was manager. Between 1919 and 1972, when it closed, more than fifteen thousand students were trained for positions in the business world. Advertised as "The School You Like," the Fayetteville Business College offered modern and practical courses in machine accounting, civil service, salesmanship, shorthand, typewriting, secretarial training, and Dictaphone. Numerous short-lived businesses have occupied this site since then.

H.O. Davis

Fayetteville Business College, 1940s

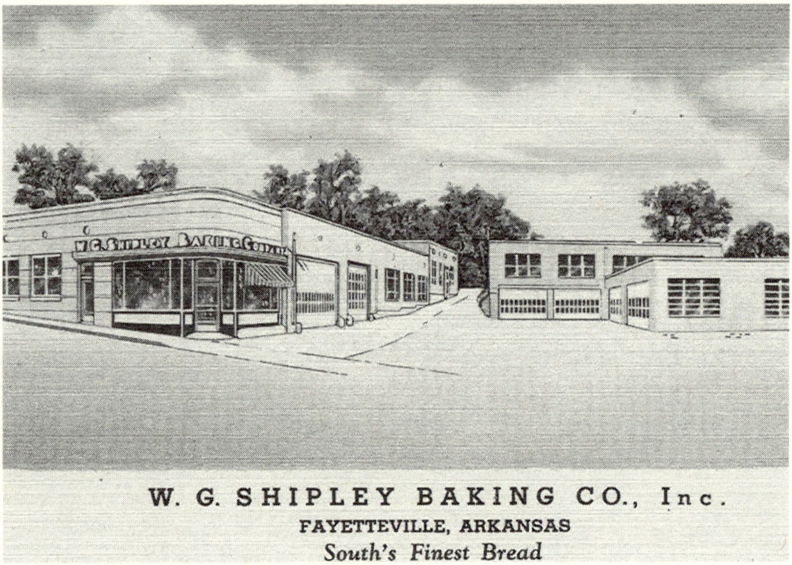

Shipley Baking Company, 1950s

311 WEST DICKSON
Shipley Baking Company

311 West Dickson became the home of Shipley Baking Company in 1937. Established in Fort Smith in 1921 by brothers Harry and Garvin Shipley, the company's Fayetteville history begins in 1926, when the Shipleys purchased the Crow Baking Company on the south side of the square. From there they moved to a plant on North School Street and in December 1937 they opened the "Model Bakery of the South" at 311 West Dickson. It was a two level "banana blend" modernistic brick building with a curved front and art-deco aluminum letters spelling out the company name. When it opened, the bakery employed twenty people and had an annual payroll of $25,000.

In 1945 the Fayetteville bakery became the property of Garvin Shipley, his wife, Grace Cotton, and their daughters, Grace Cowan and Martha Leach. In 1958 Harry Shipley of Fort Smith purchased Garvin Shipley's interests in the Fayetteville bakery. In 1962 his son Curtis took over operations in Fayetteville. For many years, Shipley Baking Company was known as the home of the Holsum Buttereg and Honey-Crust Wheat Bread. Shipley Baking Company produced a variety of specialty breads, cakes, and pies and for most of its history was the leading wholesale baker

To These Men Who Have Given So Much We Can Give So Little—A Job

CLINTON BOWLES, Baker; BUSTER BRANTLEY, Salesman; HOWARD S. COWAN, A. P. Correspondent; GREGG WILSON, Bookkeeper; FRANK S. LEACH, Asst. Manager; TRANT DAVIS, Baker; LEONARD G. LICHLYTER, Salesman; RALPH COKER, Baker

MELVIN SPENCE, Salesman; JAMES E. McCORMICK, Salesman; JAMES G. PARKS, Wrapping Machine Operator; CECIL EVANS, Utility Man; BURTON NOBLE, Baker; COY DURNING, Baker; FLOYD E. TRICE, Baker

The Lord has blessed us by returning the above 15 "Doughboys" to us safely after we had loaned them to the Services of Our Country. These men played an active part in bringing Peace to a War-Torn World, not only in England, France and in the air over Africa, but in the thousand islands of the vast hot sweltering Pacific. These "Doughboys" have returned to work and we can say so little, yet our hearts are so swelled with joy and pride that the only words we can think of is: "Thanks for a Job well done. The Lord answered our prayers for every one of you."

W. G. SHIPLEY BAKING COMPANY

311 West Dickson Street — Fayetteville, Arkansas

Shipley Baking Company ad, 1946

and bread distributor in Northwest Arkansas and Eastern Oklahoma. Their long-time slogan was "Don't Say Bread, Say Holsum."

Many Dickson Street regulars not only remember the great smell of fresh baked bread, but also recall many a day when Curtis Shipley stopped traffic while navigating large bread trucks into the bakery's loading area.

Shipley Baking Company, 1995

The Fayetteville bakery stopped production in 1991 but kept their sales and distribution offices on the site until 1997, when the property was redeveloped into a multi-purpose center featuring a bakery, a restaurant, galleries, and small shops.

313 WEST DICKSON

Esso Service Station

In 1932 the Bates Brothers opened a branch of the Standard Oil Company next door to Shipley Baking Company. In 1937 M. C. Maxwell purchased it and established the Dickson Street Esso Station. The station originally handled Esso and Essolene gasoline and Esso and Essolube motor oils. This was one of the first stations on Dickson to have a rotary lift. During the 1940s and 1950s the station was owned by Buck Spyres. During the 1950s and 1960s Lee & McWhorter owned it. In the late 1960s and 1970s it was known as Lee's Esso Service Center, and in 1973, following the changes in Standard Oil's corporate structure, Lee's Exxon Service Center. In 1990 the station affiliated with the Kerr-McGhee Oil Company. It was known as Dave's Kerr-McGee after the owner, Dave Letsch. It was demolished in 1997 to make way for the Bakery shopping complex.

Kerr-McGee gas station, 1995

Vickers Cleaners, 1923

325 WEST DICKSON
Vickers/Woodruff Cleaners

In 1911 Roy Vickers opened a small tailoring and dry-cleaning shop at 408 West Dickson. In 1922 he moved to a larger facility at 323–325 West Dickson, the present home of the Dickson Street Book Shop. In 1941 Hot Springs cleaner and launderer Preston Woodruff purchased the business.

Vicker's delivery trucks, 1940s

Shortly after they got started, the United States entered World War II, and, according to his son Ron, it was next to impossible to get replacement parts for the older equipment they had bought from Vickers. During the war Preston Woodruff often used his bicycle to make deliveries, although later he acquired a fleet of delivery trucks. Woodruff's provided the standard services of laundry and cleaning, and also tinted and dyed suede and leather jackets, laundered rugs, and cleaned hats.

Preston Woodruff

In its busiest years, Woodruff's employed as many as eighty-five people, but it was a classic family business. Ron's father, Preston Woodruff, operated the cleaning equipment; his grandfather Robert, better known as Poppy, operated the laundry equipment, and his mother Kathryn and sister-in-law Carol took care of the books. Other than time spent in the service, Ron worked as a cleaner almost literally from birth until the business closed. His brother, Preston Jr., worked as a launderer. Ron's former wife (current Washington County Circuit Clerk) Bette Stamps, also worked as a seamstress, originally from home, while caring for the couple's two children. Bette hemmed leather and suede skirts and ROTC men's pants and performed alterations and repairs. Later on, she bagged the dry cleaning. Grandmother Ina Woodruff ran the house and did the cooking. In addition to serving the general population, Woodruff's

Snowstorm, 1969

Dickson Street Bookshop exterior, 1995

did the cleaning and laundry for all of Fayetteville's motels and hospitals. Woodruff's closed in 1976.

Dickson Street Bookshop

In 1979 Donald Choffel and Charles O'Donnell opened the Dickson Street Bookshop at 318 West Dickson Street. In 1988 they moved across the street to 323–325 West Dickson, the former home of Woodruff's Cleaners. Since then, the shop has expanded southward to occupy the entire building. The Dickson Street Bookshop stocks more than 60,000 volumes, including many rare Arkansas and general-interest books and first editions and a very large collection of paperbacks. They also buy and trade books and offer out-of-print search service.

300–324 WEST DICKSON

Campbell

The family of T. Murray Campbell owned most of the property on the north side of the street until the early 1890s. Campbell was Mayor of Fayetteville in 1871 and 1872, and was the uncle of Judge Frank Campbell, who lived in the 400 block of East Dickson Street. T. Murray Campbell's house was near the present day location of Jose's.

Mayor Campbell

Choffel and O'Donnell, Dickson Street Bookshop, 1990s

300–306 WEST DICKSON
"Your Drive-In Block"

When the federal government decided in the early Thirties to build a Veterans' Hospital in Fayetteville, local developer Earle Bates believed that the town was on the verge of an economic boom. In 1932 he began construction of what he called "Your Drive-In Block" and caused this slogan to be imbedded in stone above the entrance. The new building, on the northeast corner of Dickson and Rollston, contained Needham's IGA, a succession of beauty shops, and, most recently, the D-Lux Restaurant. The yellow brick facade harmonized with other buildings on the street.

Your Drive-In Block, 1930s

300 WEST DICKSON

Needhams / King's Food Market

Originally known as Needham's IGA, the grocery at 300 West Dickson became King's Food Market in 1933. It was known as the first drive-up grocery in Fayetteville. Owned by Loyd Cate and Olive King, King's was known for their Kansas City meats and fresh vegetables. It remained on the corner of Rollston and Dickson until 1946, when the Kings moved up the street to 216 West Dickson. Goff Brothers IGA took over the location, but in 1953 they too moved out, to a new building on the northwest corner of College and Lafayette, later occupied by the Auto Zone parts store.

302 WEST DICKSON

Gingham Girl Beauty Shop

Several beauty shops operated at 302 West Dickson (which is now the upper part of the former D-Lux Restaurant.) Alice's, Janes, Gingham Girl, Chatter Box, and Lewis & Rada Beauty Salon # 2 called 302 West Dickson home until 1968, when Pat and Helen Martin expanded the Deluxe Restaurant. Alice Dorsett owned and operated Alice's Beauty Shoppe between

King's Food Market ad, 1937

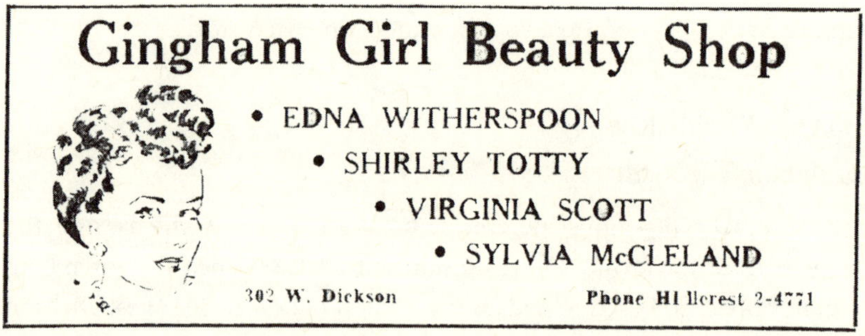

Gingham Girl Beauty Shop ad, 1947

Alice's Beauty Shoppe ad, 1941; Chatter Box Beauty Shop ad, 1962

1932 and 1941. The Gingham Girl shop had four chairs. Between 1945 and 1959, owners included Nina and Lee Little, Edna Witherspoon, and Helen Roff. Edna Witherspoon offered night time appointments; her slogan was "Large Enough for Your Needs, Small Enough to Appreciate Your Business."

306 WEST DICKSON

Deluxe Restaurant

The Deluxe Restaurant, known as the Chew & Chat between 1932 and 1934, was originally housed in a previous building at the same site. It re-opened in the present building on June 2, 1937.

To mark the event, the original owner, Jug Wheeler, offered free beer and sandwiches to his customers. This restaurant is perhaps one of the more endearing landmarks on West Dickson Street. Wheeler offered curbside service,

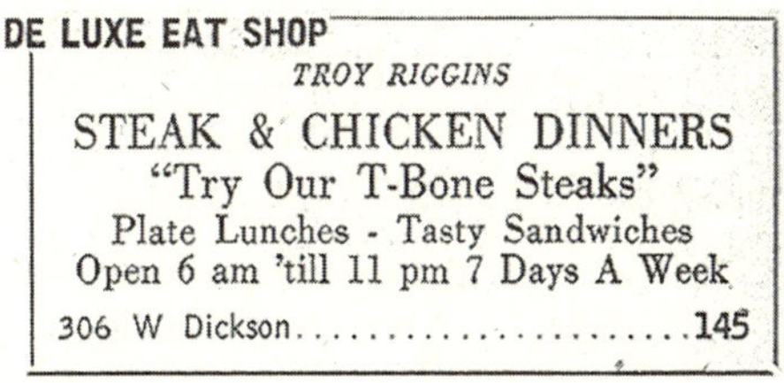

above: *De Luxe ad, 1949*
right: *De Lux ad, 1970s*

De Luxe Eat Shop Grand-Opening ad, 1937

appropriate to "Your Drive In Block," and had ample parking west of the building. In 1947 Wheeler opened Wheeler's Drive-In one door west and sold the Deluxe to Toy and Mabel Riggins.

They owned it until 1960, when Perry and Eva West purchased the business. In 1968 Pat and Helen Martin purchased the D-Lux, expanded it, taking over the space formerly occupied by the beauty parlor at 302 West Dickson, and added a game room at 300 West Dickson, the former site of King's Food Market. At some time in this interval, the spelling of the name was changed to reflect the accepted pronunciation, "dee-lux." Between the 1960s and 1980s the D-Lux was famous for its cheeseburgers, steak sandwiches, rubens, French fries and pitchers of cold beer. They also provided live musical entertainment in the basement, known as the Rathskeller. In 1986 the Martins sold the property to Anita Leflett. She established the 1936 Club and Cafe in the space formerly occupied by the game room. She sold the D-Lux and "36 Club" in 1993. Today the D-Lux is known as the Early Berlin Restaurant.

36 Club interior, 1990s

Your Drive-In Block, 1997

308–314 WEST DICKSON
Bear State Oil Company

Between 1913 and 1926, Bear State Oil Company occupied a moderate-size building at what was 314 West Dickson, selling "Bearcat Gasoline" and "Ozark Oils & Greases." Bear State's regional offices for Northwest Arkansas were in Rogers, and this company enjoyed the longest occupancy of the building. In the last known year of its existence in Fayetteville, the Bear State Oil Company was run by Hosea L. Williams, a resident of the 200 block of East Dickson. It was followed by Continental, Marathon, and Lion Oil Companies, as well as the A. B. Smith Tire Company. For a few years it housed the O.K. Taxi Company terminal. Around 1941 the Bear State Oil Company lot was demolished and replaced with a smaller building.

The Bear State Oil Company

LOCAL OFFICE--FAYETTEVILLE, ARK.
H. L. WILLIAMS, Agent
314 West Dickson St. Telephone 608

BEARCAT GASOLINE
OZARK OILS and GREASES

"QUALITY--SERVICE"

PATRONIZE A HOME COMPANY

GENERAL OFFICES
ROGERS, ARKANSAS

DISTRIBUTING STATIONS	DISTRIBUTING STATIONS
Eureka Springs	Siloam Springs
Fayetteville	Grove, Okla.
Springdale	Harrison
Gravette	Everton
Leslie	Rogers

Bear State Oil Company ad, 1922

O.K. Taxi ad, 1945

310 WEST DICKSON
Jug's/George's Brown Derby

By 1947 there were too many cars on Dickson Street for the DeLuxe to continue its curbside service. So owner Jug Wheeler constructed a drive-in on the site. Jug's was famous for hickory-smoked barbecued ribs, fried chicken, and a greasy and delicious foot-long hot dog. In addition to offering fountain service, Wheeler's was the first in Fayetteville to have tele-tray service in the parking lot. They also provided home delivery and catering. Most important, Jug's was the only eatery in Fayetteville to serve beer drive-in style. During the 1950s it was common to "buzz Jug's."

Wheeler's, 1950s

left: *Wheeler's ad, 1958;*
right: *George's ad, 1965*

According to several long-time residents, there was a certain hierarchy of parking spaces around Jug's. The hot cars and motorcycles parked in front near the street and the DeLuxe where they were headed downhill and could show off more chrome, color, engine, etc. The greasers and long-hairs parked back toward Tri-State on Campbell Avenue. The girls parked behind Jug's on the north side of the building and the college kids parked on the west side.

In 1964 Joe Hinton, husband of Mary Hinton, the owner of George's Majestic Lounge, purchased Wheeler's and renamed it George's Derby Drive-In. It was known for its broasted chicken, and barbecue. George's Derby Drive-In closed in 1969. Joe Hinton had another drive-in on College Avenue called the Top Hat, offering essentially the same menu.

Holsum Thrift Store

Between 1970 and 1997 the building at 310 West Dickson became the Holsum Thrift Store, also known as Shipley's "day-old" store, with bargains from the bakery across the street that were past their "sell-by" dates. After the bakery closed, the building was converted into office space. The property was redeveloped beginning in 2004 as Bordino's Restaurant.

Holsum Thrift Store, 1992

316–318 WEST DICKSON

City Bakery

Around 1915 the building at 316 West Dickson became known as John Seamster's City Bakery Company. By 1919 Seamster had greatly expanded, remodeled, and subdivided it into two business houses—which became known as 316 and 318 West Dickson. City Bakery, which then moved to 318 West Dickson, carried a variety of breads and pastries, including Butter-Nut Bread. It remained in operation until 1932. Original stone walls are clearly visible on the west side of this building, which is currently the home of Doe's Eat Place.

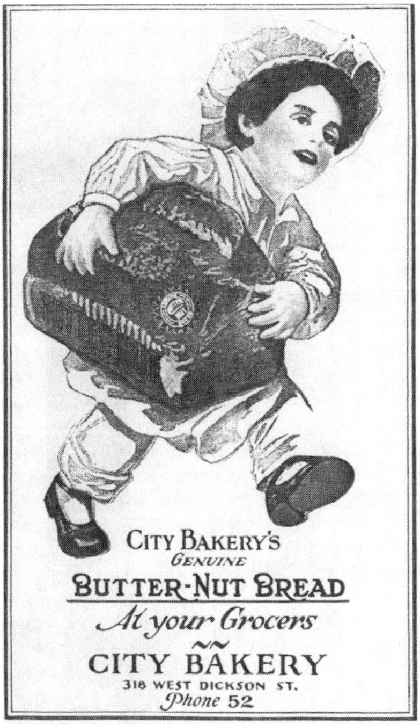

City Bakery ad, 1927

Star Grocery

The other part of the divided building, 316 West Dickson, was the site of Star Grocery between 1919 and 1937. Run by H. J. Dever, Star Grocery carried everything in the line of groceries, as well as fancy candies, cakes, and fruits. Portions of the original stone foundation and wall of the expanded building can still be seen in the area behind this address.

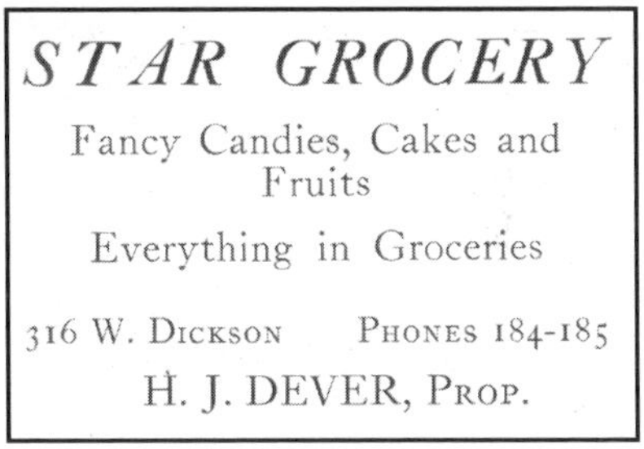

Star Grocery ad, 1922

Since the 1930s the buildings at 316–318 West Dickson have had many short-term occupants, including the medical offices of Dr. Fount Richardson and the U.S. Navy, Marine, and Army recruiting offices. The Dickson Street Book Shop started out in this location before moving across the street.

Puttin' on the Ritz second hand clothing store, 1980s

320 WEST DICKSON
McCormick Meat Market

James McCormick opened McCormick Meat Market in 1903 at 320 West Dickson, near the present location of Jose's. This meat market advertised that it handled only the freshest meats available. In 1910 McCormick sold it to H. J. Dever, who, in a few years, also would own the Star Grocery Company one door east. Dever changed the name to Arkansas Meat Market Company, and it remained at 320 West Dickson until 1925.

McCormick & McConnel

Handle only the

FRESHEST MEATS

Quick Delivery

WEST DICKSON

McCormick ad, 1909

Tri-State Sales

In 1932 Otto "Tobe" Gage founded the Tri-State Sales Company, which distributed coin-operated machines. In 1939 Gage began selling and servicing jukeboxes, radios, pinball machines, and appliances. Two years later, he moved the company to a two-story brick building at 320 West Dickson. In 1949 he added television sets to his stock. According to Gage, Tri-State sold and serviced the first television set in Fayetteville. In 1955 Gage split the company. The television sales and service were incorporated under the name of Enterprise T.V., Inc. at 320 West Dickson, where Gage remodeled the shop and added a lounge for viewing television sets. A year later this business moved to College Avenue. Gage then moved his coin-operated machine operation to 315 Rollston, just off Dickson, where it remained until the early 1990s.

TRI-STATE SALES COMPANY

Distributors of

Coin Machine – Sales Boards

Sales and Service

Electrical Appliances – Business Machines

—We Rent Music Machines For Private Parties—

320 West Dickson Phone 513

Tri-State Sales ad, 1945

324 WEST DICKSON

Northwest Arkansas Lumber Company

Around 1895 the Northwest Arkansas Lumber Company built a large brick building at 324 West Dickson, the current location of Jose's. Established in 1885 and incorporated in 1898, their main office was originally in Springdale. They acquired the property of the old Cazort Brothers lumber yard across the street at 319–325 West Dickson, but gradually built a very extensive lumber plant and storage facilities (almost three acres) in the rear of the north side of the 300 block of West Dickson. This yard included much of the property between Dickson and Watson Streets, where patrons of Jose's and other current Dickson Street establishments frequently park. The Northwest Arkansas Lumber Company, originally owned by C. W. Phelps, J. P. Deaver, and R. H. Johnson, was the largest wholesale and retail dealer and manufacturer of lumber, mill work, and glass in Northwest Arkansas. One of the company's specialties was the manufacture of wooden boxes for packing fruit grown by local farmers. In the 1920s, it employed as many as twenty-five people who were dedicated to the company's slogan: "We Make It Right."

Northwest Arkansas Lumber Company ad, 1904

Kelley Brothers Lumber Company

In 1921 the Kelley brothers, Roy, Clarence J., and Harry, purchased the Northwest Arkansas Lumber Company. They had started out in Madison County in 1914 and had mills in Clifty, Huntsville, and Springdale, and the Hill City Lumber company in Fayetteville. One of their longtime slogans was "Kelley Kwality." They provided customers with all of their lumber and building needs, such as millwork, cabinets, roofing, insulation, paint, cement, and glass. From Day One, Kelley Brothers also were distributors of Sherwin-Williams Paints. They moved to North Gregg Street in 1965, where they were later bought out by Meeks Lumber Company.

above left: *Homecoming float, 1936*

below left: *Kelley Brothers Lumber Company ad, 1942*

324 West Dickson
Kelley Brothers Building Burns

Between 1969 and 1971 the former Kelley Brothers building was occupied by Dennis Home Furniture. In 1971 the Oldham Furniture Company occupied the building until August 30 of that year, when fire devastated the seventy-five- year-old building and the neighboring building at 320 West Dickson Street. Damage was estimated at $100,000. The fire also damaged the roof of the neighboring Fashion Shop Cleaners and was so hot that it shattered the glass panels of Lee's Esso Station and Woodruff's Cleaners across the street. To the satisfaction of many who opposed the war in Vietnam, the fire also threatened the neighboring military recruiting offices. Firefighters were booed when they saved these buildings. Firefighters battled the fire, which was believed to have been the work of an arsonist, for nearly six hours. A large crowd gathered to watch, which reportedly gave the neighboring Hob Nob Liquor Store one of its best nights in years.

Minute Man/Speakeasy

In 1973 Fred Bourbon and Dick Gray opened the Minute Man Restaurant at 324 West Dickson. A franchise of the Minute Man Restaurant in Little Rock, this pre-dated McDonald's arrival in Fayetteville. The burgers were much larger here and the Minute Man had a pool room. In addition to the

Speakeasy ad, 1975

Minuteman ad, 1973

owners, long-time Fayetteville attorney John Logan Burrow and retired SWEPCO employee Tracy Menifee ran the restaurant. The Minute Man and the short-lived Speakeasy occupied the site until 1980.

Jose's

Joe Fennel opened Jose's on March 5, 1980, as an 82-seat Mexican restaurant employing eleven people. Jose's was considered by many the best place in town for live bands, beer, and cheap Mexican food. Until the mid-80s, Jose's and Flying Possum Leather co-sponsored an annual "Suds 'n' Sandals" party, featuring beer and Birkenstocks. Bands including Jed Clampit, the Ozark Plantation Band and Cookbook played every night. In 1983, Fennel introduced the killer margarita, which became the restaurant's signature drink.

In 1992, Fennel added an outdoor patio and later started serving Italian food in a small restaurant at the rear of the building. One year after its opening, Il Patio was renamed Bordino's and subsequently became an entirely separate operation east of Jose's on the site of Jug Wheeler's drive-in. In 1997 Fennel's outdoor patio area was reborn as Jose's Streetside. Neal Crawford, longtime employee and partner, is the present owner of Jose's.

right: *"Enjoying the Band" at Jose's, 1982*
below: *Jose's, 1995*

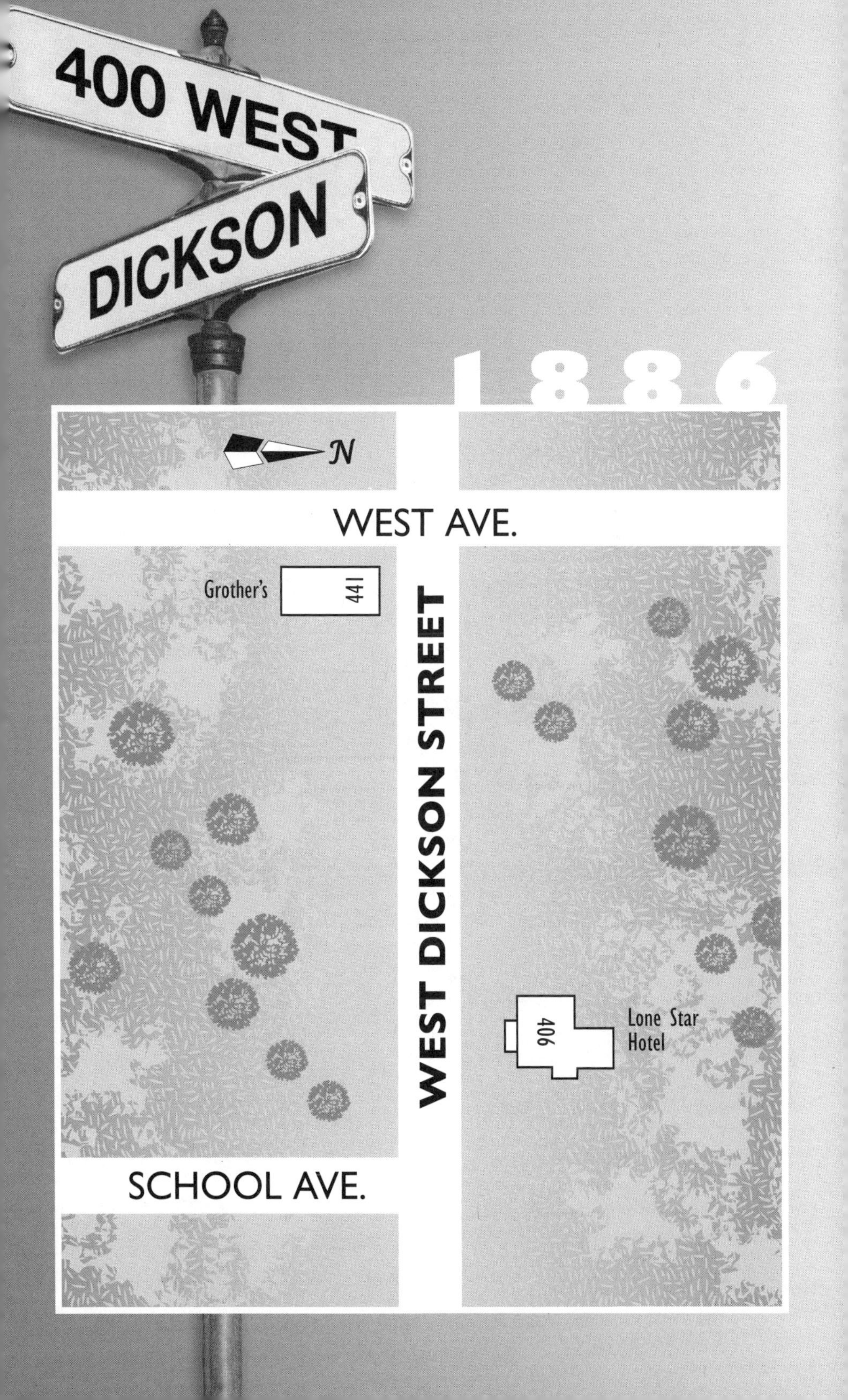

400 WEST
DICKSON
1886
N
WEST AVE.
Grother's
441
WEST DICKSON STREET
406
Lone Star Hotel
SCHOOL AVE.

400 WEST
DICKSON

1908

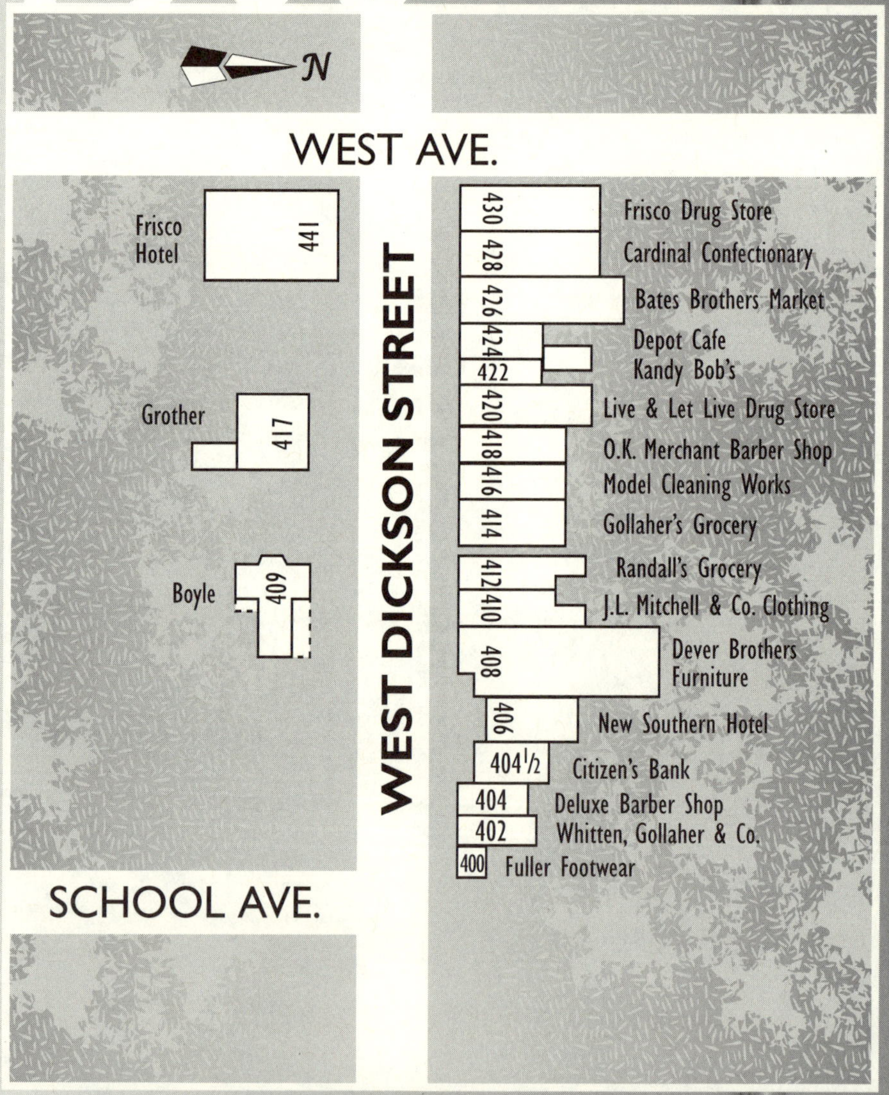

N
WEST AVE.
WEST DICKSON STREET
SCHOOL AVE.
Frisco Hotel
441
Grother
417
Boyle
409
430 Frisco Drug Store
428 Cardinal Confectionary
426 Bates Brothers Market
424 Depot Cafe
422 Kandy Bob's
420 Live & Let Live Drug Store
418 O.K. Merchant Barber Shop
416 Model Cleaning Works
414 Gollaher's Grocery
412 Randall's Grocery
410 J.L. Mitchell & Co. Clothing
408 Dever Brothers Furniture
406 New Southern Hotel
404½ Citizen's Bank
404 Deluxe Barber Shop
402 Whitten, Gollaher & Co.
400 Fuller Footwear

400 WEST
DICKSON

1948

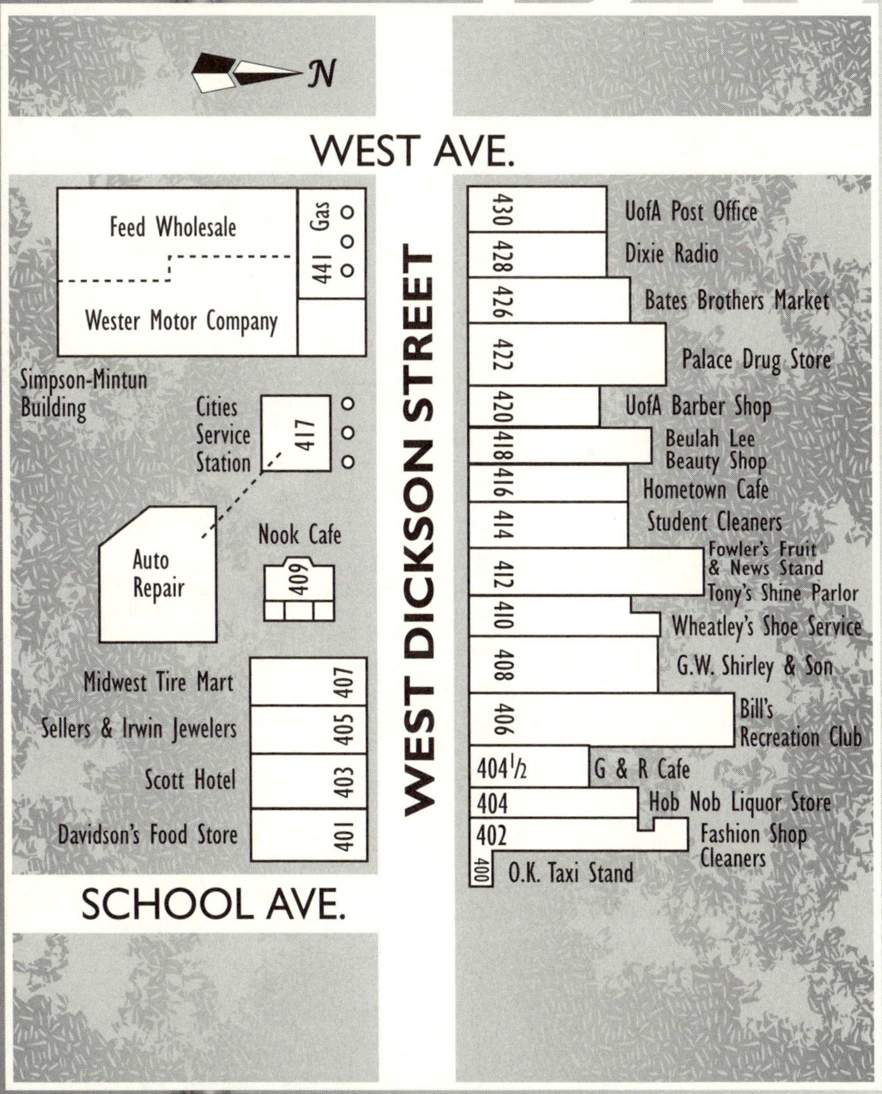
N
WEST AVE.
WEST DICKSON STREET
SCHOOL AVE.
Feed Wholesale
Wester Motor Company
441
Gas
Simpson-Mintun Building
Cities Service Station
417
Auto Repair
Nook Cafe
409
Midwest Tire Mart
407
Sellers & Irwin Jewelers
405
Scott Hotel
403
Davidson's Food Store
401
430 UofA Post Office
428 Dixie Radio
426 Bates Brothers Market
422 Palace Drug Store
420 UofA Barber Shop
418 Beulah Lee Beauty Shop
416 Hometown Cafe
414 Student Cleaners
412 Fowler's Fruit & News Stand
Tony's Shine Parlor
410 Wheatley's Shoe Service
408 G.W. Shirley & Son
406 Bill's Recreation Club
404½ G & R Cafe
404 Hob Nob Liquor Store
402 Fashion Shop Cleaners
400 O.K. Taxi Stand

400 WEST
DICKSON

1995

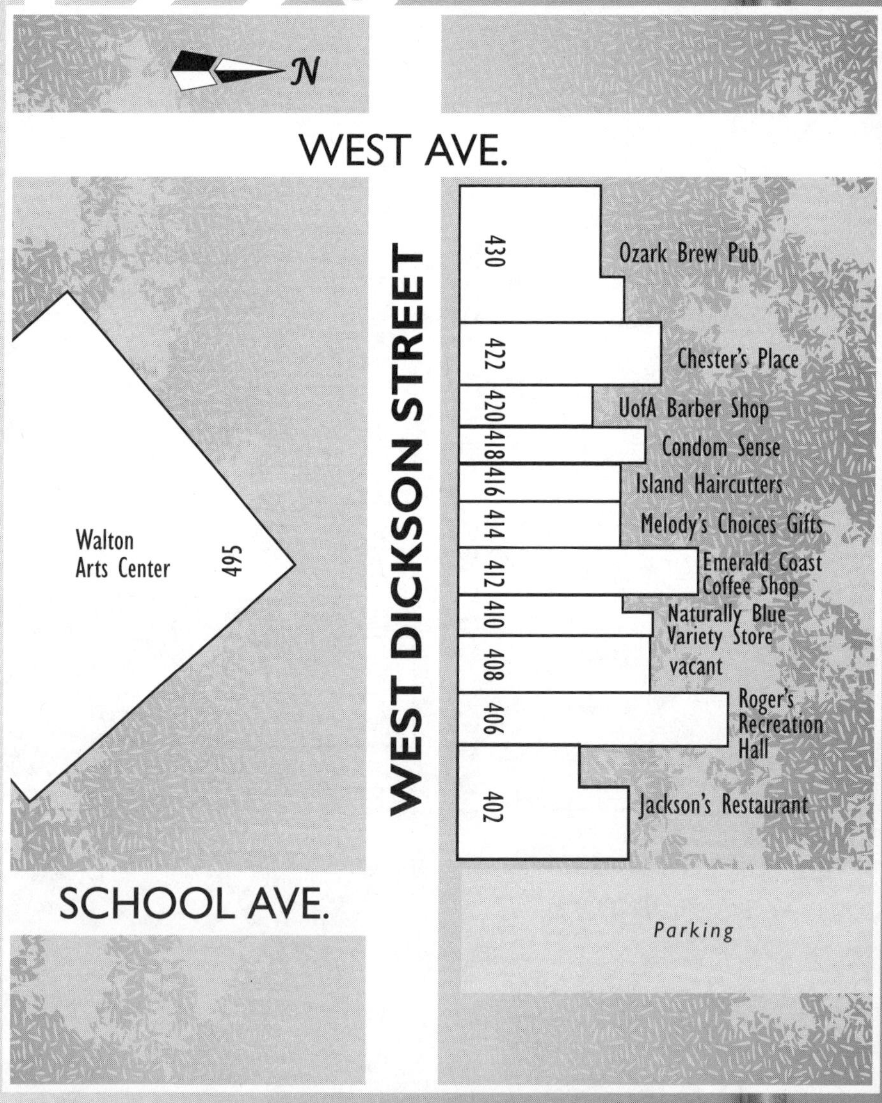

N
WEST AVE.
WEST DICKSON STREET
SCHOOL AVE.
Walton Arts Center
495
430 Ozark Brew Pub
422 Chester's Place
420 UofA Barber Shop
418 Condom Sense
416 Island Haircutters
414 Melody's Choices Gifts
412 Emerald Coast Coffee Shop
410 Naturally Blue Variety Store
408 vacant
406 Roger's Recreation Hall
402 Jackson's Restaurant
Parking

Perhaps the most famous block of Dickson Street is the 400 block. Here Dickson Street makes it final descent to Town Creek. Until the mid-1880s and early 1890s, the area consisted of undeveloped pasture. The T. Murray Campbell family, who resided in the 300 block, owned much of the property on the north side. Several families, including those of Wilburn D. Reagan, Dr. A. S. Gregg, and Henry Grother, owned property on the south side of the street. Shortly after the arrival of the Frisco Railroad, the 400 block began to develop into a small commercial district catering to travelers arriving at the depot one block west. A hotel and grocery were the first businesses to locate here, both established by 1886.

The 400 block experienced a boom in the 1890s and early 1900s, when it began to develop into the commercial district it is today. Businesses on the north side of Dickson during this period included a bank, two barber shops, three clothing stores, two laundries, two shoe stores, three feed stores, a bakery, three groceries, two drugstores, and five restaurants. The south side of the street included two large rooming houses. Some of the early occupants included the Southern Hotel, Frisco Hotel, Frisco Drug, Citizens Bank, Mitchell & Company, OK Merchant (U of A) Barber Shop, Live & Let Live (Palace) Drugstore, and Bates Brothers Market. A few of these remained on Dickson for several decades, most lasting into the 1940s and 1950s. The U of A Barber Shop did not leave Dickson until 1998!

400 WEST DICKSON

U of A Cafe

John C. Martin, George E. Elderton, and W. Elbert Martin opened the U of A Cafe at 418 West Dickson in 1918. If it was good to eat, the U of A Cafe had it. The cafe offered both regular meals (plate lunches) and short orders (sandwiches) and was open twenty-four hours a day. In 1921 the cafe moved to 412 West Dickson. In 1922 Roy Marshall purchased it and temporarily renamed it the White Way Cafe to honor the installation of street lights down Dickson Street (see earlier description of the White Way). James Campbell purchased the cafe in 1925 and moved the U of A Cafe to a *very* small square building at 400 West Dickson. (This building

400–404 West Dickson, 1995

was most recently used for Springfest activities until being demolished in 1994.) Between 1930 and 1945, when it closed, Ben Shiley ran the cafe. According to long-time residents, the U of A Cafe had stools and a built-in counter on one side of the building. The other side had a stove and grill where the cook prepared short order meals.

402–404 WEST DICKSON
Fashion Shop Cleaners

Guy W. Pinkerton opened the Fashion Shop Cleaners at 402 West Dickson Street in 1922. He and his brother, Ralph, ran it until retiring in 1974 and 1975, respectively. Fashion

The Fashion Shop ad, 1926

Shop tailored, dry and steam cleaned, pressed, altered, and dyed all types of fine clothing. The Fashion Shop also had prompt and courteous delivery. Their motto was "Not How Cheap, But How Clean." Before closing in the 1970s, the Fashion Shop cleaners also rented costumes.

Hob Nob Liquor Store

W. T. Adams opened the Hob Nob Liquor Store at 404 West Dickson in 1935, two years after the repeal of prohibition. Between the 1940s and 1970s it was owned by Guy W. Pinkerton, who also co-owned and operated the Fashion Shop Cleaners one door east. The Hob Nob, "where high spirits prevailed at low prices," carried moderately priced imported and domestic wines and liquor, gin, cognac, champagne, and brandy. The Hob Nob, one of Fayetteville's most popular liquor stores, also had cold beer to go. Before closing in 1983, the Hob Nob was also owned by James House and Evelyn Hileman. Since the 1970s and 1980s 402–404 West Dickson has been home to numerous short-lived restaurants and clubs.

Hob-Nob ad, 1940s

404½ WEST DICKSON

Citizens Bank

In 1907 Jay Fulbright, along with several other business people, opened a bank at 404½ West Dickson Street. Built by A. M. Byrnes, the original Citizens Bank building has been the bar portion of several restaurants and clubs, including the Dugout, Lily's, Jackson's, Art's Place, and now The

Dickson Street at night, 1977

Gypsy. Citizens Bank catered to the University of Arkansas community and other businesses in Shuler Town. By encouraging many residents to invest their money in building up their homes, Citizens Bank was an important factor in the development of Fayetteville. In 1925 Citizens Bank moved to 414 West Dickson Street, the current home of Melody's Choices. At that time Roberta Fulbright was president and Jobelle Holcomb was vice-president of the bank. Around 1942 Citizens Bank merged with First National Bank of Fayetteville, now part of the Bank of America.

During the 1930s and 1940s 404½ West Dickson was the home of Ozark Barber Shop. Dawn's Flowers was here during the 1960s and 1970s. A number of short-lived bars and clubs, including Lily's, shared space with 404 West Dickson since that time.

THE CITIZENS BANK

ONE YEAR OLD JUNE 3rd

The history of its first year's growth told in plain figures

Statement of condition at close of first day's business June 3rd, 1908

Resources		Liabilities	
LOANS	$ 500.00	Capital paid in	$ 10,000.00
Cash	11,641.13	Deposits	2,141.13
	$12,141.13		$12,141.13

SIX MONTHS LATER

Statement of condition at close of business December 3, 1908

Resources		Liabilities	
Loans	$21,085.43	Capital paid in	$10,000.00
Overdrafts	227.82	Int. and exchange	684.31
Furniture and Fixtures	605.00	Rediscount	2,500.00
Expense	1,152.98	Deposits	20,096.40
Cash	10,209.55		
	$33,280.78		$33,280.78

ONE YEAR LATER

Statement of condition at close of business June 2nd, 1909

(June 3rd having been a holiday)

Resources		Liabilities	
Loans	$28,613.53	Capital paid in	$10,000.00
OVERDRAFTS	79.48	Int. and exchange	2,060.68
Furniture and fixtures	780.00	Deposits	52,971.27
Expenses	1,952.21		
CASH	33,606.73		
	$65,031.95		$65,031.95

I, Guy Phillips, cashier of the above named bank, do solemnly swear that the above statement is true and correct to the best of my knowledge and belief; that no item contained therein has been enlarged for statement purposes; that none of the officers or directors or anyone else has given this bank any note or notes and have taken credit for same for the purpose of making the deposits appear larger than they actually are. The loans and deposits are all bona fide.

Guy Philips, Cashier.

Subscribed and sworn to before me this 3rd day of June, 1909.

E. L. Nettleship, Notary Public

My commission expires Dec 19, 1910.

63 per cent of the deposits in cash. Overdrafts less than 100 dollars. Deposits five times the paid capital. Increase of over 150 per cent in deposits in last six months. We ask your critical examination of the above statement and on the strength of it we solicit your patronage. No deposit is too small for us to receive. Watch us grow.

J. C. WHITE, *President* R. L. TAYLOR, *Cashier* RAY B. TILLEY, *Asst. Cashier*

Citizens Bank of Fayetteville

CAPITAL AND SURPLUS $20,000

The Most Convenient Bank for University Folk
Always Ready to Serve

4% Paid on Time and Savings Deposits

ON DIXON STREET

above: *Citizen's Bank financial statement, 1909*

left: *Citizen's Bank of Fayetteville ad, 1922*

Lily's, 1980s

406 WEST DICKSON
Southern Hotel

Operated by Leon Matney, the Lone Star Hotel opened in 1886. It was located in Mrs. Fane's old house at what would be known as 406 West Dickson, the current site of Roger's Rec. It is not certain what, if any, connection this hotel had with Texas. "Everything was clean and comfortable and their table was second to none." Rates at the Lone Star Hotel were $1.00 to $1.50 a day. By 1890 the Lone Star was known as the Southern Hotel. Around 1903 it was enlarged substantially and became the New Southern Hotel. Although the "new" was dropped after a few years, the Southern Hotel remained a stopping-off point for travelers arriving in Fayetteville via the Frisco. In 1911 the two-story, seventeen-room brick hotel was owned by John A. Lisko and boasted of city water, baths, and electric lights. It could accommodate twenty-five boarders. After twenty years rates were still $1.00 a day! The Southern Hotel remained at 406 West Dickson until 1929, when it burned.

Southern Hotel, 1911

Roger's Rec

Located at 406 West Dickson since 1947, Roger's Recreation Hall was originally known as Bill's Recreation Club, and then, between 1952 and 1954, as Dutche's Recreation Parlor. In 1954 Roger Koetter bought the pool hall and renamed it Roger's Rec. Since 1986 it has been owned by Bob "Swifty" Reynolds. Roger's has been known as the cheapest place in town to shoot a game of pool, play dominoes or shuffleboard, and drink ice cold beer. The walls of the long, narrow building are lined with beer posters, most featuring scantily clad women. Rogers appeals to a mix of people, including students, professors, bikers, lawyers, and ex-hippies reminiscing of days gone by.

Roger's Rec, 1980s

Tree Protest # 2

In 1900, the City of Fayetteville wanted to repair the sidewalks on West Dickson Street. One obstacle was the large elm tree in front of the Southern Hotel. Legend has it that the tree was a Fayetteville landmark and was mentioned in nineteenth- century land abstracts. The city insisted the tree had to be removed to keep the sidewalk from buckling. However, under protest from the proprietors of the Southern Hotel, as well as other Fayetteville residents, the city compromised. The owners of the Southern cut the roots of the tree so the sidewalk would not buckle and then were allowed to erect a decorative stone wall around the tree. This helped maintain a shady walk and helped keep the hotel cool during the summer.

For five years after fire destroyed the Southern Hotel, the tree remained. In 1934, J. A. Jones, a local contractor, constructed a new building near the former site of the Southern Hotel. He was very sensitive to the emotions aroused by saving the tree. Jones apologized to local residents for not being able to save the decorative wall but was able to save the beloved tree. The large tree remained until 1947, when it was cut down to make way for Bill Bartle's new Recreation Hall (currently Rogers Rec).

City Landmark To Be Uprooted

"We think that you shall never see this tree (pictured above) again" might well be the Fayetteville version of Kilmer's poem, but the fact that the huge elm is being cut down to make room for a business house is not the only reason why the photographer took the picture. This big timber on Dickson Street is a Fayetteville landmark dating from 'way back when, and probably is one of the city's most famous trees. The elm is mentioned in land abstract deeds, drawn up by Fayetteville pioneers as far back as 1834, which marked off property so many "posts from the old elm tree." But the city's progress necessitated the uprooting of the more-than-a-century old tree. Bill Bartle plans to build a new business building where the tree now stands. (Ed Puska Photo)

Tree at 406 West Dickson, 1947

408 WEST DICKSON

Acme Typewriter Exchange

David J. Feibleman opened Acme Typewriter Exchange at 407 West Dickson in 1948. In 1951 he bought out the Taylor Typewriter Service, which was also on Dickson Street. A few months later, Feibleman sold the business to Bill Weatherford, who moved Acme across the street to 408 West Dickson in 1964 and operated it until 1983. Between 1986 and 1989, when it left Dickson Street, the business was known as Northwest Office Equipment. Acme Typewriter Exchange sold and serviced Royal, Underwood, Smith Corona, and Remington Typewriters, as well as Victor adding machines and printing calculators. New, used, and portable typewriters were also available for rent.

Local Clubs Accused of Illegal Gaming

On April 4, 1968 a few Dickson Street merchants were arrested on charges involving gambling payoffs on pinball machines located in their businesses in the 400 block. One merchant was also charged with keeping a gaming house and betting on horses. Fayetteville police confiscated two pinball machines each from the Idle Hour Club, Paul's Recreation Club, and the Razorback Bowl. No pinball machines were taken from Rogers Recreation Hall, perhaps the most popular beer-only club on Dickson at the time.

Gambling raid, 1968

Acme Typewriter Exchange ad, 1955

410 WEST DICKSON
J. L. Mitchell/Simmons Brothers

In 1904 J. L. Mitchell, a son of J. C. Mitchell of the 300 block, opened a clothing store at 410 West Dickson. Mitchell was famous for his up-to-date line of gentlemen's furnishings and haberdashery. The store was an agent for the J. W. Losse tailoring company of St. Louis and the Nettleton & Thompson Shoe Company.

In 1918 Mitchell died of the Spanish influenza. After his death, Julian, Malcolm and Charles Simmons opened Simmons Brothers, another fine clothing store. They carried Wilson Brothers Shirts and Furnishings, Phoenix Hosiery, Mallory and Stetson Hats, and Thompson Brothers Shoes. In 1929 Simmons Brothers became the Razorback Toggery, which remained at this location until 1931.

February Clearance Sale

The Sale you have been waiting for opens

Thursday, Feb. 17th

With as many bargains as you have ever been able to enjoy. You can profit by taking advantage of this *Money Saving Opportunity*

ALL GOODS HAVE BEEN REDUCED—TERMS OF SALE CASH

Men's Shirts

LOT NO. 1—All Men's $2.00 and $2.50 Shirts; Clearance Sale Price.... $1.65

LOT NO. 2—All Men's $1.50 Wilson Bros. Shirts; Clearance Sale Price ... $1.05

LOT NO. 3—All Men's $1.50 Pleated Bosom Shirts; Clearance Sale Price 95c

LOT NO. 4—All Men's $1.00 Wilson Bros. Shirts; Clearance Sale Price 80c

LOT NO. 5—25 dozen assortment of Men's Shirts, worth up to $1.00; Clearance Sale Price 48c

Men's Neckwear

All $1.00 Neckwear; Clearance Sale Price 65c

All 50c Neckwear. Clearance Sale Price 40c

Spalding Sweaters

Reduced 20 per cent.

Men's Shoes

All Stetson $6.00 Shoes, Black or Tan; Clearance Sale Price $4.85

All Thompson Bros. $5.00 Bench Made Shoes; Clearance Sale Price $4.35

All Thompson Bros. $4.00 and $4.50 Shoes; Clearance Sale Price $3.25

All $3.00 and $3.50 Men's Shoes; Clearance Sale Price $2.55

130 pairs Shoes, no two pair alike, of Stetson, Nettleton and Thompson make; Clearance Sale Price $2.25

Men's Hosiery

All Wilson Bros. 50c Silk Hose; Clearance Sale Price 40c
(3 pair for $1.00)

All 25c Silk and Lisle values, any color; Clearance Sale Price 19c

Large assortment Men's Hose, grey, blue, tan, black, 15c, 2 for 25c values; Clearance Sale Price 7c

Men's Underwear

LOT NO. 1—All Cooper's Ribbed Wool Union Suits, $2.50 and $3.00 values; Clearance Sale Price ... $2.25

LOT NO. 2—All Cooper's and Wilson Bros. Pat. Closed Crotch Union Suits, worth $1.50; Sale Price $1.15

LOT NO. 3—All Wilson Bros. $1.00 Union Suits; Sale Price 80c

LOT NO. 4—All 2-piece garments go in this sale at
25 Per Cent Off

Men's Hats

All $3 Mallory Hats; Clearance Sale Price ... $2.35

All $2 Hats, any color; Clearance Sale Price ... $1.50

All Frank P. Heid $1.50 and $2.00 Caps; Clearance Sale Price ... $1.35

All $1.00 Heid Caps; Clearance Sale Price 75c

Remember the best always goes first—Come early
Terms of Sale Cash—We need the money, not the goods

J. L. MITCHELL

410 WEST DICKSON

J. L. Mitchell ad, 1916

University of Arkansas

These Three Sons of Alma Mater are Proud of Your Success in Service to the State. May Your Usefulness Continue and Magnify Until Time Ends.

Simmons Brothers

Men's Furnishing — West Dickson Street

University Home Comers Are Cordially Invited To Come In And Renew Old Ties

Simmons Brothers ad, 1922

Wright's=Shoe Repair Shop=Wheatley's

W. B. Wright sold and repaired shoes at many different locations on Dickson Street from the early 1900s until he retired in 1935. He catered to students and working class customers. Known as Wright's Electric Shoe Shop and Wright's Shoe Hospital, Wright claimed to repair shoes until they were right, and "You can't go wrong at Wright's."

Frank Wheatley purchased the business in 1935. In 1940 he moved it to 410 West Dickson, where it was known as Wheatley's Shoe Service. A native of Oklahoma, Wheatley was in the shoe business in New York, Milwaukee, and St. Louis before settling in Fayetteville. He retired in 1968. Today 410 West Dickson is part of an expanded Common Grounds Coffee House.

When your shoes are not *Right*
See WRIGHT
He will make them *Right*

328 West Dickson St. Fayetteville, Arkansas

W. B. Wright's
SHOE HOSPITAL
We make old shoes look like new
SHINE PARLOR
Wear a Tony shine found at all functions

The STUDENTS' Repairman
You can't go wrong at
Wright's Electric Shoe Shop
404 W. DIXON PHONE 675W

Wrights Shoe Shop ads, 1915–22

Wheatley's ad, 1940s

412 WEST DICKSON

Tony's Shine Parlor x 2

Tony White, a resident of Rogers, opened Tony's Shine Parlor at 328 West Dickson in 1916 and remained on Dickson until the 1920s. He appears to have been closely associated with W. B. Wright. In 1929 Anthony Chiabotti, an Italian immigrant, operated Tony's Shine Parlor at 412 West Dickson Street and was at this location until 1948. According to long-time residents, Tony never failed to greet persons making their way through Shuler Town. "A Tony's shine always made shoes look like new."

Fowler's Fruit & News Stand/Razorback News Stand

Mr. and Mrs. W. Allen Fowler opened a small news stand at 328 West Dickson in 1931. In 1941 they moved it to 412 West Dickson. Fowler's was advertised as "The Big Little Store." In 1951, Mrs. Fowler sold the newsstand to Carmen Read. In 1953 Fowler's became the Razorback News Stand. In addition to newspapers, these businesses sold magazines, drinks, candies, a small line of groceries, and school supplies. Several persons operated this business until its closing in 1973. Today 412 West Dickson is the home of Common Grounds Coffee House.

above: *Fowler's ad, 1948*
right: *Sidney's, with trees, 1980s*

414 WEST DICKSON

Gollaher's

Around 1907 E. Clifford Gollaher opened a small grocery at 414 West Dickson Street, the present site of Melody's Choices. Gollaher sold candies, cookies, and fruit. For several years, Gollaher was the only grocer to sell gasoline. Gollaher remained in business at that location until 1921.

Student Cleaners

In 1937 the Blackmon Brothers (Lingle P., E. B., Shelly, and Joel) opened the Student Cleaners at 407 West Dickson Street. The name had a surprising double meaning, for in addition to serving a student clientele, the Blackmons, natives of Siloam Springs, were law students. In 1943 Lingle Blackmon moved the cleaners across the street to 414 West Dickson. It closed in 1956.

Dream Merchant

Cedric Neal, Jr. opened the Dream Merchant gift shop at 414 West Dickson Street in 1973. For many years, the Dream Merchant was known for its alternative gifts, including tie-dyed fabrics, psychedelic posters, and

Merchant, 1990

1911 Fire

On March 27, 1911, fire destroyed part of the north side of the 400 block. According to newspaper accounts, damages were estimated at $20,000 and it was considered Fayetteville's worst fire in twenty years. It started in a cafe near the present location of Chester's and destroyed most of the buildings not constructed of brick or stone, which at that time were 414, 416, 418, 420, and 422 West Dickson. Water pressure was so low that the firefighters used dynamite to help put out the fire. Two buildings constructed of brick and stone suffered some damage but were not totally destroyed. Today, they house the brew pub at the end of the block.

The 400 block rapidly recovered from the 1911 fire. The business houses at 412–422 West Dickson were all rebuilt by 1912. Most pre-1911 businesses remained on the block in or nearby their original locations.

1911 fire, looking east

1911 fire, looking west

412–416 West Dickson, 1995

drug paraphernalia. Since 1992 the business has been Melody's Choices, after the current owners, Steve and Pamela Melody.

416 WEST DICKSON

DeLuxe Barber Shop

The DeLuxe Barber Shop was at 404 West Dickson from around 1897 until 1911, when owner Bill Lisko moved it to 416 West Dickson. In 1915 the DeLuxe was owned by J. W. Ballard who ran "a strictly up-to-date, sanitary shop, using antiseptic sterilizers and electric hair dryer and massage." The Deluxe Barber Shop left Dickson Street in 1920.

Hometown Cafe

Edith Karnes opened the Hometown Cafe at 416 West Dickson in 1946.

Hometown Cafe ad, 1946

From the time it opened in 1942 at 316 West Dickson, the Hometown Cafe specialized in home cooked meals. It was a favorite eating place for many Dickson Street merchants until it closed in 1964.

Island Haircutters

Barbering came back to 416 W. Dickson with the arrival of Quincy Jones Haircutters. In 1979 H. C. Gilliam opened the Island Haircutters, also known as Fantasy Island Haircutters, and was at this address until 2000.

418 WEST DICKSON

Hodges Cafe

The Hodges Brothers, Thomas and Floyd, ran a number of cafes in the 400 and 500 blocks of West Dickson from the 1910s to the 1930s. The Hodges family were pioneer restaurateurs in Fayetteville. Around the turn of the century, their father, Robert K. Hodges, owned the Blue Moon Cafe on the Fayetteville square, which continued well into the twentieth century. According to one of my sources, Ed McCormick, the Hodges brothers learned to cook while serving in the U. S. Army during the First World War. The Hodges left Dickson around 1939, when they were at 418 West Dickson, the current home of Condom Sense.

Hodges Cafe ad, 1925

Beulah Lee Beauty Shop

Beulah Lee Batson opened the Beulah Lee Beauty Shop at 418 West Dickson Street in 1940. Originally housed in the Simpson-Mintun Building,

Beulah Lee Beauty Shop ad, 1957

Mrs. Batson specialized in "hair cutting and styling." She was also open evenings by appointment. The Beulah Lee Beauty Shop closed in 1975.

Rock Bottom Used Book Store

In 1976 Wilda L. Hardin opened the Rock Bottom Used Bookstore, which, until 1995, was at 418 West Dickson Street. It specialized in used paperbacks and collectible comic books.

420 WEST DICKSON

O. K. Merchant Barber Shop

In 1897 J. F. Goss opened the Parlor Barber Shop in a small frame building at 418 West Dickson. The Parlor was "first class in every respect and had a bath room in connection." Toll Ladd purchased it around 1908 and renamed it the O.K. Merchant Barber Shop. In 1911 Ladd built a new shop at 420 West Dickson. He owned it until 1916, when Bullet and Clint Murphy purchased it and renamed it the U of A Barber Shop.

U of A Barber Shop

The U of A Barber Shop claimed to be the most up-to-date barber shop on Dickson. It had all kinds of electrical devices for clipping, massaging,

O. K. Merchant Barber Shop

Carrying a Nice Line of Toilet and Tonique, Also Fine Razors and Strops.

Caters strictly to student trade. Union Card and Union Barbers. *BATHS.*

G. T. LADD, Proprietor

First Shop East of Depot

O. K. Merchant Barber Shop ad, 1912

and shampooing. In 1924, the U of A Barber Shop became one of the first, if not the first, unisex shops in Fayetteville. Run by Mrs. Jim McCann of Ft. Smith, the U of A Barber Shop's ladies department offered marcelling, water waving, and curling. In the early years Clint and Bullet Murphy catered strictly to student trade. However, by the 1960s, when the Murphys sold the shop, many of their student clientele were alumni who had remained in Fayetteville. The Murphy Brothers' clientele then included the larger Fayetteville community. In 1967 Wally Scranton began cutting hair with then owner Bill Lazenby. Eventually, Wally bought out Lazenby and ran the U of A Style Shop at the same location until selling it at the end of 1998. At that point, the O. K. Merchant/U of A Barber Shop/ U of A Style Shop had the distinction of being the oldest continuously-operating

400 block of West Dickson, 1990

Above, *O. K. Merchant Barber Shop;* below, *interior, 1910*

U of A Barber Shop ad, 1943

business on Dickson. With neighboring Chester's Place and the Rock Bottom Book Store, it also has the distinction of being located on the former site of the Live and Let Live Drug Store, which gave birth to Shuler Town.

418–422 WEST DICKSON
Birthplace of Shulertown
Live & Let Live Drug Store

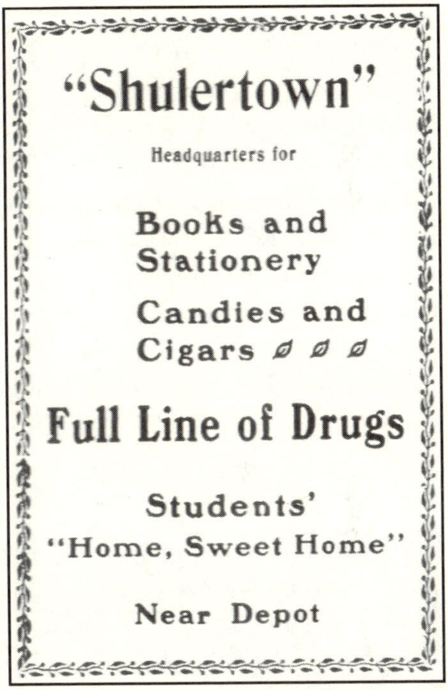

Shulertown ad, 1906

In the fall of 1901, A. C. McAdams, resident of the 200 block of East Dickson, opened a depot branch of his Live & Let Live Drugstore at 420 West Dickson, the main drugstore being on the southwest corner of the square. In addition to medicines, the Live & Let Live carried books, school supplies, stationery, paints, oils, and glass, as well as candy and cigars. Like most early drugstores, it also had a very popular soda fountain. T. Fred Shuler, a former A.I.U. student who had been employed by McAdams since 1898, ran the "Depot Town" drugstore. So popular was Shuler with the students that they eventually called the whole area around the Live & Let Live "Shuler Town." Shuler left for Colorado in 1905 for the sake of his wife's health. They ended up in Missouri, where, in 1931, Shuler was appointed to the Missouri State Pharmacy Board. Although Shuler was in Fayetteville for only a few years, he made a lasting contribution to Fayetteville's rich history.

Palace Drug Store

After the 1911 fire A. C. McAdams rebuilt his drug store at 418 West Dickson and renamed it the Palace Drug Store. In 1912 he sold it to Gus Bridenthal, who ran it until the 1920s. Other owners included W. G. Ownbey (1930s), W. F. Porter (1940s), and Henry I. Caudle (1950s). In 1918 Bridenthal moved the Palace Drug Store to 422 West Dickson, the current home of Chester's. Over the years, the Palace Drug Store had a soda fountain and also sold drugs, cosmetics, stationery, school supplies, magazines, film, and a large selection of candy. In 1955 Henry Caudle moved the Palace Drug Store to a much larger building at 624 West Dickson, the present home of Campus Bookstore.

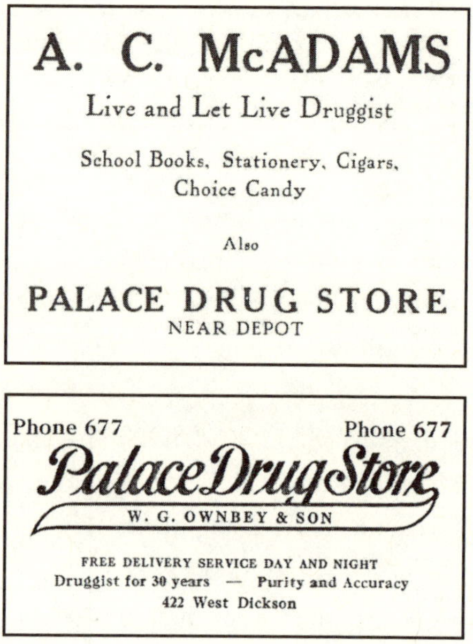

Palace Drug Store ads, 1912 and 1928

"Hanging Out at Palace Drug," 1917

418–422 West Dickson, 1992

422 WEST DICKSON

Library Club

In 1967 Doyle Morgan opened the Library Club at 422 West Dickson. The Library Club burned in 1982 but re-opened the following year. Between 1971 and 1993, when it closed, the Library Club was owned by Richard "Dicky" Poole. For many years the Library had a very dark décor. Customers sat on church pews around long wooden tables. Among the many bands who played at the Library were Zorro and the Blue Footballs.

Chester's Place

In 1993 Margie and Bu Waggoner, former co-owners of George's Majestic Lounge, purchased the Library Club at 422 West Dickson and opened Chester's, an upscale nightclub. Chester's was named after Margie Waggoner's cat. The walls of the club were tastefully decorated with imported rugs and cat memorabilia. Chester's Place regularly hosted live bands ranging from Washington County's own Cate Brothers to Kansas City's Nace Brothers. Chester's also sponsored many musicians not regularly appearing in Fayetteville. Chester's was so popular that it was nearly

right: *Library Club bar menu, 1993*

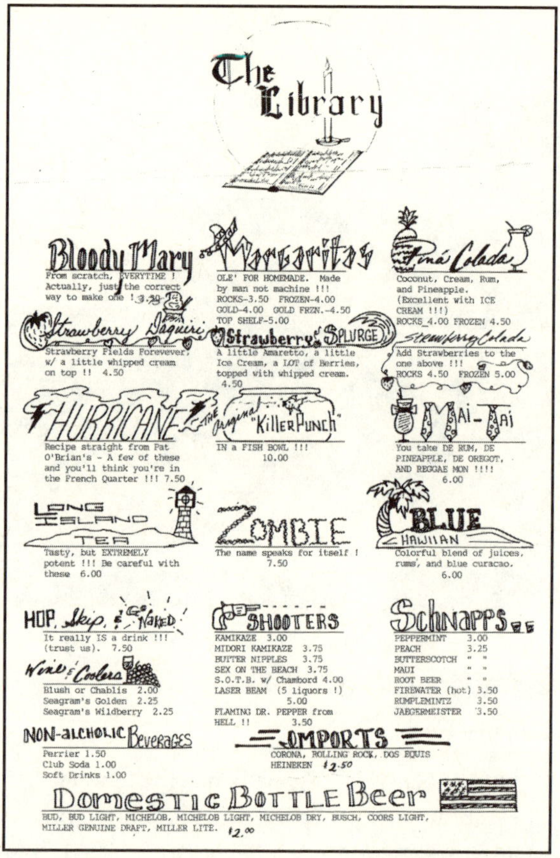

The Library

Bloody Mary
From scratch, EVERYTIME ! Actually, just the correct way to make one ! 3.50

Margaritas
OLE' FOR HOMEMADE. Made by man not machine !!!
ROCKS-3.50 FROZEN-4.00
GOLD-4.00 GOLD FRZN.-4.50
TOP SHELF-5.00

Piná Colada
Coconut, Cream, Rum, and Pineapple. (Excellent with ICE CREAM !!!)
ROCKS 4.00 FROZEN 4.50

Strawberry Daquiri
Strawberry Fields Forevever, w/ a little whipped cream on top !! 4.50

Strawberry Splurge
A little Amaretto, a little Ice Cream, a LOT of Berries, topped with whipped cream. 4.50

Strawberry Colada
Add Strawberries to the one above !!!
ROCKS 4.50 FROZEN 5.00

Hurricane
Recipe straight from Pat O'Brian's - A few of these and you'll think you're in the French Quarter !!! 7.50

The Original "Killer Punch"
IN a FISH BOWL !!!
10.00

Mai-Tai
You take DE RUM, DE PINEAPPLE, DE OREGOT, AND REGGAE MON !!!!
6.00

Long Island Tea
Tasty, but EXTREMELY potent !!! Be careful with these 6.00

Zombie
The name speaks for itself !
7.50

Blue Hawiian
Colorful blend of juices, rums, and blue curacao.
6.00

Hop, Skip, & Go Naked
It really IS a drink !!! (trust us). 7.50

Wine & Coolers
Blush or Chablis 2.00
Seagram's Golden 2.25
Seagram's Wildberry 2.25

Shooters
KAMIKAZE 3.00
MIDORI KAMIKAZE 3.75
BUTTER NIPPLES 3.75
SEX ON THE BEACH 3.75
S.O.T.B. w/ Chambord 4.00
LASER BEAM (5 liquors !) 5.00
FLAMING DR. PEPPER from HELL !! 3.50

Schnapps
PEPPERMINT 3.00
PEACH 3.25
BUTTERSCOTCH " "
MAUI " "
ROOT BEER " "
FIREWATER (hot) 3.50
RUMPLEMINTZ 3.50
JAEGERMEISTER 3.50

Non-Alcholic Beverages
Perrier 1.50
Club Soda 1.00
Soft Drinks 1.00

Imports
CORONA, ROLLING ROCK, DOS EQUIS
HEINEKEN $2.50

Domestic Bottle Beer
BUD, BUD LIGHT, MICHELOB, MICHELOB LIGHT, MICHELOB DRY, BUSCH, COORS LIGHT, MILLER GENUINE DRAFT, MILLER LITE. $2.00

below: *Chester's Place/U of A Style Shop, 1995. "Birthplace of Shulertown"*

impossible to find a table on Friday and Saturday evenings once the music had begun.

426–430 WEST DICKSON
Bates Brothers

Bates Brothers Market ad, 1955

James and Joe Bates, the Bates Brothers, along with cousin Earl, started selling groceries in 1897 from a small frame building on Dickson Street. That year they built a sandstone building at 410 West Dickson, the upstairs portion of Common Grounds. By 1899 business had grown so much that they rented space in a two- story sandstone building at 430 West Dickson, which now houses the brewing tanks of the brewpub on the corner. In 1904 the Bates Brothers constructed a two- story red brick building at 426–428 West Dickson, which now houses the restaurant part of the brew pub. They remained in business until 1955, shortly before Joe Bates's death. The Bates Brothers were known for quality merchandise. They carried the best staple and fancy groceries in town. Although prices were sometimes higher than their competitors, persons wanting assurances of quality would most often pay the higher price at the Bates Brothers Market. Canned goods, imported pickles, table dressings, a big line of cigars, tobacco, stationery, candies, and notions lined their shelves. The Bates Brothers also offered delivery service and included the University of Arkansas Infirmary on their route.

426–428 WEST DICKSON
Bill & Lil's
Swinging Door/White Water Tavern

M. B. Tichenor opened Bill and Lil's Steak House at 426 West Dickson and Bill and Lil's Lounge next door at 428 West Dickson in 1967. The steak

Above, *Bates Brothers Market, ca. 1898*. Below: *Bates Brothers Market interior, ca. 1898*

A Note on the Bates Brothers Building Site

A few long-time residents of Fayetteville commented that the Bates Brothers had problems with rats in their basement. Workmen who renovated the building for the Ozark Brewing Company may have discovered the source of the Bates Brothers' rat problem. About twenty years before the building was constructed, the site was in an undeveloped part of town and was apparently used as a dump and landfill. Remains of a fire were also excavated during the recent construction. It is believed that these remains were dumped on the Dickson Street site after a fire that devastated the Fayetteville square in 1880.

house moved to College Avenue in 1970. In 1973 David Barrow, Bill and Lil's manager, purchased the steakhouse and expanded it one door east. Shortly thereafter, he renamed it the Swingin' Door, and it remained a fixture on West Dickson until it closed in 1980. Its trademark was a

Left, *Bill & Lil's ad, 1968.*
Right, *Swingin' Door ad, 1975*

X-Ray Strike of 1913

In 1912 U of A students organized a club called the Iconoclasts. They published a newspaper, *The X-Ray,* on February 24, criticizing the indifference, incompetence, and unfairness of some professors and the rigidity of student discipline. The town of Fayetteville came under attack also, for the high prices charged students and for the "nastiest, muddiest, filthiest, dirtiest, and most ill-kept streets in the country," which obviously included Dickson Street. When the publishers of *The X-Ray* were dismissed, U of A students struck. Wearing green and white arm bands, waving pennants, and accompanied by a band, they marched down Dickson Street toward the Fayetteville square. After a visit by Governor Donaghey on March 2, 1912, the situation was resolved and campus life returned to normal.

X-Ray strikers in front of Bates Brothers, 1913

Swingin' Door, 1970s

large cowboy painted on the front of the building above the entrance. For many people, the Swingin' Door was the first "club" on Dickson Street whose only attractions were alcohol and live music. It had a couples and group room (with red carpet and velvet drapes), and two game rooms. The live music included such bands as The Ozark Plantation Band, Jed Clampit, and Lloyd Marley They also played at the Swinging Door's successor, the Whitewater Tavern, which was at the same location between 1981 and 1984. Between 1985 and 1987, it was the home of Reunion Station, a short-lived gay bar.

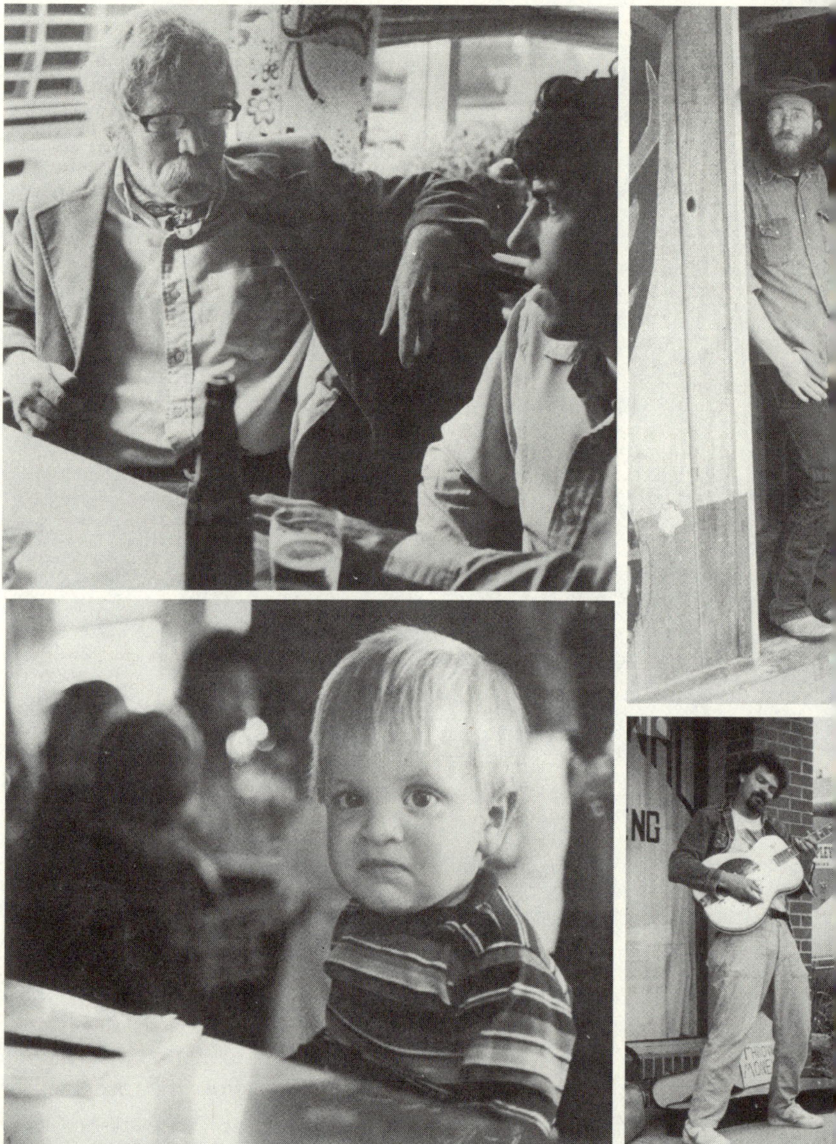

Bar scene, 1980

Dickson Street Murders, 1980–1981

On October 16, 1980, the body of Charles Shipp, a Madison County resident, was found in the Holsum Thrift Store parking lot. He had apparently been shot twice in the back and head with a 20 gauge shotgun. Doug Treadway, a former U of A student, was arrested and charged. He was convicted of second degree murder and served a suspended fifteen-year sentence at Cummins. Treadway claimed Shipp was a dope dealer who openly sold dope on Dickson and regularly ripped off buyers. He later blamed the demise of Dickson Street on the after-hours bars, which he said attracted rats, roaches, and leeches who preyed on innocent Dickson Street patrons. In 1981 a man standing at a pool table at the Whitewater Tavern was killed by a bullet fired from across the street. Apparently the shooter was angry at having been thrown out of the tavern and decided to shoot out one of their expensive leaded glass windows. Also in 1981, after a fight which started in the Library Club, a man was found stabbed to death between two cars parked behind the club. In 1982, in an effort to curb violence on West Dickson, the City of Fayetteville passed an ordinance prohibiting the sale of alcohol between 2:00 am and 10:00 am.

Bar scene, 1980

Pedaling east on Dickson, 1980s

430 WEST DICKSON

Frisco Drug Store

Jessie C. Williams opened the Frisco Drug Store in 1905 at 430 West Dickson Street. The Frisco Drugstore was the place to buy all your drugs, patent medicines, school books and tablets, and Parker Lucky Curve fountain pens. The Frisco also claimed to have the most complete line of cigars and tobaccos in the city. Upon Williams' death in 1912, neighboring merchants said, "Uncle Jessie's death removes the brightest face from Dickson Street." Several persons operated the Frisco Drug Store before it closed

Frisco Drug Store ad, 1906

SIGMA PHI EPSILON

To those students who have been wondering during the entire year whether or not the S. P. E.'s have a chapter here, we direct attention to the above cut.

Frisco Drug Store sketch, 1919

U of A Post Office, 1950s

Dickson Street looking east, 1992

in 1927. Between 1931 and 1937 430 West Dickson was the home of the Cardinal Drug Store.

U. S. Post Office University Station

In order to handle the enormous amount of University of Arkansas mail, the U. S. Post Office opened a substation at 601 West Dickson Street in 1925. In 1937 the post office relocated it to 430 West Dickson, the current home of the Hog Haus brew pub. The U of A sub-station was there until 1962, when it was consolidated with the new post office at 14 West Dickson Street.

426–430 WEST DICKSON

Ozark Brewing Company

After spending millions of dollars to renovate the old Bates Brothers buildings, John Gilliam opened the Ozark Brewing Company, a microbrewery and restaurant, at 430 West Dickson in 1994. The two-story structure, two buildings joined into one, occupies the sites formerly housing Bates Brothers, the University Post Office station, Bill and Lil's, the

Ozark Brew Pub prior to renovation, 1992

Swinging Door, and the Whitewater Tavern. The Ozark Brewing Company, known as the Brew Pub, made beer for consumption on the premises. It has a three-story brew house, a pub that seats about eighty people, a dining room that seats about ninety, and a balcony that seats about twenty. The 11,000-square-foot building features extensive decorative woodwork and large expanses of glass through which patrons can check the brewing operation. In 2004 The Brew Pub changed hands and was renamed Hog Haus, but its services continued substantially the same.

401–405 WEST DICKSON
Scott Hotel

One of the long-term businesses on the south side of the street was the Scott Hotel. The eastern portion of the Walton Arts Center now occupies this site. Constructed in 1913, the hotel occupied space on the second story of the Edward Green Building. The Green Building was at 401–405 West Dickson; the hotel lobby was at 403 West Dickson. Operated by H. M. Scott, it was advertised as a well-equipped European-style hotel with seventeen spacious, nicely furnished rooms. Over its 56-year history, the Scott Hotel became a favorite rooming house for traveling businessmen and newcomers. During the years preceding World War II rates were only

Scott Hotel ad, 1920

$1.00 a day. While the upper floor contained the hotel, many other businesses occupied street-level space in the Green Building. There were groceries, cafes, doughnut shops, beauty shops, dress shops, shoe shops, and jewelry stores. By the 1960s, rooming hotels such as the Scott began to fall out of favor. By 1969, when the Scott Hotel was demolished, it had a reputation as a flop house. During the 1970s and 1980s the site was occupied by a Burger Chef restaurant and Mountain Man Pawn.

401 WEST DICKSON

Winchester's Cash Grocery

In 1913 James F. Winchester opened a grocery at 401 West Dickson Street; its entrance was on the School Street side of the Edward Green

Scott Hotel, 1960s

building. Winchester's "had nothing to wear but had everything to eat. It was "a good place to spend money because it was a good place to save money." Winchester's had fresh meats, groceries, vegetables, and fruits. They also had a good supply of pickles. According to one of my sources, Ann Sugg, a childhood neighbor of Winchester, the shop consisted of one room with some storage at the back. The meat counter stood in the back and was presided over by Mr. Winchester, who as butcher, wore the mark of the profession with several fingers missing from his left hand. Winchester's closed in 1943. Between 1944 and 1946 two groceries, Shamblin's and Val's, occupied the space. Winchester's, along with the Scott Hotel, was demolished in 1969.

James F. Winchester

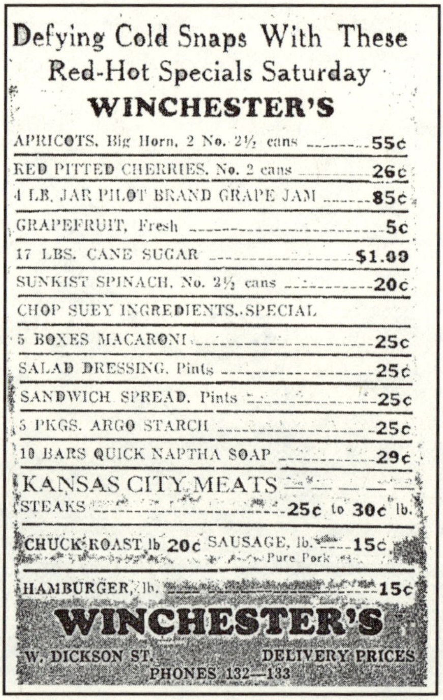

Winchester's ad, 1931

409–441 WEST DICKSON

Rooming Houses

On the south side of the street on the western

half of the 400 block were the Boyle and Grother Rooming Houses, both constructed in the 1890s. Arthur and Mary Boyle owned a rooming house at 409 West Dickson between 1903 and 1939 and at 417 West Dickson between 1891 and 1919. Both houses disappeared by the early 1940s.

Frisco Hotel

In 1883, two years after the arrival of the Frisco Railroad, Henry and Mary Grother also had constructed a two-story frame building on the westernmost part of the south side of the street. The first floor contained a grocery and the second floor was known as the Frisco Hotel. It was torn down around 1922.

409 WEST DICKSON

Nook Cafe

Charles Bird opened the Nook Cafe in 1947. The Nook Cafe was similar in concept to the White Castle fast food chains in the North. It was a pre-fabricated building of black and white enameled steel panels. Jim and Anna Lauderdale, of the 800 block of West Dickson, ran it until retiring in 1972.

Bulls-Eye Pub

Glen T. Brewer opened Ken's Pizza at 409 West Dickson in 1969. Ken's closed in 1977. In that year, Mike Womack opened the Bulls-Eye Pub, which advertised itself as "the only pub in town." It was a very popular meeting place for young adults, including University students. Several pool tables, a dart board, foozball tables, and TV sets supplemented the long wooden tables on which customers enjoyed their pizza and beer.

Bulls Eye Pub ad, 1981

Camera Shop and Bulls-Eye Pub, prior to demolition, 1980s

Joel Henderson ran it in the early 1980s and for a few years, the pub offered free live entertainment. The Bulls Eye Pub remained in business until 1988, when the City of Fayetteville condemned the property for preparation of the Walton Arts Center site.

417 WEST DICKSON

Cities Service Station

M. C. Price, owner of Price Oil Company, opened a service station at 417 West Dickson in 1936. By 1937 Jesse W. and James H. Brashears were operating a Cities Service Station here. Cities Service offered a one-stop shop for quality gasoline and oils, lubrication service, and tire sales. The Brashears also had a large lot behind their building, where they offered free parking for shoppers. In 1946, they opened a Motor Service Company next door, in the rear portion of 409 West Dickson. Shirley Ogden bought the station in 1951 and ran it until 1965, when it closed. This building was torn down in 1988.

Simpson-Mintun Company

In 1923 William Simpson and Arthur Mintun constructed what was then the largest commercial building in Fayetteville. It was located at 439–441 West Dickson, the western portion of the Walton Arts Center site. It housed the Simpson-Mintun Company, which was formerly

Evening rush hour, (note Cities Service Station), 1946

located on West Center Street. The upstairs portion of the building housed several additional businesses, including the Beulah Lee Beauty Shop and a photography studio.

Simpson-Mintun originally were wholesalers of fruits, seeds, and flour. However, by the 1930s they were better known as wholesalers of gasoline and oil. In addition, they carried a full line of automobile accessories including tires, tubes, batteries, and greases. Simpson-Mintun also had an automobile storage business on the site. Arthur Mintun managed the Simpson-Mintun Company until retiring in 1931. In 1934 Wallace Wester joined the firm as assistant manager. He purchased the business in 1936 and by 1941 it was known as Wester Motor Company.

Simpson-Mintun ad, 1926

Homecoming Parade. (note Simpson-Mintun and Ozark Grocer on left), 1920s

Wester Motor Company

Wallace Wester purchased the stock of the Simpson-Mintun Wholesale Company in 1936 and until 1957 operated the Wester Motor Company at 441 West Dickson. While maintaining Simpson-Mintun's reputation as a dealer in gas, oils, and automobile accessories, Wester also was a dealer for Studebaker cars and trucks.

Wester Motor Company ad, 1947

Fayetteville Linen Supply

In 1962 Howard Bass converted the Simpson-Mintun/Wester Motor Company building at 441 West Dickson into the Fayetteville Linen Supply Company. This company specialized in quality uniforms for use in food processing plants, industrial plants, restaurants, drug and variety stores,

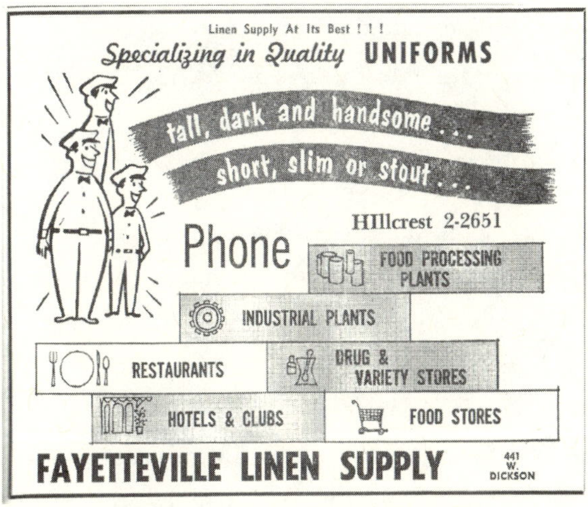

Fayetteville Linen Supply ad, 1961

hotels and clubs, and food stores. In 1985, Carl Holt purchased the company and it became a part of the Cintas Linen & Supply Company. They moved to Springdale in 1987. During the 1960s and 1970s, the second floor of the building was home to Don's Studio. Don specialized in formal portraits as well as photographs of University of Arkansas student parties. Early in his career E. Fay Jones, later a world-famous architect, occupied another upstairs office. Not long after Cintas Linen left, the building was demolished for construction of the Walton Arts Center.

407–409 West Dickson, prior to demolition, 1988

Dickson Street or Main Street?

In 1922 there was a movement among many of Dickson Street's more prosperous merchants, including the Bates Brothers, to rename the street Main Street. This would allow persons new to Fayetteville to recognize it as one of the city's primary business streets. Many of Fayetteville's older residents, including Gus Lewis of the 500 block, fervently argued against it. They argued that Dickson Street was named after one of Fayetteville's earliest and most beloved families, and that changing the name to Main Street would dishonor their memory. It would also disturb those persons throughout Arkansas for whom Dickson was the street most associated with their time at the University of Arkansas. Besides, according to Lewis, Fayetteville already had a Center Street on the square, which indicated the main business center for Fayetteville. Having both a Main Street and a Center Street could be confusing. Upon recognizing the fondness Fayetteville residents had for Dickson Street, the merchants supporting the change quickly backed down and the Dickson Street name was retained.

On-street parking on Dickson, 1915

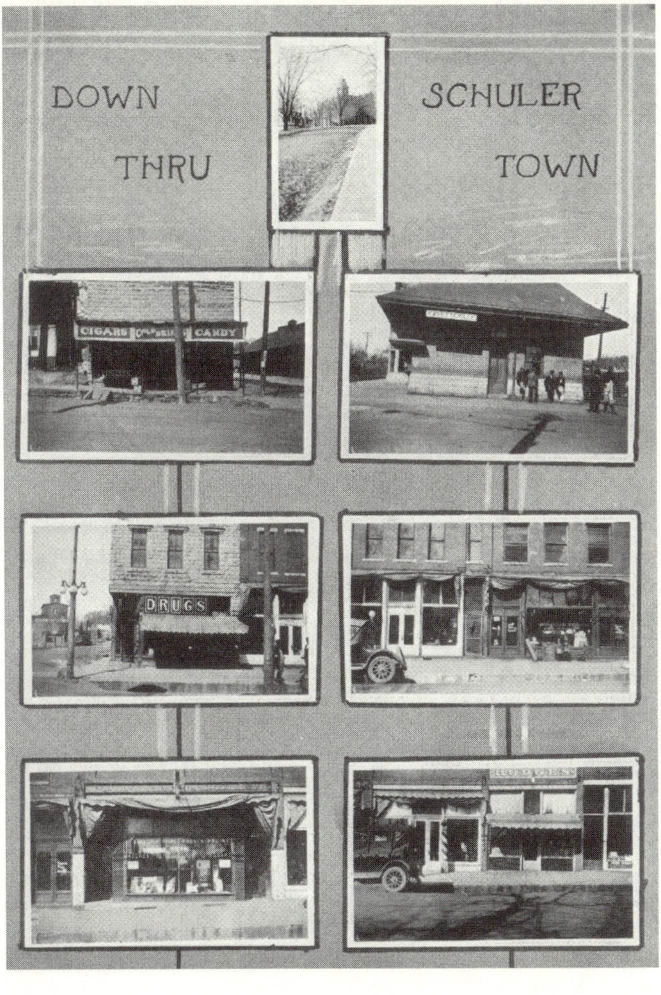

"Down Thru Shuler Town," 1920

Springfest

Since 1984 the Pride in Dickson Street Merchants Association has sponsored Dickson Street's annual Springfest in April or May. In recent years, the annual celebration has begun with a pancake breakfast at the Ozark Mountain Smokehouse. Musicians perform country, folk, blues, and rock music throughout the day. In addition to the arts and crafts booths and food and drink vendors that line the street, several children's events transpire. The Dickson Street bed race is usually scheduled around noon, and for several years it was followed by the traditional Springfest parade. Springfest usually winds up around 5:00 or 6:00 in the evening. Some Springfest celebrants, including the author, have been fooled by the cool springtime weather and have obtained their worst sunburns of the year while enjoying the festivities.

Springfest Bed Race, 1980s

Roger Koetter "King of Dickson Street," 1987

Mary Hinton "Queen of Dickson Street," 1987

Walton Arts Center, 1992

495 WEST DICKSON
Walton Arts Center

Beginning in 1977, the City of Fayetteville set aside extra revenues from the city's "hamburger tax" to build an arts center. In 1981 Fayetteville city leaders, more firmly convinced of their desire to build such a center, set aside an additional fraction of a 1% sales tax for that purpose. In that year Sam and Helen Walton, founders of Bentonville-based Wal-Mart, donated five million dollars to the University of Arkansas to build an arts and business center. The City of Fayetteville and the University of Arkansas soon realized they were seeking the same goal and began discussing the possibility of sharing the costs of building an arts center.

The City wanted to build the arts center near the square and the University of Arkansas wanted to build it on campus. The two entities agreed that Dickson Street was the perfect compromise. Although this was a perfect solution for government leaders, selection of the Dickson Street location disturbed many local merchants and residents. They feared that building the arts center on West Dickson would cause property values and taxes to rise so sharply that many long-term property owners would be forced off Dickson Street and out of the surrounding neighborhood (this in fact did happen). The City of Fayetteville, as well as some merchants, counter-argued that an arts center on Dickson would automatically improve the street by removing some of the bikers' and teenagers' hangouts. The arts center would also attract more "upscale" businesses to the street and consequently obliterate the bad image that had plagued Dickson Street for the previous decade (this in fact did also happen, although both teenagers and bikers returned later).

The City of Fayetteville won the battle and preparation for the arts center began in the fall of 1988 with the dozing of Bull's Eye Pub and the Nearly Famous Restaurant (which the author frequented quite regularly). Soon after, the Camera Shop and the Blood Plasma Center, which was briefly located in the old Burger Chef building on the corner of School and Dickson, came down. The last building to be demolished on Dickson was the Cintas Linen and Supply Company, originally the Simpson-Mintun Company Building. This building proved difficult to tear down. When demolition was complete an extremely large crater, which filled with water and debris, occupied the site for nearly two years. Disgruntled residents referred to the eyesore as the fenced-in lake on Dickson.

After several delays, construction of the arts center began in 1990 and the building finally opened in May 1992 as the Walton Arts Center, Northwest Arkansas' Center for the Arts or simply the Walton Arts Center, with Bill Mitchell as its first director. It consists of more than 55,000 square feet and contains three performance halls. The main hall contains a stage surrounded by twelve hundred seats, some rising on the floor and some in the balcony. The center also contains a 2500-square-foot visual arts gallery, a 250-seat theater with flexible seating, and a rehearsal and meeting room

Walton Arts Center resident, 1995

with 125 seats. The grounds of the Walton Arts Center include a 125- seat amphitheatre terraced with native stone, grass, and trees. Nearby is a memorial rose garden.

The Ozark Stageworks Production Company presentation of Athol Fugard's "Road to Mecca" was the first arts center production. Under the direction of Carlton Woods, the North Arkansas Symphony Orchestra presented the arts center's first concert "Celebrating a New Beginning." More than 350 public events occur annually at the Walton, including music and dance performances, operas, plays, lectures, and community and private gatherings. At present approximately fifteen art exhibits are mounted in the gallery spaces each year. Walton Arts Center serves more than 25,000 students and teachers from thirty school districts each year in its education programs

Many, but not all, residents have overcome the hard feelings aroused during the initial demolition and construction stages. The Walton Arts Center has helped revitalize Dickson Street and business there is quite good. However, it is ironic to note that the grounds of the Walton Arts Center have become, at least in the summertime, quite a pleasant hang-out for skateboarders and other teenagers.

NAAC Basketball Championship Celebration

Dickson Street saw perhaps one of its largest crowds ever on Monday night, April 4, 1994, after Nolan Richardson's Arkansas Razorbacks defeated Duke University for the NAAC Basketball Championship. According to Fayetteville Police Chief Richard Watson, several thousand students gathered on West Dickson Street near the Walton Arts Center shortly after the game. Students and other Razorback fans partied on Dickson Street from around 9:00 P.M. until 1:00 A.M. According to Watson, however, only seventy-nine alcohol-related arrests were made. Watson said the police log showed several reports of loud people and horn-blowing. Watson said Fayetteville's reaction to the Hogs' title victory was a welcome change from the response in other cities whose sports teams have won national titles, citing riots in Chicago and Dallas after teams from those cities won NBA and NFL championships.

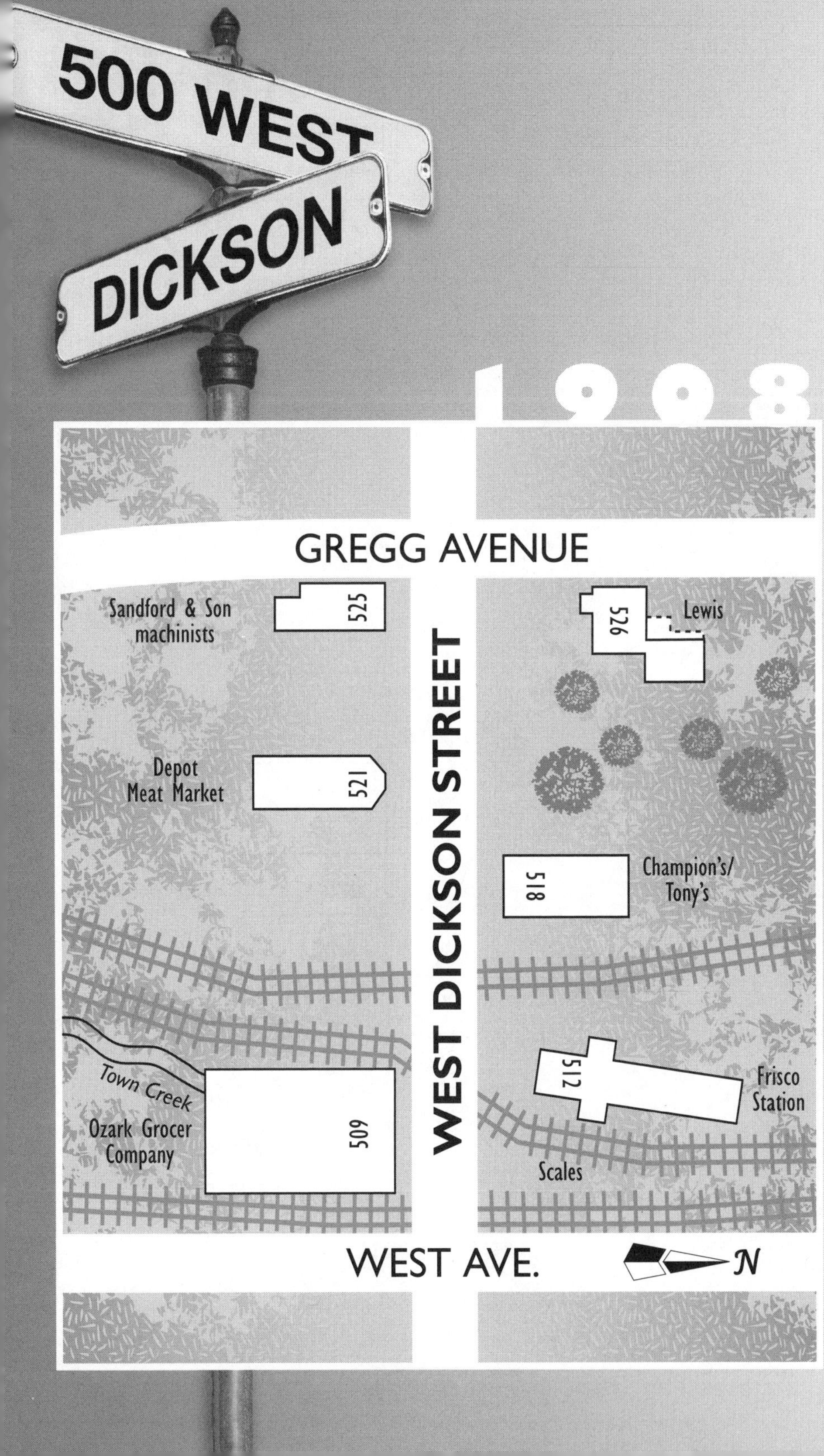
500 WEST
DICKSON
1908
GREGG AVENUE
WEST DICKSON STREET
Sandford & Son
machinists
525
Lewis
526
Depot
Meat Market
521
518
Champion's/
Tony's
Town Creek
Ozark Grocer
Company
509
512
Frisco
Station
Scales
WEST AVE.
N

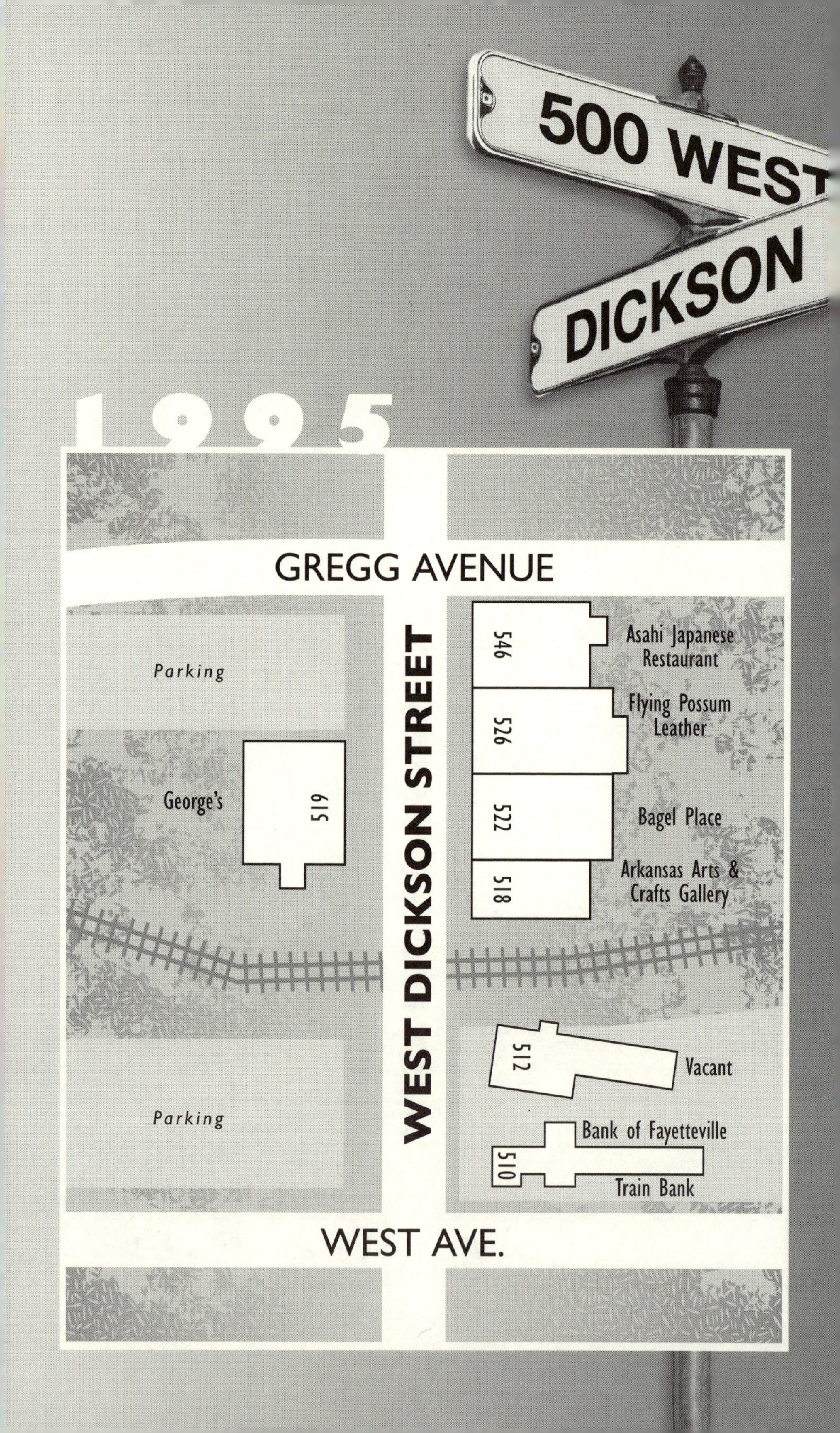
500 WEST
DICKSON
1995
GREGG AVENUE
WEST DICKSON STREET
Parking
George's
519
546
Asahi Japanese Restaurant
526
Flying Possum Leather
522
Bagel Place
518
Arkansas Arts & Crafts Gallery
512
Vacant
Bank of Fayetteville
510
Train Bank
Parking
WEST AVE.

500 BLOCK

At the 500 block, West Dickson Street bottoms out at Town Creek. Until the early 1870s, this block consisted of undeveloped pasture land. With the exception of Gus Lewis' store (which appeared shortly after the U of A did), the 500 block did not begin to develop until after the arrival of the Frisco Railroad in 1881.

510–512 WEST DICKSON

St. Louis & San Francisco Railway

On June 1, 1881, the St. Louis & San Francisco Railroad Company, nicknamed the Frisco, laid track near what is now North Gregg Avenue north of North Street, outside the northern limits of the town. On July 4, 1881, amid great fanfare, the first passenger train arrived from Pierce City, Missouri. In order to get to Fayetteville proper, tracks had to be laid across the watershed extending from Mt. Nord to Arkansas Industrial University. It took a few more months for laborers to work through the slate deposits in the Fayetteville Fault area, afterward known as the "Cut." On November 26, 1881, the first passenger train arrived on Dickson Street.

The original depot was built in 1881. It burned in 1897. A second brick depot, with a low tower on the track side, was then constructed. It was used until 1925, when, in an effort to standardize their depots, the Frisco replaced it with a new building having a southwestern motif. While this station was under construction, a temporary station existed on the south side of the street near the Ozark Grocer.

For many years, the lot between the depot and West Street was used as a wagon yard and produce scales. One of the many dignitaries to arrive at the Fayetteville Depot was former President William Howard Taft, who visited Fayetteville in November, 1917. He had a speaking engagement at the Ozark Theatre; his topic was the war in Europe (World War I) and the proposed league to enforce the peace. After Taft arrived at the depot, J. C. Futrall escorted him, via Dickson Street, to the Futrall residence on College Avenue. A crowd of about a thousand people gathered along Dickson to wish the ex-President well.

Frisco Station, 1897

"X-Ray Strikers" at the Frisco Station, 1913

Goodbye to Passenger Trains

September 18, 1965, was a sad day for Fayetteville. A large crowd came to the depot to bid the Frisco farewell. Later the abandoned train station was leased from the railroad by John Lewis, of the Bank of Fayetteville, and a group of businessmen. Rumors have circulated for years about plans for redevelopment of this property. On occasion, it is a stopping-off point for the Arkansas & Missouri's Excursion train between Springdale and Van Buren. In 1992, while running for President, Governor Bill Clinton made a campaign stop at the station. The author happened to witness the event and actually had the opportunity to shake hands with the candidate.

World War I Exhibition Train ad, 1918

Frisco Station, 1940s

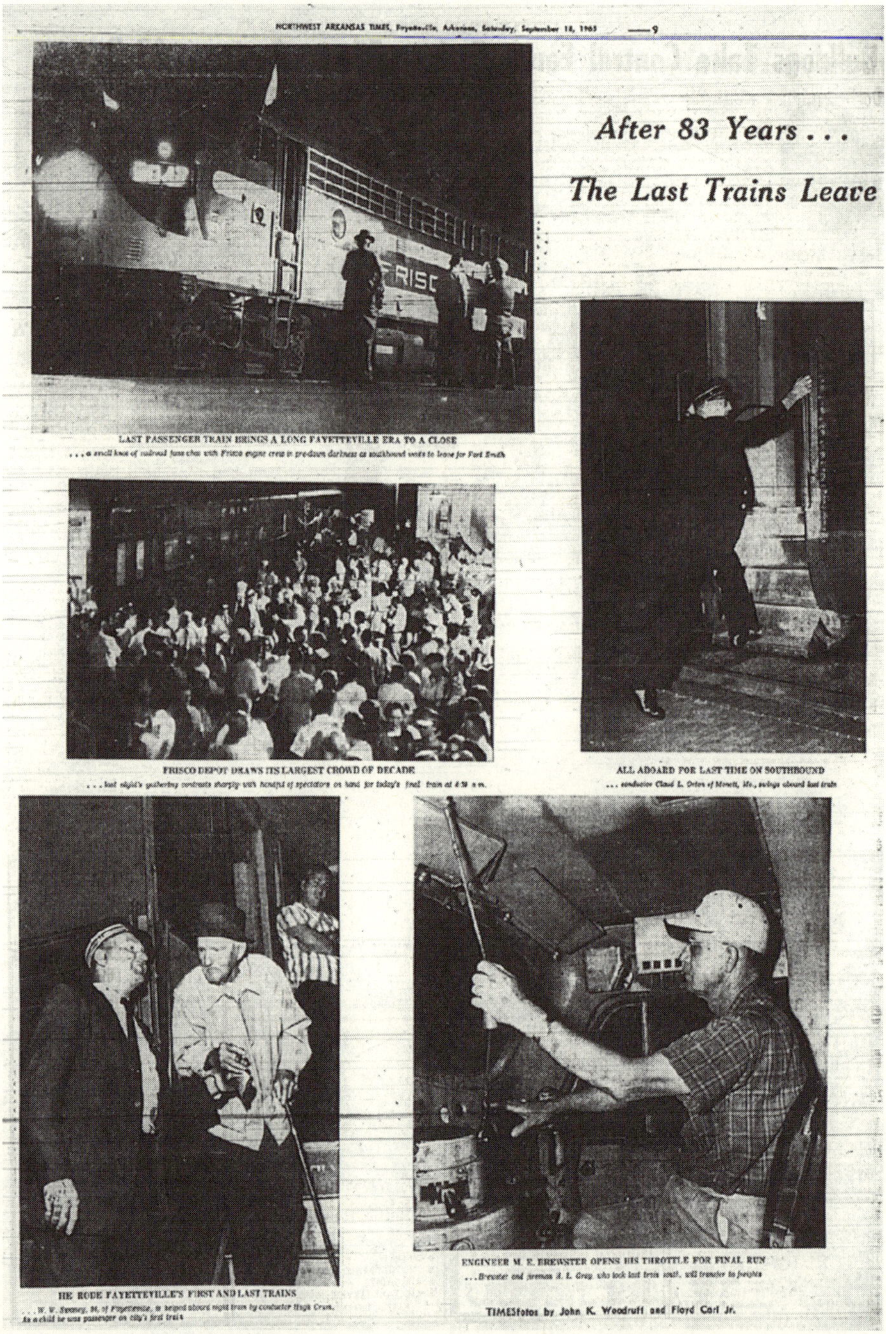
NORTHWEST ARKANSAS TIMES, Fayetteville, Arkansas, Saturday, September 18, 1965 — 9

After 83 Years . . .

The Last Trains Leave

LAST PASSENGER TRAIN BRINGS A LONG FAYETTEVILLE ERA TO A CLOSE

. . . a small knot of railroad fans chat with Frisco engine crew in predawn darkness as southbound waits to leave for Fort Smith

FRISCO DEPOT DRAWS ITS LARGEST CROWD OF DECADE

. . . last night's gathering contrasts sharply with handful of spectators on hand for today's final train at [illegible] a.m.

ALL ABOARD FOR LAST TIME ON SOUTHBOUND

. . . conductor Claud L. Orton of Monett, Mo., swings aboard last train

HE RODE FAYETTEVILLE'S FIRST AND LAST TRAINS

. . . W. W. Sweeney, [illegible], of Fayetteville, is helped aboard night train by conductor Hugh Crum. As a child he was passenger on city's first train

ENGINEER M. E. BREWSTER OPENS HIS THROTTLE FOR FINAL RUN

. . . Brewster and fireman A. L. Gray, who took last train south, will transfer to freights

TIMESfotos by John K. Woodruff and Floyd Carl Jr.

Goodbye to passenger trains, 1965

Frisco Station and Train Bank, 1995

510–512 WEST DICKSON
Bank of Fayetteville

John Lewis

In 1990 the Bank of Fayetteville opened a Dickson Street branch on the northwest corner of West and Dickson. The bank is comprised of two beautifully restored turn-of-the-century railroad cars and a caboose. According to John Lewis, President of the Bank of Fayetteville, there is no other "train bank" in the country. The Bank of Fayetteville bought the caboose from John Gill of Little Rock, who had bought and restored it in the 1970s as an anniversary present for his wife. According to Gill, the caboose was originally owned by the Cotton Belt Railroad.

518 WEST DICKSON
Tony's

Just one step west of the tracks was Champion's News Stand, which was better known as Tony's Confectionery or simply Tony's. In 1907 Oscar L. Champion and Tony Sowder purchased the recently constructed Lewis Brothers News Stand and confectionery at 518 West Dickson. Champion's was "the proper place" to buy reading material. In addition to twelve leading newspapers, the news stand carried many popular magazines and dime novels. Tony's, "Where Good Fellows Get Together," was a very popular hangout for University of Arkansas coeds. It was the place to buy all kinds of cakes, candies, fruits, nuts, popcorn, cold drinks, cigars, and tobacco. Champion's and Tony's were considered the best source in town for Razorback (formerly Cardinal) booster material. In 1929 Linn L.

It's Tony's this and Tony's that,
It's Tony's every time you're broke,
It's Tony's this and Tony's that
And Tony's for a *Koke.*

Tony's ads, 1920 and 1924

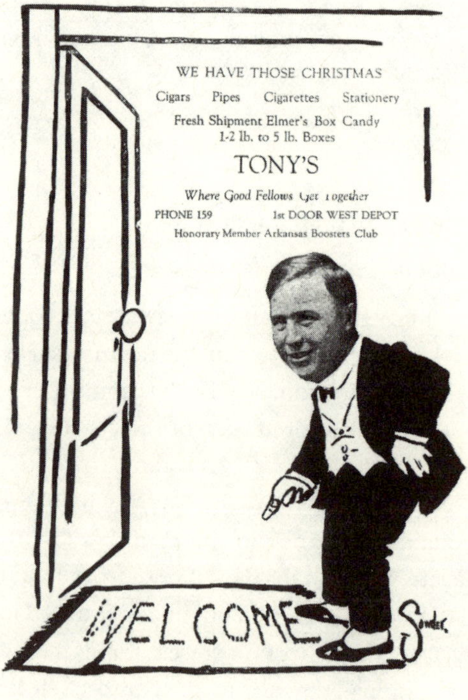

and Lamar Lewis, sons of Uncle Gus Lewis, purchased Tony's and renamed it the Varsity Shop. In 1937 the Lewis brothers closed the Varsity Shop and opened the Varsity Shop Restaurant at 526 West Dickson. Neither it nor its successor, the Bill & Belle Cafe, remained in business for more than two years. Apparently the Depression and the competition from the Majestic Cafe, which would open across the street in 1927, were too much for them.

House of Books

The House of Books bookstore opened in 1962 in Tony's old place of business at 518 West Dickson. Several owners, including Philip H. and Thelma Rosenbach (1974–1981) and Bill Baker (1981–1983) ran the House of Books until 1983, when it closed.

House of Books ad, 1962

Bill Baker

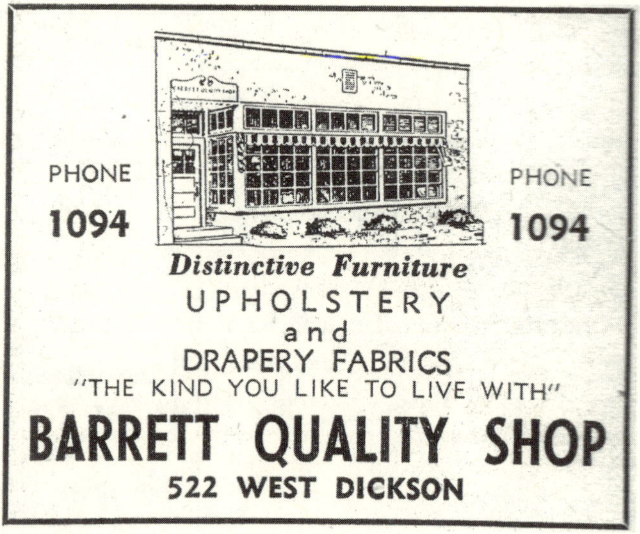

Barrett Quality Shop ad, 1949

522 WEST DICKSON

Barrett Quality Shop

Paul L. and Bertha L. Barrett were the first tenants of 522 West Dickson, which was constructed around 1946. They opened the Barrett Quality Shop at this location. This interior design business had a distinctive selection of upholstered chairs and sofas, occasional tables and lamps, and drapery fabrics. The Barrett Quality Shop closed in 1961. Since the 1980s many short-lived businesses, including several small restaurants, have occupied 518 and 522 West Dickson.

524–546 WEST DICKSON

Gray

Professor Gray

Around 1875 Oliver Crosby "O. C." Gray and his wife, Virginia Davis, built a home on the northeast corner of Dickson and Gregg Streets. Born in Maine in 1832, Gray graduated from Colby College in 1855. Four years later he moved to Princeton (Dallas County), Arkansas, where he was principal of a female seminary. In 1875 Gray became professor of mathematics at Arkansas Industrial University and taught at A.I.U. until 1885. Between

1886 and 1888 Gray was mayor of Fayetteville. Professor Gray was an ardent supporter of the Frisco Railroad. He donated much of his property to the railroad for the Frisco yard and depot, which was developed in 1881. Until her death in 1886, Mrs. Gray taught art at Arkansas Industrial University. She helped decorate the Naomi Williams Private School, which was across the street at 607 West Dickson. In 1889 O. C. Gray remarried. His second wife was Mrs. Beattie. She was a teacher and matron at the Deaf & Mute Institute in Little Rock. The Grays remained at this location until 1895, when they moved to Little Rock.

Lewis

In 1895 Augustus B. Lewis, more affectionately known as "Uncle Gus," and his wife, Rebecca Hewitt, purchased the Gray home and lived there until about 1919. Born in Hempstead County, Arkansas, in 1835, Lewis was educated at Arkansas College in Cane Hill. He moved to Fayetteville in 1855 and opened a store on the Fayetteville square. In 1872 Lewis was elected Treasurer of Washington County for a four-year term, but served only two years because of the change of the state constitution. In 1875 he

Augustus B. Lewis

"X-Ray Strikers" near Lewis residence. Tony's and depot to east, 1913

Varsity Cafe, 1940

opened a small mercantile at 519 West Dickson, near the current site of George's. It closed in 1907.

After 1919 Gus and Sophia Lewis lived with their daughter, Lena Lewis Sharp, who resided at the southeast corner of Dickson and Duncan. Lewis was known as a local historian and great weather enthusiast, as apparently he could predict the weather quite accurately. At the time of his death in 1928, Lewis was the last of the antebellum merchants. His house was torn down around 1935. Around 1937, the Lewis family constructed two commercial buildings on the property. The one on the corner of Gregg and Dickson was built with a Southwestern flavor to harmonize with the nearby Frisco Railway station. The earliest tenants, like some more recent ones, were restaurants, including the short-lived Varsity Cafe, and many barber and beauty shops. Mrs. Lewis died in 1940.

524–526 WEST DICKSON
Beauty & Barber Shops

A number of beauty and barber shops occupied 524 and 526 West Dickson Street between 1937 and 1974. In 1937 Lorene Waggoner opened the College Beauty Shop at 524 West Dickson. She carried a line of Theo Bender Cosmetics. In addition to permanents, her "6 competent operators" did facials. The College Beauty Shop was at the same address until 1948, when long-time barber and beautician, Orin and Florence Stapleton, pur-

College Beauty Shop grand-opening ad, 1939

Lorene's College Beauty Shop ad, 1941

chased the business and renamed it Stape's Beauty and Barber Shop. The beauty shop was at 524 and the barber shop was at 526 West Dickson. In 1964 Dennis A. Fuller purchased Stape's Beauty Shop and renamed it Mr. D's Beauty Salon. He remained at this location until 1968. In 1959 Frank D. Steele purchased Stape's Barber Shop and renamed it City Barber Shop. Between 1962 and 1966 Thomas Spicer ran it and the shop was known as Spicer's City Barber Shop. Several other barbers worked at City Barber Shop until it closed in 1974.

518–546 West Dickson, 1995

Flying Possum Leather

In 1975, Jim Nelson opened a leather shop at 526 West Dickson. He owned it until 1976, when Bruce Walker purchased the business and renamed it Flying Possum Leather. Known for its line of Birkenstock sandals, Flying Possum also carries a line of leather goods, including belts, purses, and hats. Flying Possum Leather was the first Birkenstock dealer in Northwest Arkansas. Introduced in the U. S. in 1966, the German-made sandals have become very popular in recent years and are now sold by mail order companies such as L. L. Bean. Walker witnessed the exodus of businesses from Dickson in the 1970s and early 1980s but was confident of Dickson Street's renaissance and has remained committed to its well-being.

540–546 WEST DICKSON

Fayetteville Floor Company

In 1945 Proctor F. Johnson opened the Top Hat Antique Shop at 546 West Dickson. In 1953 his son Martin Johnson opened the Fayetteville Floor Company. It sold the finest inlaid linoleum, asphalt and wood tile, and Formica counter tops. It remained at this location until 1973.

Bruce Walker, proprietor of Flying Possum Leather, with customer, 1980

Fayetteville Floor Company ad, 1954

Christian Science Reading Room

In 1965 the former Varsity Shop Cafe building at 546 West Dickson Street was divided in two. The eastern half of the building, known as 540 West Dickson, became the Christian Science Reading Room. Several different librarians, including Edna Rumsey, Grace Newfield, Elizabeth Fleener, and Marge Hughes, ran the reading room until 1988, when they moved to the Fayetteville square.

For many years Polly's Cafe occupied the western portion of the building. A succession of other small restaurants has followed.

540–546 West Dickson, 1992

509 WEST DICKSON

Ozark Grocer

In 1883, two years after the arrival of the Frisco, A. J. Rhea opened a small wholesale grocery store on the south side of the block. In 1886 he built a large two-story stone building on the lot known as 509 West Dickson. The new and expanded grocery had a series of private railroad switch yards and loading docks alongside West Street. In the early 1890s Rhea sold his interests to the Fayetteville Grocer Company, which was founded in 1890. In 1907 the Fayetteville Grocer Company absorbed the capital of Conner Wholesale Grocer, owned by Caleb C. Conner, who lived in the 200 block of East Dickson. It then became the Ozark Grocer Company. Throughout its history, the Ozark Grocer Company was the leading wholesale grocery house in Northwest Arkansas. It sold Sun-Kist fruits and vegetables, Burt-Olney Canned Vegetables, University Oats and hand-made Ozark Cigars. The Ozark Grocer Company was also a main distributor of beer. During Prohibition, they distributed "near-beer." In 1954 the McCord Wholesale Grocery Company purchased the Ozark Grocer. At that time, E. H. Froning was McCord's President. The officers of the Ozark Grocer included Walter E. McWhorter president, Paris Green, vice-president, Sam Wheeler secretary, Walter Miller, treasurer,

Ozark Grocer, 1910s

and board members Herbert Lewis, Sr., Harvey Jones, Jeff Baggett, and W. C. Whitfield. The Ozark Grocer Company closed in 1968. For a few years Ruble Transfer and Storage occupied the building. The historic building burned in 1974.

Ozark Grocer ad, 1933

Town Creek Drowning

In May 1929, Tom Pickell, a water-polo star at the University of Arkansas, fell into a pool of water at the southwest corner of Dickson and West Street and drowned before anyone could help him. According to Gene Warren, operator of the Simpson-Mintun service station, Pickell was hurrying to get to the University of Arkansas before the bell, when he stepped off the curb, lost his footing, and fell into the turbulent Town Creek, which was swollen from heavy rains. Warren, believing Pickell could swim, did not go to his assistance. He claimed he was busy waiting on a customer and their motto was "Always Business Before Pleasure." Garth McMillan, a fellow student, tried to save Pickell, but was too late.

Tree Protest # 3

During the 1970s and 1980s many native trees, shrubbery, and other plant life took over the creek bed and the vacant lot formerly occupied by the Ozark Grocer Company. In 1992, shortly after the Walton Arts Center was completed, an effort was made to turn this area into a historic park. However, because of the rugged terrain, concerns about possible mischievous activity at the site, and the need for parking, the City of Fayetteville overruled the park enthusiasts, arguing that elderly patrons needed convenient access to the Walton Arts Center. The site was cleared, the ravine filled in, and a parking lot constructed. Some of the ruins of the Ozark Grocer Company foundation were saved and used for a nicely landscaped reflecting pool on the southeast side of the parking lot.

Excavating Walton Arts Center parking lot, 1992

Walton Arts Center parking lot, 1995

519–525 WEST DICKSON

Lewis & Sharp

In 1875 Gus Lewis and A. L. Sharp opened a small mercantile near the present location of George's Majestic Lounge. Known as Lewis & Sharp, this mercantile was apparently the first business on Dickson Street to cater expressly to university students. Legend has it that the sign on the west side of the building read "First Chance," so that students coming from A.I.U. would stop here first before heading to the square. A sign on the east side read "Last Chance" so that students would stop to make last-minute purchases before walking the final few blocks west to campus. Lewis closed his business in 1907 when the Frisco condemned the property for their use. Shortly thereafter, he built another similar business house across the street at 518 West Dickson. Originally Lewis Brothers News Stand, this business was later known as Tony's and Champions. It was also very popular with the university crowd. Lewis & Sharp has the distinction of being the only known business on Dickson Street before the arrival of the Frisco.

Sandford & Son

In 1898 the Sweitzer Wagon Company built a shop at 525 West Dickson, the present-day site of George's parking lot. In 1905 Samuel Sandford purchased the capital of Sweitzer Wagon Company and opened Sandford & Son; not a junk yard, but a machine shop. He and his son, Claude H. Sandford, operated at this location until 1933, when they relocated to West Street. Sandford & Son was an early version of an auto repair shop. Initially specializing in overhauling and repairing wagons, they gradually moved on to automobiles and other vehicles. They were proud of the fact that they did work in the least possible time because they were able to duplicate broken parts. Their catchy slogan was "We Mend Everything But A Broken Heart."

519 WEST DICKSON

Majestic Cafe/George's

In 1926–1927 Len Lewis, a third son of Uncle Gus, constructed a small brick building near the site of the old Lewis & Sharp Mercantile. On February 1, 1927, without any fanfare, Greek immigrants by the name of

George Pappas

Tellas, John, and George Pappastavian, Pappas for short, and George's cousin, Theodore Kantas, opened the Majestic Cafe, which seated seventy-five. George was cashier, and John was chef. Until the end of prohibition, George's was a cafe only. In 1934, one year after prohibition ended, Pappas constructed a summer beer garden at the rear of the building. The Majestic was a major student hangout, and because of George's liberal credit, almost went out of business during the depths of the Depression. One of the students who hung out at the Majestic was Bill Fulbright. It is said that he distrusted the highly seasoned Greek dishes and always ordered Campbell's tomato soup. U of A President John C. Futrall got his afternoon coffee and his El Roi Tan cigars at the Majestic. According to Walter Lemke, during World War II a troop train pulled to a stop at the depot. In spite of the presence of the Military Police, the soldiers poured out of the rear cars of the train, trampled the beer garden, insulted all the male customers (4-F) in the place, and devastated the interior of the restaurant.

In 1947 Mary Hinton purchased George's from Pappas. During Mary's tenure as George's owner, the famous landmark was the scene of many Fayetteville firsts—color TV, pizza, submarine sandwiches, restaurant/tavern integration, and live music. According to Mary, the first live music at George's was performed in 1955 by "Cowboy Ray Thornton," a law

Majestic ad, 1951

student running for student body president at the U of A, and the Seldom Fed Seven, a band consisting mostly of football players. Other acts over the years have included local jazz musicians Buddy Hays (1950s), Ronnie Hawkins, and the Cate Brothers (1970s–1990s).

Mary is also credited with making the beer garden a cool place to be during the hot summer months. In the early 1960s a box elder sprouted amidst the garden's picnic tables. Mary took pity on it for having the gumption of growing in such a crowded place and began nurturing it. Over the next twenty-five years the box elder

Cowboy Ray Thornton

George's Majestic Lounge, 1995

grew to such proportions that it became the garden's centerpiece. On May 22, 1989 a powerful storm that wrought havoc on Fayetteville destroyed the beloved box elder. Before the tree was removed from the garden, several patrons held a memorial service for the fallen landmark.

Between 1987 and 1993 Marjorie and Bu Waggoner, along with William and Betty Harrison, owned George's. Beginning in 1993 the Harrisons greatly enlarged and renovated George's, uncovering the original brick walls of the seventy-year-old building and almost doubling the capacity of the original Majestic Cafe. They also expanded the beer garden and enclosed it with large sound barriers to comply with city noise ordinances. Although George's no longer serves meals, it continues to be one of the most popular hangouts for residents and University of Arkansas students alike, especially in the summer months when they can enjoy live music in the beer garden.

Mary Hinton, the beloved long-time owner and operator of George's died February 12, 2001, at the age of 80. In honor of her memory, Mayor Dan Coody proclaimed Valentine's Day, February 14, as Mary Katherine Hinton Day. According to Alderman Swifty Reynolds and others, Mary was the sweetheart of Dickson Street.

Vietnam Moratorium Day

On October 16, 1969, about six hundred persons marched east on Dickson toward the Fayetteville square protesting the war in Vietnam. Coordinator of the Vietnam Moratorium Day March, Dr. Otto Zinke, a professor of physics, believed the march brought the reality of the war to the attention of the people of Fayetteville. Art Hobson, another moratorium leader, believed the march exceeded all expectations of the group and was quite pleased with the turnout, comparing it to the public's lack of interest in the small war protests on the corner of Storer and Maple in 1967. Most of the protestors were University of Arkansas faculty and students; however, many persons not affiliated with the university participated.

War Supporters

Approximately one hundred fifty veterans marched in support of President Richard Nixon's attempt to end the war in Vietnam. Jim McGhee, a veteran of the Korean War, organized the veterans' march. The Veterans' group stated that they were not opposed to responsible dissent, since that was what they had fought for; however, they believed the Moratorium Day activities verged on irresponsible dissent and that the demonstrators worked against President Nixon's attempt to end the war more quickly. They carried signs reading "Back the U. S., Not the Moratorium, "Bomb Hanoi," and "Protest the Protestors."

Vietnam War protestors, 1969

Backers of the war, 1969

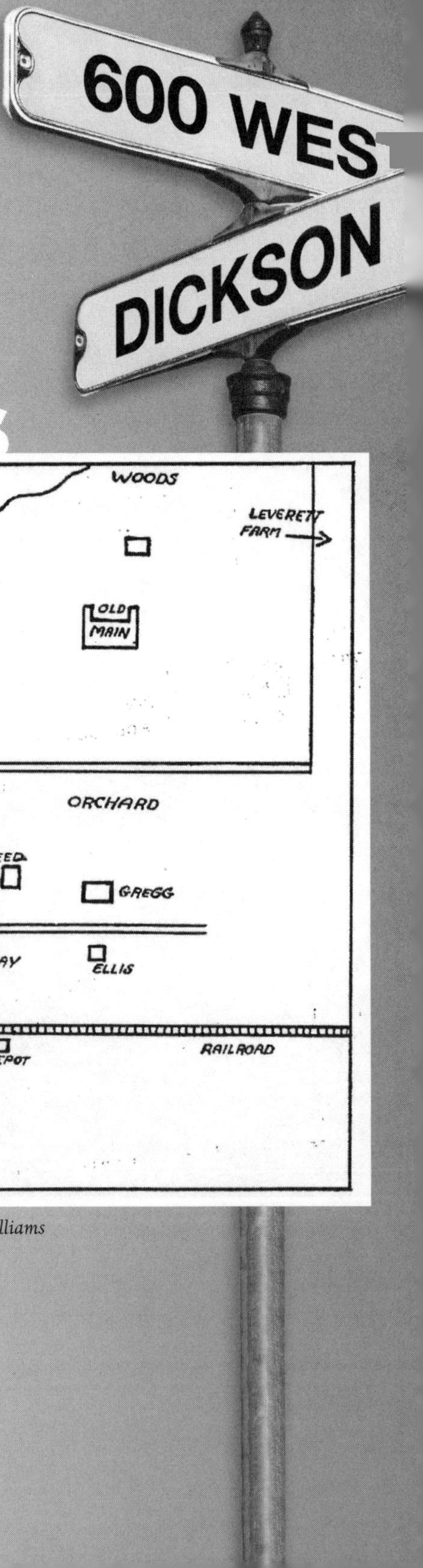

1880s

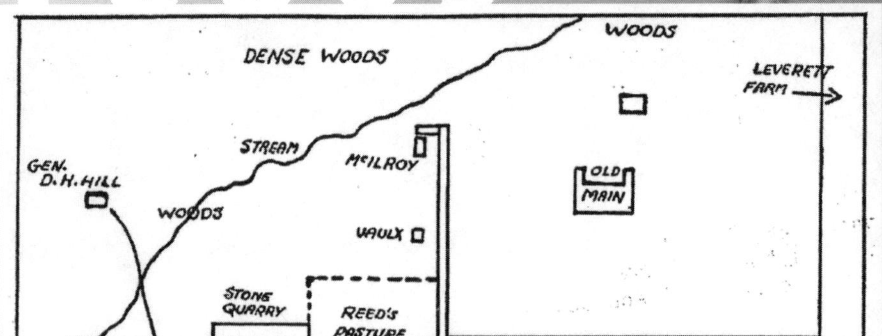

West Dickson Street, 1880s, from map by Miss Hattie Williams

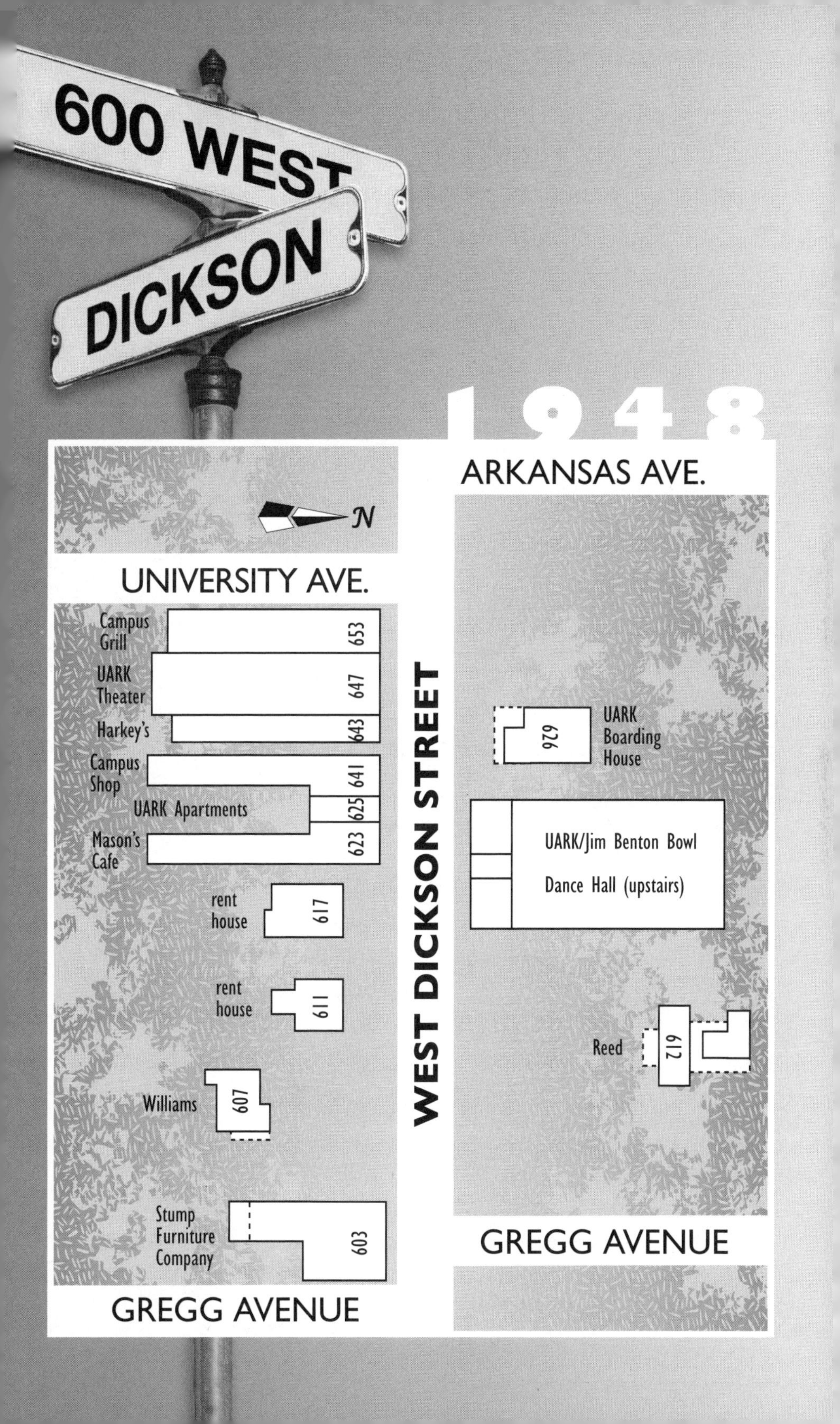
600 WEST
DICKSON
1948
ARKANSAS AVE.
N
UNIVERSITY AVE.
Campus Grill
653
UARK Theater
647
Harkey's
643
Campus Shop
641
UARK Apartments
625
Mason's Cafe
623
rent house
617
rent house
611
Williams
607
Stump Furniture Company
603
WEST DICKSON STREET
UARK Boarding House
626
UARK/Jim Benton Bowl
Dance Hall (upstairs)
Reed
612
GREGG AVENUE
GREGG AVENUE

600 WEST
DICKSON

1995

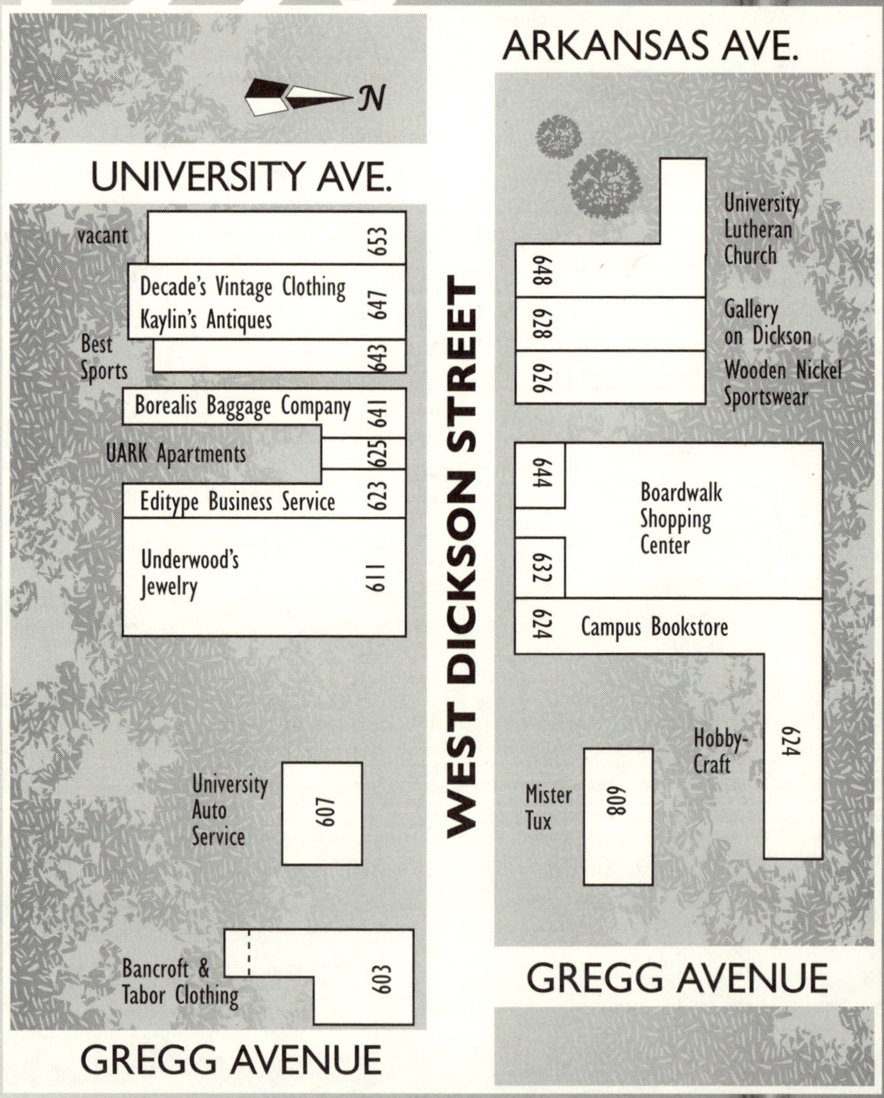
ARKANSAS AVE.
N
UNIVERSITY AVE.
WEST DICKSON STREET
vacant 653
Decade's Vintage Clothing
Kaylin's Antiques 647
Best Sports 643
Borealis Baggage Company 641
UARK Apartments 625
Editype Business Service 623
Underwood's Jewelry 611
University Auto Service 607
Bancroft & Tabor Clothing 603
University Lutheran Church 648
Gallery on Dickson 628
Wooden Nickel Sportswear 626
644
Boardwalk Shopping Center
632
624 Campus Bookstore
Hobby-Craft 624
Mister Tux 608
GREGG AVENUE
GREGG AVENUE

600 BLOCK

Dickson Street begins its uphill trek toward the University of Arkansas in the 600 block. The Reed and Williams families owned most of the property here until the 1940s.

601–611 WEST DICKSON
Williams

Around 1881 James H. Williams built his home at what would become 607 West Dickson, just east of what is now Underwood's. Born in Tennessee in 1839, Williams married Louisa A. Alderson. They moved to Fayetteville in 1872 so that their children could attend the Arkansas Industrial University. For many years, Williams was a distributor of feed, grain and wood. Mr. and Mrs. Williams lived at 607 West Dickson until their deaths in 1911 and 1923, respectively.

Naomi Williams

Naomi J. and Hattie Williams, two of the Williams daughters, also lived at 607 West Dickson. Born at Bull's Gap, Tennessee, in 1861, Naomi received her education at Arkansas Industrial University and at the University of Michigan. In 1882 she opened a private school at her father's newly constructed residence. Tuition was $1.50. In 1888 Williams, affectionately known as Miss Naomi, accepted a position as a Latin and history teacher in the Preparatory Department of Arkansas Industrial University. One of her students was Joe T. Robinson, later U. S. Senator from Arkansas. She taught in the Preparatory Department until 1910, when that department was abolished. Miss Naomi then taught in the Fayetteville and Fort Smith high schools. She was in Fort Smith when a close friend and colleague, Ella Carnall, died. Miss Naomi died in 1943.

Born in 1879, Hattie also lived at 607 West Dickson until 1953. Not much is known about her life. However, I am grateful for her unknowing contributions to this project. Her stories about Fayetteville and about

Miss Naomi, published in *Flashback,* the journal of the Washington County Historical Society, have been of enormous assistance. Her map is reproduced in this book.

601–603 WEST DICKSON

Goddard/Griffin Grocer Company

In 1900 the opening of the Ozark & Cherokee Central Railway into Oklahoma Territory created an expanded market for wholesale groceries in Fayetteville. In 1901, the Northwest Arkansas Lumber Company began construction of a new wholesale grocery at 601 West Dickson. J. T. Evins and Joe D. Wilson, the principals of the new business, had formerly been affiliated with the Fayetteville Grocer Company. The Evins-Wilson Grocer Company served western Arkansas, Oklahoma Territory, and southwest Missouri. In 1907 they sold the business to Jesse W. Goddard, who operated the Goddard Grocer Company until 1922. In 1927 the Griffin Grocer Company of Muskogee, Oklahoma opened a store here. They were in business until 1936. Between 1925 and 1937 the U of A substation of the U. S. Post Office occupied the eastern portion of the building. Between 1939 and 1948 the Vita-O-Ray Milling Company occupied the building.

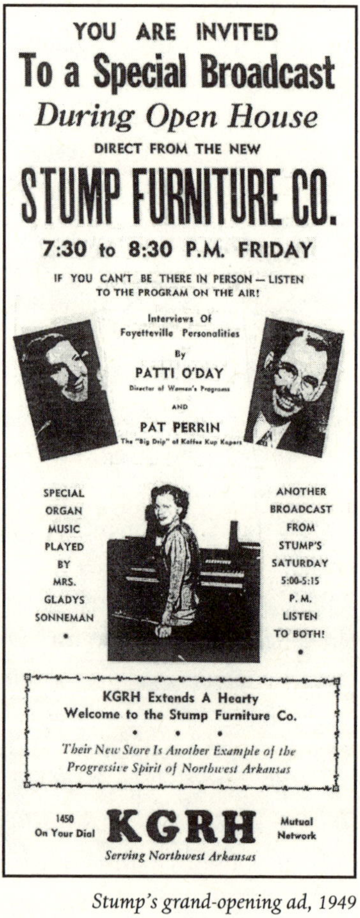

Stump's grand-opening ad, 1949

Stump/Polk Furniture Company

In 1949 Charles and Daisy Stump of Muskogee, Oklahoma, leased the Goddard Grocer building at 603 West Dickson and opened their third Stump Furniture Company store. Tom Edmonston was manager. This store had fifteen thousand square feet of display space. Stump's carried

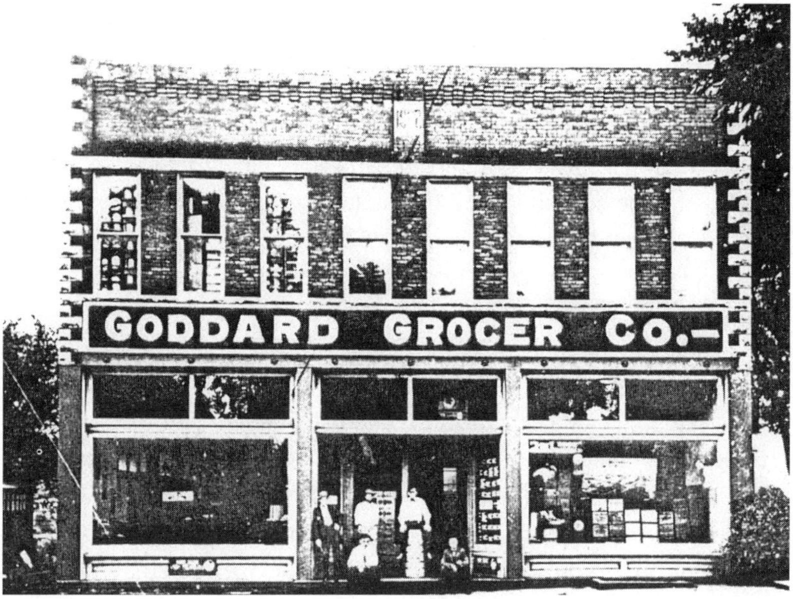

Goddard Grocer Company, 1910s

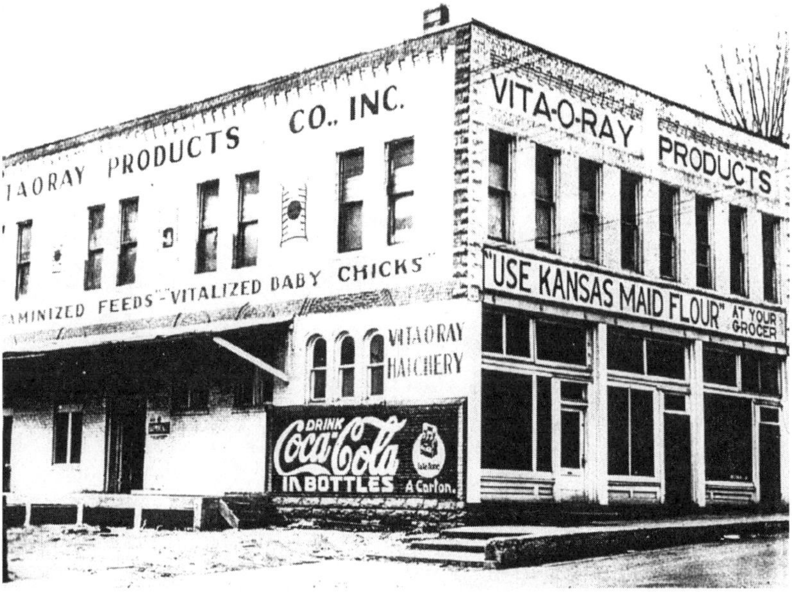

Vita-O-Ray Milling Company, 1940s

furniture for every room, including popular furniture brands such as Kroehler, Pullman, Tomlinson, Drexel, and Simmons.

In 1959 Stump's became the Polk Furniture Company. Their advertisement asked, "Why pay retail when you can buy at Discount Prices?" In addition to furniture, both Stump and Polk Furniture carried radios, ranges, and linoleum. Between 1974 and 1984, when it moved to Springdale, Polk Furniture was managed by Bill Ames.

607 WEST DICKSON

University Auto Service

Probably motivated by the rapid encroachment of commercialization around her residence, Hattie J. Williams sold the Williams house at 607 West Dickson in 1953 and moved to a less congested part of town. The Williams house was demolished around 1954. In 1958 Fred Hanna and Fred Hanna, Jr. constructed a Gulf Station on the lot. Open seven days a week, this service station provided road service,and minor tune-up and brake service in the shop. In 1972 Donald Dingledine purchased the station. In 1987 he got rid of the gasoline tanks and changed the name to University Auto Service. In addition to all kinds of auto repairs and tune-ups, University Auto was a state inspection station and an agent for Ryder Trucks. It moved to North College Avenue in 1997. Now owned by Underwood's, the site is undergoing development.

607 West Dickson, University Auto Service, 1995

611 WEST DICKSON
Underwood's

Around 1897 James H. Williams constructed two rent houses at 611 and 617 West Dickson. Bill Underwood demolished the houses in 1966 to make way for the present Underwood's Jewelry Store building. Bill Underwood, whose business was at that time at 623 West Dickson (later home of Editype), needed additional space. Local architect Fay Jones, who was just beginning his career, also needed space. Neither could afford it, so the two struck a deal. Jones designed the new Underwood's building in exchange for five years' free rent. The Underwood building is the only known commercial building that now world-famous architect Fay Jones designed. The Underwood showroom includes artful wood and glass display cases enhanced by special lighting.

Underwood's was named the best single jewelry store in the United States, and its staff has been recognized with prestigious awards from the industry. Underwood's has specialized in custom design of jewelry with diamonds and other precious stones. Tom Weishaar, Underwood's master goldsmith, is the nation's first Certified Master Bench Jeweler.

Underwood's, 1995

Underwood's ad, 1966

623–653 WEST DICKSON

Rent Houses

653 *West Dickson, 1911*

In 1885 T. P. Harrison purchased the property at the corner of Dickson and University Avenue. He built two rent houses that were demolished by 1940 to make way for the UARK Theater.

UARK Theatre Complex

In 1940, Seligman, Missouri, native Bill Sonneman, one-time owner of the Ozark and Victory Theaters on the Fayetteville square, purchased the old Harrison properties and replaced them with the UARK Theatre building. Designed by Fayetteville architect Paul Young, this property is now known as 643, 645, and 653 West Dickson. The UARK, advertised as the "most modern theatre in Arkansas, and one of the finest in the South" was at 645 West Dickson. "The Haunted Honeymoon," with Robert

UARK Theatre, Williams rent house to east, 1941

GRAND OPENING

UARK THEATRE

THURSDAY

• • •

THE MOST MODERN THEATRE IN ARKANSAS, AND ONE OF THE FINEST IN THE SOUTH

• • •

You Are Invited

• • •

THURSDAY--FRIDAY--SATURDAY

News--Popeye--Other Selected Shorts

Sunday, Matinee & Night 2:30 & 9p.m.

The Current Ozark Show Moves to This Theatre--When Ozark Admission Prices Govern

• • •

Open House Thursday

Night—Organ 6 P. M. to 7:00 P. M. PICTURES——7 and 9 P. M.

INSPECTION OF

HARKEYS — CAMPUS GRILL— ROOF GARDEN AND CARRIE LEE'S Where Coffee and Doughnuts will be Served to All. Before, during Show and After

• • •

UArk Admission Prices

ADULTS 26c—Defense Tax 3—State 1 . . . . Total 30c

THESE PRICES SIX NIGHTS A WEEK—OZARK PRICES ON SUNDAY

• • •

After The Show—

Come In

SCHRAMM'S

INC.

Campus Grill

Catering to the University of Arkansas Students

Most Modernly Furnished Soda Grill In Northwest Arkansas

In the UARK Building

Carrie Lee

Invites you to come in and Eat with the Students . . .

Serving Regular Dinners
Catering to Private Parties

We Serve Meals Not Only to Regular Diners, But Conduct Our Business Like Any Other Restaurent

Plan to Eat Here Whenever You Go Out

CARRIE LEE'S

ON UNIVERSITY ST.

In rear of UARK building

harkey's *Feminine Fashions*

We Invite YOU To Attend Our . . .

FORMAL OPENING

Thursday Evening, Jan. 16th

UARK BUILDING

OUR FASHIONS WILL SURPRISE YOU. COME IN AND LOOK THEM OVER.

UARK Theatre grand-opening ad, 1941

Campus Grill ad, 1941

Fount Allen, 1949

Montgomery, opened the UARK on January 16, 1941. Admission price for adults was 30 cents. After the show, patrons, mostly U of A students, were encouraged to stop next door at the Campus Grill, the "most modernly furnished soda grill in Northwest Arkansas."

Run by former Palace Drug fountain manager Fount Allen, the Campus Grill was one door west and Harkey's Fine Fashions was one door east of the theatre. Of the three new businesses, the UARK Theatre remained in business the longest. Until the early 1960s blacks were not allowed to attend the UARK, as there was no balcony to segregate them. It closed in 1976. Harkey's closed in 1952. The Campus Grill closed in 1968.

623–641 WEST DICKSON

Sonneman Enterprises Grow

In 1947 Bill Sonneman constructed a large commercial building at what is now 623 and 641 West Dickson. The front contained shops and the rear portion, at 625 West

UARK Theater Revival

Shortly after the original UARK Theatre closed, several attempts were made to revive it. Richard Sherin and Jeffery Seidensticker made the first attempt; they showed classic films and scheduled a few musical programs. After this attempt failed, Allan Hickman, Bill Sleeper, and Marvin Davis converted the rear ballroom of the theatre into Fayetteville's first disco—"42nd Street." It provided an alternative to the heavy-metal and country rock that had become popular on Dickson. 42nd Street also helped solidify the UARK's reputation as an entertainment alternative by showing cult classics such as *Rocky Horror Picture Show* and *Pink Flamingos.* It was also known for a brief time as Colonel Smucker's, which was Fayetteville's only New Wave club. Before closing for the last time in 1981, the UARK was known as the UARK Arts Center. Run by Dickson Street entrepreneuse Anita Leflett, it included a coffee house and sponsored a wide range of music including blues, swing, punk rock, and classical. Since that time the UARK has housed many short-lived businesses.

Dickson, was and continues to be the UARK Court Apartments. The first known tenant of 623 West Dickson was the College Jewelry Store, which moved here in 1956. In 1958 Bill Underwood purchased it and renamed the business Underwood's Jewelry. 623 West Dickson was for many years the home of Editype Business Services. Between 1947 and 1977, 641 West Dickson was the home of the Boston Store's Campus Shop. During the 1980s and early 1990s it was occupied by Borealis Baggage Company.

623 WEST DICKSON

Editype

Founded by Stephanie Meehan Eifling , Editype has been on Dickson Street since 1980 and at 623 West Dickson since 1987. Editype offers typing, word processing, and résumé service. Stephanie's writings on Dickson Street published in *The Grapevine* during the 1970s and 1980s have been of enormous assistance with this project.

Dickson Street at night, 1982

611–643 West Dickson, 1995

Dickson Street from the U of A, 1970

643 WEST DICKSON

Best Sports

Best Sports opened at 643 West Dickson in 1979. It sold all kinds of individual and team sporting goods, including monogrammed jackets, uniforms, and shoes. Best Sports also carried a full line of clothing with fraternity and sorority emblems. The business moved off Dickson around 2000.

653 WEST DICKSON

Arkansas Book Store

The Arkansas Book Store, owned by Sterling Anders,opened in 1969. It carried a large stock of textbooks and school supplies. In 1987 Anders merged the Arkansas Book Store with his other business, the Campus Book Store, across the street.

608–648 WEST DICKSON

Reed

The George W. M. Reed family lived on the north side of the 600 block for nearly 100 years. Built in 1851 by A. M. Wilson, the Wilson-Reed house was at 612 West Dickson and was used during the Civil War as a hospital for Union soldiers.

George W. M. Reed was a prominent antebellum merchant and was associated with Barnard, Putnam and Ferguson. Born in 1830 near Rosedale (Franklin County), Arkansas, Reed was a city councilman, a postmaster, and Circuit Clerk. He died in 1897. His wife, Mary Jane Ferguson died in 1925.

612 West Dickson, 1934

George and Mary Jane Reed

Born in 1862 Lina Xantha Reed was the daughter of George and Mary Jane Reed and the sister of John A. Reed, who lived on the northeast corner of College and Dickson. She obtained her formal education from Arkansas Industrial University, Harvard University, and Cornell University. She taught in the Preparatory Department of the Arkansas Industrial University, where she was a colleague of her neighbor Miss Naomi Williams. Reed also served as principal of the Muskogee, Oklahoma, school. An artist, she took lessons from Mrs. Gray, another neighbor. Miss Reed died in 1951.

Before being demolished in 1954, the Wilson-Reed house and the large lot on which it stood were one of the most pleasant landmarks students and faculty passed on their way to the University of Arkansas. The site is currently occupied by Wallace's Campus Bookstore and Hobby-Craft Shopping Center.

608–624 WEST DICKSON
UARK Center

In 1954, three years after Lina Reed's death, J. F. Palmer purchased the Reed house, demolished it, and constructed a service station and a commercial strip called the UARK Center. Unlike other businesses on Dickson Street, the UARK Center at 624 West Dickson had ample parking space. Designed by local architect Paul Young and built by the Tune

Lina X. Reed with niece

612 West Dickson before demolition, 1951

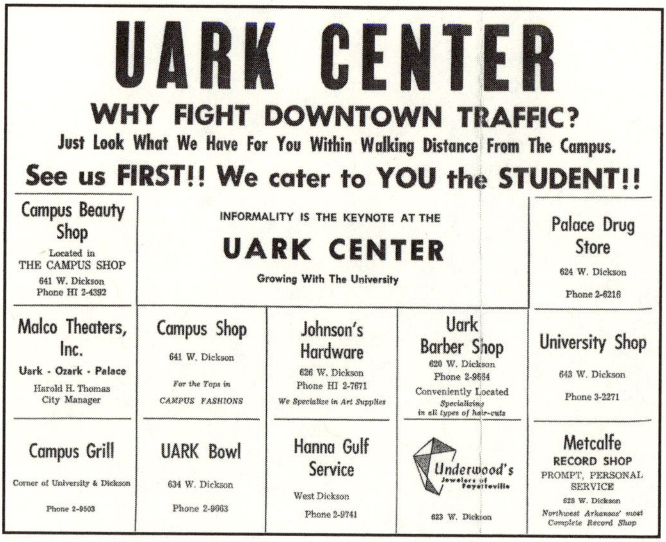

UARK Center ad, 1962

Homecoming parade float. UARK Center at left, 1957

and Fraser construction companies, the "L" shaped shopping center cost approximately $250,000. Many long-time residents consider it Fayetteville's first strip shopping center. In addition to the gas station, the UARK center comprised a drugstore, dime store, grocery store, and space for two smaller businesses. Between September, 1954, when the first tenant moved to the new UARK Shopping Center, and 1981, the anchors were Palace Drug Store, formerly of 422 West Dickson, Piggly Wiggly Grocery Store, and the Mobile service station.

Mobil Oil Station

On February 4, 1955, Dick Steele opened the Mobil Oil Station on the northwest corner of Dickson and Gregg. This station had several owners, including Robert Phelan, who owned it between 1959 and 1968. Open 7 days a week between 7:00 am and midnight, the UARK Mobil was here until 1974.

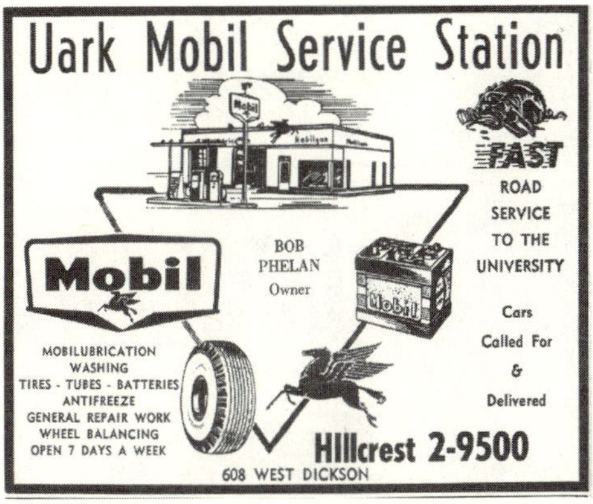

UARK Mobil ad, 1965

Palace Drug Store

The new Palace Drug Store, a Walgreen agency, was the first tenant of the UARK Shopping Center. It had twenty employees and was located immediately east of the UARK Bowl. The Palace Drug Store was the "home of personalized service." In addition to prescription medicines, Henry I. Caudle's new store carried baby necessities, sick room supplies, crutches and cosmetics. They also advertised a complete tobacco department, Whitman, King, and Pangburn Candies, a soda fountain, and a magazine section. The new Palace Drugstore also carried small electrical appliances, radios, television sets, and toys. In 1966 Ray Huff purchased the drugstore. He owned it until 1982, when it closed. One morning in 1974, his partner Joe Bruce was shot while sitting at his desk, apparently a victim of a drug-related robbery. This murder remains one of Fayetteville's unsolved crimes.

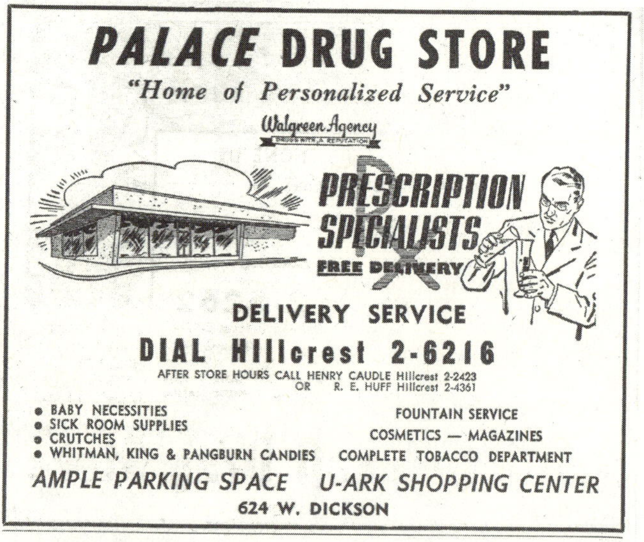

Palace Drug Store ad, 1955

UARK Food Center ad, 1955

UARK Food Center/Piggly Wiggly

Hoyt Greenwood and E. M. Silcott opened the UARK Food Center at 604 West Dickson the first week of June, 1955. In 1957 the UARK Food Center became affiliated with the Piggly Wiggly chain of super-markets. It closed in 1972.

Piggly Wiggly ad, 1957

Mr. Tux, 1995

Mr. Tux

Various persons have operated Mr. Tux, a tuxedo and formal gown rental agency since 1975,when it moved to 608 West Dickson Street, former location of the Mobil Oil Station. While this book was in preparation, Mr. Tux moved to Joyce Plaza in north Fayetteville.

Campus Bookstore

The Campus Bookstore occupies the former Palace Drug Store building at 624 West Dickson. Sterling Anders opened it in 1982. In 1987, after acquiring the stock of the Arkansas Book Store at 653 West Dickson, Campus Bookstore almost doubled in size. This store sells textbooks, school supplies, magazines, and Razorback sportswear.

Hobby-Craft

Hobby-Craft occupies the former Piggly Wiggly site at 612 West Dickson. Various individuals have operated it since its opening in 1983. Throughout its history, Hobby-Craft has been well known for custom picture framing work. They also have a large selection of arts, crafts, and hobby supplies.

Campus Bookstore, 1995

Hobby-Craft, 1995

Downtown Dickson ad, 1970s

U-ARK Bowl ad, 1948

632–644 WEST DICKSON

UARK Bowl

In 1947 Bill Sonneman developed a large parcel of the Lina Reed property on the north side of the street, matching in style and materials his properties on the south side. A two- story white brick building, at what is now 644 West Dickson, housed the UARK Bowl on the street level (also known as Jim Benton's and Razorback Bowl) and a dance hall upstairs. The bowling alley had twelve lanes, AMF automatic pin spotters, billiard tables, and a snack bar. Many business and student leagues bowled there. The UARK Bowl closed in 1971, reopened for a short time and closed for good in 1976. The dance hall closed around 1955 and was replaced by the UARK Bowl Hall, one of Fayetteville's early meeting halls. During the 1950s and 1960s civic organizations such as the Kiwanis, Lions, and Rotary clubs met here.

Boardwalk Shopping Center

By 1979 the former UARK Bowl building was converted into a small indoor shopping center, the Boardwalk. Three of the longest-lasting tenants were the Boardwalk Cafe, the Record Exchange, and Rainbow

Jim Benton's Bowling Lanes ad, 1950s

Graphics. Since the 1970s the second story has housed businesses including barbers, insurance agents, realtors, and photographers. Toward the end of the 1990s the upstairs meeting hall was refurbished for use for upscale entertaining and events.

Boardwalk Cafe, 1995

626 WEST DICKSON
Boarding House

Around 1940 the Reeds sold a lot behind what would become the UARK Bowl Building, and a boarding house was built there. It was originally run by Mrs. Carrie Lee Bivens, the former operator of the Campus Cafeteria, a predecessor of the current Arkansas Union Servery on the campus. When the UARK building opened across the street, Mrs. Bivens advertised her business, Carrie Lee's, in that location. During the mid-1940s Carrie Lee's boarding house was known as the UARK Annex and during the 1950s it was known as the Metcalfe House. The house was torn down in the 1970s.

U-ARK Annex, 1949

Metcalfe Record Shop, 1950s

626–628 WEST DICKSON

Metcalfe Record Shop

The second Sonneman building, a three story structure at what is now 628 West Dickson, was built in 1947 next door to Carrie Lee Bivens' boarding house. The second and third floors contained apartments, and the street level was occupied by Bill Sonneman, Jr.'s U of A Record Shop. In 1951 Edward and Dorothy Metcalfe, natives of Chicago, purchased the fledgling store and renamed it Metcalfe's Record Shop. According to Dorothy Metcalfe, the inventory then consisted almost entirely of 78-rpm records, with only five long-playing records in the entire store. The Metcalfe Record Shop originally concentrated on classical music; however, as time passed, it carried a good selection of jazz and rock 'n' roll records. Its outstanding stock of classical music albums attracted clients from as far away as Missouri and Oklahoma. Metcalfe's also had a soundproof listening booth for previewing recordings. Metcalfe Record Shop sponsored a variety of touring

Metcalfe's, note UARK Annex in rear, 1970s

Wooden Nickel Sportswear, 1995

musical groups, including the Kingston Trio, who, before the days of live music on Dickson Street, played at the University of Arkansas Gymnasium. In 1979, after nearly thirty years in the record business, Mr. and Mrs. Metcalfe sold the store. It closed shortly thereafter.

Around 1962 the Sonneman building at 628 West Dickson was expanded to the east. The addition was known as 626 West Dickson. And like the former Metcalfe Record Shop building, it has housed many businesses, including the Jet Inn Ice Cream Parlor, Editype, Kinkos Copies, and Wooden Nickel Sportswear.

648 WEST DICKSON
University Lutheran Church

The Lutheran Church is a comparative late-comer to Fayetteville among the mainstream Christian denominations. Its modern history begins in September 1943, when the Reverend William Ludwig, pastor of the Salem Lutheran Church of Springdale, began preaching regularly in Fayetteville. On June 5, 1944, Fayetteville Lutherans organized St. John's Lutheran Church. Then they conducted a drive to build a church near the University of Arkansas campus. They selected a site near what was once the Reed property on the corner of West Dickson and Arkansas Avenue. Their architect was Fayetteville resident T. Ewing Shelton. On March 19, 1950, a few months before the completion of the church, the Reverend

St. John's Lutheran Church

The Lutheran Student Chapel at Arkansas University

Building Fund Contributions
1946-1950

Lutheran Women's Missionary League—Western District	$2,500.00
Trinity Lutheran Church, Pine Bluff, Ark.	7.00
Mr. and Mrs. F. I. Kuehnert	10.00
St. John's Lutheran Church, Stuttgart, Ark.	175.00
Mr. and Mrs. A. E. Lussky	19.00
Katherine Lussky	1.15
John Lussky	1.00
Mr. and Mrs. A. J. Peterson	100.00
Miss Margaret Frick	40.00
Lutheran Women's League, First Lutheran Church, Little Rock, Ark.	10.00
Zion Lutheran Church, Waldenburg, Ark.	83.81
First Lutheran Church, Little Rock, Ark.	601.02
Mr. and Mrs. W. L. Ahlemeyer	5.00
St. Matthew's Lutheran Church, Corning, Ark.	39.41
St. Paul's Lutheran Church, Gillett, Ark.	195.46
Memorial Wreath (Mr. Paul McKimm)	15.50
Mrs. Guy Christie	10.00
Immanuel Lutheran Church, Alexander, Ark.	58.90
Mr. C. H. Ahrens	982.60
Zion Lutheran Church, Avilla, Ark.	30.13
Trinity Lutheran Church, North Little Rock, Ark.	45.00
Trinity Lutheran Women's League, North Little Rock, Ark.	15.00
Zion Lutheran Church, Ulm, Ark.	7.95
L. W. Osiek	5.00
Miss Olga Springer	5.00
Lutheran Women's League, Immanuel Lutheran Church, Joplin, Mo.	56.88
Miss Frieda Hill	10.00
Lydia Guild, Bethel Lutheran Church, Little Rock, Ark.	5.00
Mr. Norby	50.00
Lutheran Women's Missionary League—Arkansas-West Tennessee Zone	125.00
Paul Bollinger	1.00
Mrs. Jose Herrera	20.00
Mr. and Mrs. W. J. Derenbecher	5.00
Mrs. Paul McKimm	5.00
Mrs. Cleo Kelley	25.00
Dwight Pattison	2.00
Miss Shirley Brunkhorst	5.00
Mrs. F. G. Reichel	5.00
Mr. George Lussky	25.00
Mr. and Mrs. H. O. Davis (for pews)	1,000.00
Mr. Harry Bollinger	100.00
Friendship Bible Class, Lutheran Church, Hanover, Pa.	25.00
Mr. and Mrs. Henry Rubach	2.00
Miss Clara Maahs	150.00
Mr. and Mrs. Jack Phillips (altar candlesticks)	30.00
First Lutheran Church, Fort Smith, Ark. (for pews)	534.08
Mr. and Mrs. Otto Hennig and family	Hammond Organ
Von Bora Circle, Trinity Lutheran Church, Memphis, Tenn.	100.00

St. John's Lutheran Church dedication, 1950

The Wall at St. John's Lutheran Church, 2000

Marcus Lang officiated at the cornerstone laying ceremony. The cornerstone was laid not in the wall of the church, but in the altar as a reinforcing symbol that the altar is the focal point of the church. In 1986 St. John's moved to Northeast Fayetteville, but continued to sponsor a university center on Dickson Street until 1997. Today the building houses Christ on Campus Ministries. It is now used by several denominations providing worship services to students and others affiliated with the University of Arkansas.

The Wall

According to long-time Dickson Street patron and Vietnam War Veteran, Mike Dameron, during the late 1960s and early 1970s the stone wall fronting University Lutheran Church was a Dickson Street landmark. Hippies used it as a hangout and spare change center when hippiedom first arrived in Fayetteville. Of course, most of the area's merchants were not pleased with this. Several unsuccessful attempts were made to disband the hippie hangout, including dumping a large pile of cow manure on the site. Eventually, hippiedom passed on, but the near-fabled wall remains.

Beat Texas Week

Beat Texas Week was a-long standing celebration for University of Arkansas students when the U of A, as a member of the Southwest Conference, had an annual rivalry with the University of Texas. Every student has memories of at least one Beat Texas Week. Beat Texas Week made the newspaper in 1971. Students attended a well-organized pep rally at the Chi Omega Greek Theatre, which was to be followed by a dance at the UARK Bowl Hall. However, the rally just moved down the street to a huge bonfire that had been erected on the corner of Arkansas Avenue and West Dickson. By 8:30 that evening the street was impassable, as hundreds of cheerful, excited, and probably inebriated students marched down Dickson toward the square, calling the Hogs and singing the Razorback fight song as they passed each intersection. Needless to say, the planned dance at the UARK Bowl was not as exciting as the events transpiring outside.

Beat Texas Week festivities, 1971

Congestion on Dickson Street, 1971

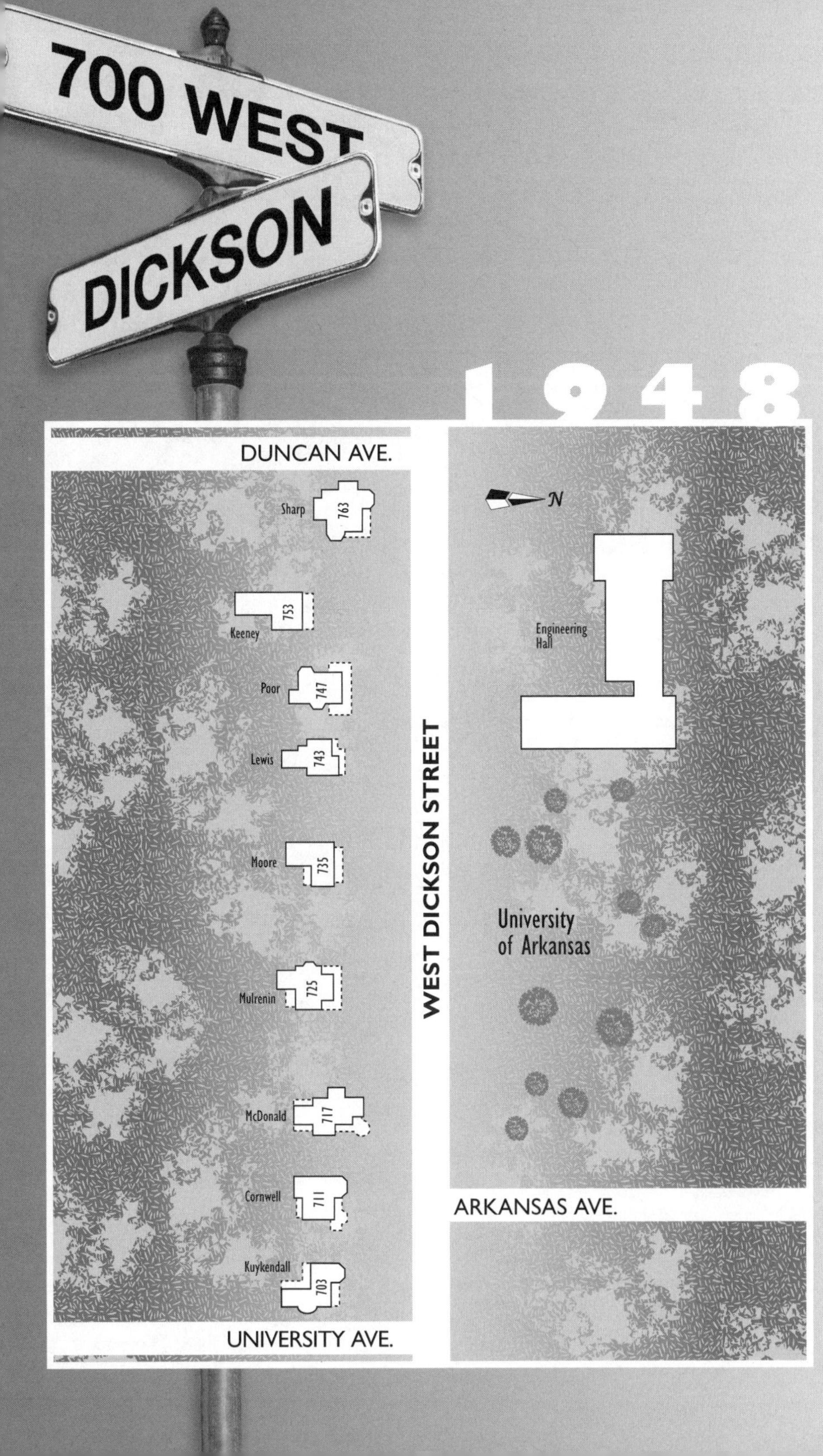
700 WEST
DICKSON
1948
DUNCAN AVE.
Sharp 763
753 Keeney
Poor 747
Lewis 743
Moore 735
Mulrenin 725
McDonald 717
Cornwell 711
Kuykendall 703
UNIVERSITY AVE.
WEST DICKSON STREET
N
Engineering Hall
University of Arkansas
ARKANSAS AVE.

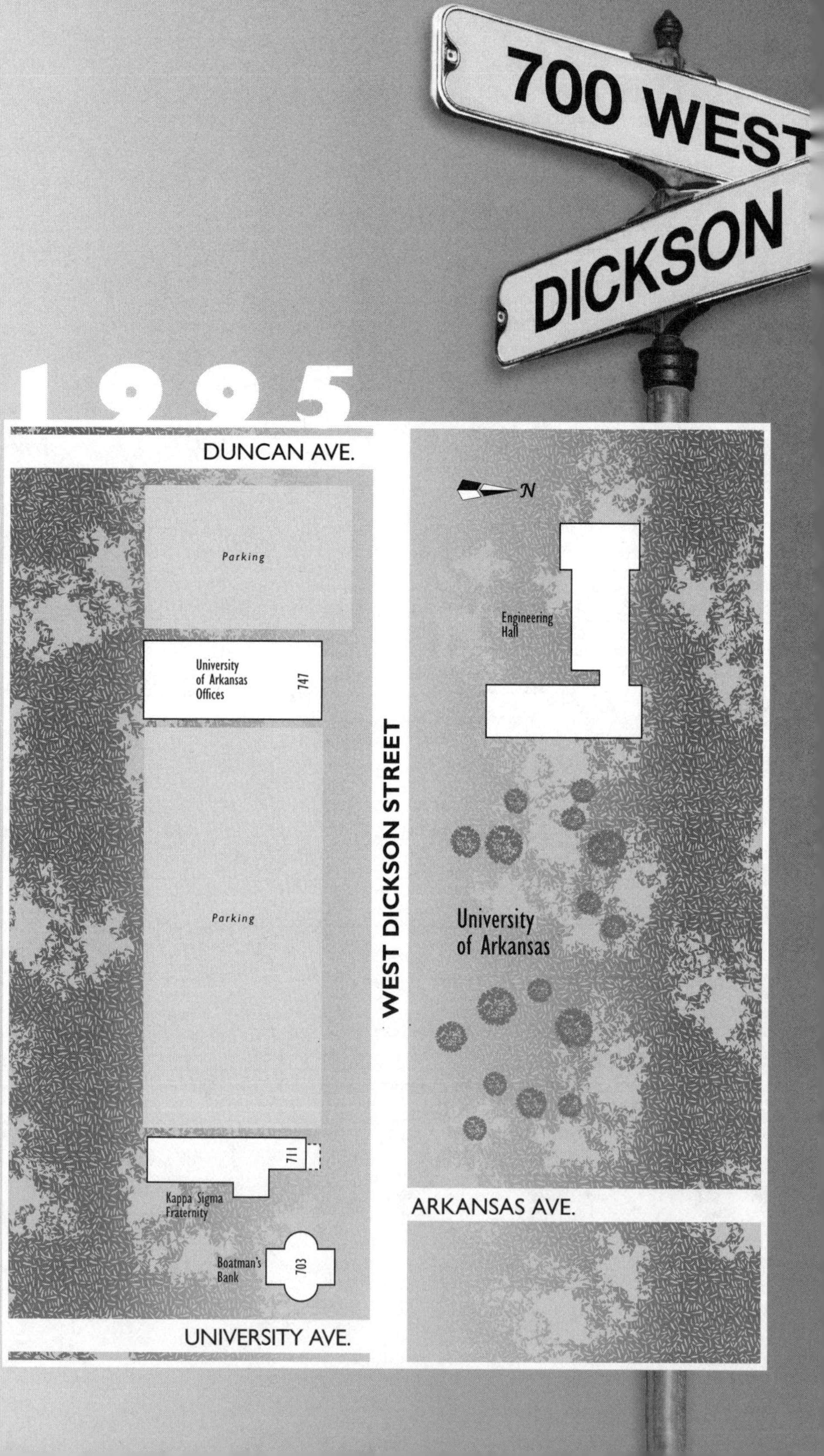
700 WEST
DICKSON
1995
DUNCAN AVE.
Parking
University of Arkansas Offices
747
Parking
711
Kappa Sigma Fraternity
Boatman's Bank
703
UNIVERSITY AVE.
WEST DICKSON STREET
N
Engineering Hall
University of Arkansas
ARKANSAS AVE.

700 BLOCK

Dickson Street continues to climb uphill toward the U of A in the 700 block. Between 1868 and 1897 the eastern half of the block was known as "Reed's Pasture," named for its owner, George W. M. Reed, resident of the 600 block. The western half was owned by the William McIlroy family, who lived in the last block of West Dickson Street. In 1897, the year of Mr. Reed's death, both the Reeds and the McIlroys began selling the undeveloped property to individuals interested in locating near the university. By 1908 the 700 block of West Dickson contained large two-story

Dickson Street looking east from the 700 block, 1952

Dickson Street at the southeast entrance to the University of Arkansas, 2000

Dickson Street from the southeast entrance to the University of Arkansas, 1983

frame houses across the street from the university's front lawn. Many of the families owning these houses provided room and board for university faculty and students. A few families also sold or rented all or portions of their homes to fraternity and sorority groups.

703 WEST DICKSON

Boarding House

Many tenants, including Circuit Clerk Millard Croxdale, the Kappa Kappa Gamma Sorority, and the Future Farmers of America, rented a house at the southwest corner of Dickson and University. Before being demolished in 1964, it was known as the Tedford Rooming House.

703 West Dickson, 1932

Bank of America

The only business in the 700 block is . . . well, they changed its name four times since I began this project!! When constructed in 1965, the auto bank on the corner of Dickson and Arkansas Avenue was known as First National Bank. In 1992 Worthen Bank of Little Rock purchased First National's assets. In 1995 Boatmen's Bank of Arkansas bought it. In 1997 it was acquired by Nationsbank. Since 1998 it has been known as Bank of America.

1st NATIONAL BANK

FAYETTEVILLE, ARKANSAS

"The Friendly Bank"

OFFICERS

HERBERT A. LEWIS
CHAIRMAN OF THE BOARD

ELLIS E. SHELTON
PRESIDENT

EVERETT SKELTON
VICE PRESIDENT

ALLEN W. DOWELL
VICE PRESIDENT

GEORGE L. DOCKERBY
VICE PRESIDENT
and TRUST OFFICER

DANIEL EPPERLY
ASST. VICE PRESIDENT

PAUL GAYER
ASST. VICE PRESIDENT

KEITH ROBBINS
CASHIER

LOYD SWOPE
ASST. CASHIER and
FARM REPRESENTATIVE

BARBARA MITCHELL
ASST. CASHIER

WARREN LANGHAM
ASST. CASHIER

WARREN LITTLE
ASST. CASHIER

DAN HUDSPETH
ASST. CASHIER

DIRECTORS

JEFF BAGGETT
MAUPIN CUMMINGS
BILL DALTON
HAL DOUGLAS
J. E. DOWELL
VINCENT O. LESH
HERBERT A. LEWIS
RALPH LEWIS
ELLIS E. SHELTON
CLINT WALDEN

UNIVERSITY BRANCH

EVELYN HILLS
SHOPPING CENTER
BRANCH

DIAL
HI llcrest 2-2347

Established 1904

1st National Bank ad, 1968

Boatmen's Bank, 1995

711 WEST DICKSON

Cornwell

Charles H. Bell, a long-term resident of 6 West Dickson, constructed a house at 711 West Dickson around 1897. Between 1904 and 1921 it was the home of William A. and Allie Cornwell. Born in Findlay, Ohio, in 1865 Cornwell was in the lumber business in Ohio and Iowa. He married Allie Utterback in 1889. She was born in Delta, Iowa, in 1869. They moved to Arkansas in 1904. Cornwell was the manager of the Fayetteville Lumber and Cement Company.

Kappa Sigma Fraternity

In 1921 the Kappa Sigma Fraternity purchased the Cornwell house. Founded in 1869 at the University of Virginia, Kappa Sigma is the oldest fraternity on the University of Arkansas campus. The Xi Chapter, which claims to be the largest and most celebrated chapter of Kappa Sigma, was established here in 1890. One of the first initiates was John C. Futrall, a football coach at the time, and the longest-serving President of the

711 West
Dickson, 1928

Kappa Sigma
Fraternity
House, 1995

University of Arkansas. In 1929 the Kappa Sigmas tore down the old Cornwell house and replaced it with a larger brick house. By 1972 the house was worn out and was condemned. However, the Kappa Sigmas decided to renovate the property and returned to the house in 1976. Today the Kappa Sigma house stands as the sole reminder of the many houses that once graced the 700 block of West Dickson.

717 WEST DICKSON

McDonald

Oliver P. McDonald

Oliver P. McDonald and his wife, Hattie J. Whorton, lived at 717 West Dickson between 1906 and 1923. Born in Grinnell, Iowa, in 1864, McDonald obtained his education at Iowa State University in Ames. For several years afterward, McDonald taught school in Iowa and California. He practiced law at Carroll, Iowa, for fifteen years before moving to Fayetteville in 1906. Upon moving here, McDonald was first associated with John Mayes in the practice of law and later with J. W. Grabiel. McDonald died in 1920. Mrs. McDonald left 717 West Dickson in 1923.

717 West Dickson, 1940

Kappa Alpha Fraternity

In 1924 Mrs. McDonald sold her house to the Kappa Alpha Fraternity, which occupied the residence until 1939. Founded in 1865 at Washington and Lee University, the Kappa Alphas established the Omicron Chapter at the University of Arkansas in 1895. The Kappa Alphas aimed to foster and maintain the customs, manners and ideals of the old colonial south. Before folding in 1959, the Kappa Alphas also rented the Bell house at 6 West Dickson Street between 1949 and 1953.

725 WEST DICKSON

Mulrenin

John F. and Mary Mulrenin lived at 725 West Dickson between 1900 and 1961. Mulrenin was a conductor for the St. Paul Branch of the Frisco Railroad until his death in 1937. The Mulrenins were natives of St. Louis, Missouri, and were members of St. Joseph's Catholic Church. Mrs. Mulrenin was also a member of the Tuesday Musical Club.

735 WEST DICKSON

Field

Julius H. Field

Julius H. Field and his wife, Minnie A. Dies, moved to 735 West Dickson in 1933. Field, a photographer, established his studio at this location. Born in Waupun, Wisconsin, in 1869, Field was one of the best art photographers in the United States, his work appearing regularly in the *New York Times.* Field credited his move to Fayetteville to an article for which he made the illustrations, William R. Lighton's back-to-the-land piece, "An Arkansas Farm," which appeared in *The Saturday Evening Post* in 1910. In the early 1900s, Field was in partnership with

C. L. Dunlap. Field was so dedicated to his desire to capture local color and scenery that once he walked the twenty-two miles to Winslow snapping photographs of subjects he encountered on the way. His photographs have immortalized the University of Arkansas, as well as the University of Oklahoma and the University of Wisconsin. Field died in 1936. Mrs. Field stayed at 735 West Dickson until 1961.

743 WEST DICKSON

English

James A. and Dove English lived at 743 West Dickson Street between 1925 and 1957. Born in 1878 in Dutch Mills, Arkansas, English was a vice-president of the Bank of Lincoln. He was also a farmer and orchardist. Mrs. English was a native of Texas. In 1933, eight years after moving here, Dove English died. James English died in 1957.

747 WEST DICKSON

Poor

Dr. Thomas C. Poor, a well-known physician, and his wife, Ruth A. Shelby, moved from Farmington to 747 West Dickson in 1903. He died in 1911. Born in 1851, Mrs. Poor was a native of St. Louis County, Missouri. She married Dr. Poor in 1880 and died in 1926. Mrs. Poor won second place in the *Fayetteville Democrat's* 1916 "Who's Who" contest in which contestants were given clues with which to guess the names and addresses of sixty-five businesses in the city. After Mrs. Poor's death, her niece, Merle Champion, and her husband, Oscar L. Champion, also lived at 747 West Dickson until 1949, when they moved to Miami, Florida. Champion was in the insurance business. He and Tony Sowder established Champion's News Stand and Tony's at 520 West Dickson in 1908. Mrs. Champion was first-place winner in the same contest her aunt entered.

753 WEST DICKSON

Keeney

Dr. J. C. and Haseltine Keeney moved to 753 West Dickson in 1897. Born in 1847 Keeney practiced medicine at Hindsville until retiring to

753 West Dickson, 1928

Fayetteville. He died in 1907. Hazeltine Forrester Keeney was born in 1858 at Lee Creek (Crawford County). She married Dr. Keeney in 1876 and lived at 753 West Dickson until 1922.

Sigma Phi Epsilon Fraternity

The Arkansas Alpha chapter of Sigma Phi Epsilon Fraternity occupied the Keeney house between 1931 and 1937 and between 1950 and 1959. The chapter was established in 1907, shortly after the fraternity was organized in 1901. Sigma Phi Epsilon declares that it was founded on the cardinal principles of Virtue, Diligence, and Brotherly Love. The local chapter became inactive in 1939 and was reactivated in 1948.

763 WEST DICKSON
Sharp

Between 1909 and 1953, 763 West Dickson was the home of Lena Lewis Sharp, the daughter of Uncle Gus and Sophia Lewis. A great history enthusiast, Lena Lewis Sharp was a popular speaker at the first

Sigma Phi Epsilon

EDWARD CAREY, President

Founded Nationally: Richmond College, November 1, 1901.
Colors: Purple and Red
Flowers: American Beauty Rose and Purple Violet

Through the years Sigma Phi Epsilon has become known as "The Fraternity with a Heart." The distinctive golden heart pin worn by generations of Sig Eps is symbolic of the spirit and ideals which helped to carry the twelve original founders through their first few adverse years.

At Arkansas, the life of a Sig Ep is a full one. Besides intramural sports and other school functions, social events such as the Golden Heart Formal and the Spring Outing, as well as the Moonshiner's Ball and April Fool's Masquerade, are looked forward to by each Sig Ep.

The Arkansas Chapter residence at 753 West Dickson shares one thing with all other chapter houses across the United States — the traditional red door. Behind these doors are men with a common purpose, preserving and furthering the traditions that have built Sigma Phi Epsilon.

Officers:	1st Semester	2nd Semester
President	Ralph Martin	Edward Carey
Vice-President	John Selig	Jim Skillen
Secretary	Ray McMillan	Bob Zierak
Treasurer	Lawrence Schmitz	Bill Love

MOONSHINER'S Ball is an annual occasion at the Sigma Phi Epsilon house. The festival attracts all varieties of weirdly-bedecked distillers and their dates.

Sigma Phi Epsilon fraternity, 1956

763 West Dickson, 1969

Fayetteville and Washington County Historical Society, which was founded in 1927 in anticipation of Fayetteville's centennial celebration the following year. 763 West Dickson was also the last home of Uncle Gus and Sophia Lewis, who died in 1928 and 1940, respectively.

717–763 WEST DICKSON
Ample Parking Space

Between the 1940s and 1960s the houses in the 700 block that were not already rented to fraternities or sororities were converted into apart-

KUAF National Public Radio, 1995

Parking at Dickson and Duncan, 1995

ments and boarding houses. All but the Kappa Sigma Fraternity House were demolished by the 1970s and replaced by a massive parking lot on the south side of the street. In 1965 Dr. Poor's house was demolished and replaced by a brick structure housing the Francesca Apartments. In 1976 the University of Arkansas purchased the property. Today it houses some University offices and KUAF, the local affiliate of National Public Radio.

800 WEST
DICKSON

1948

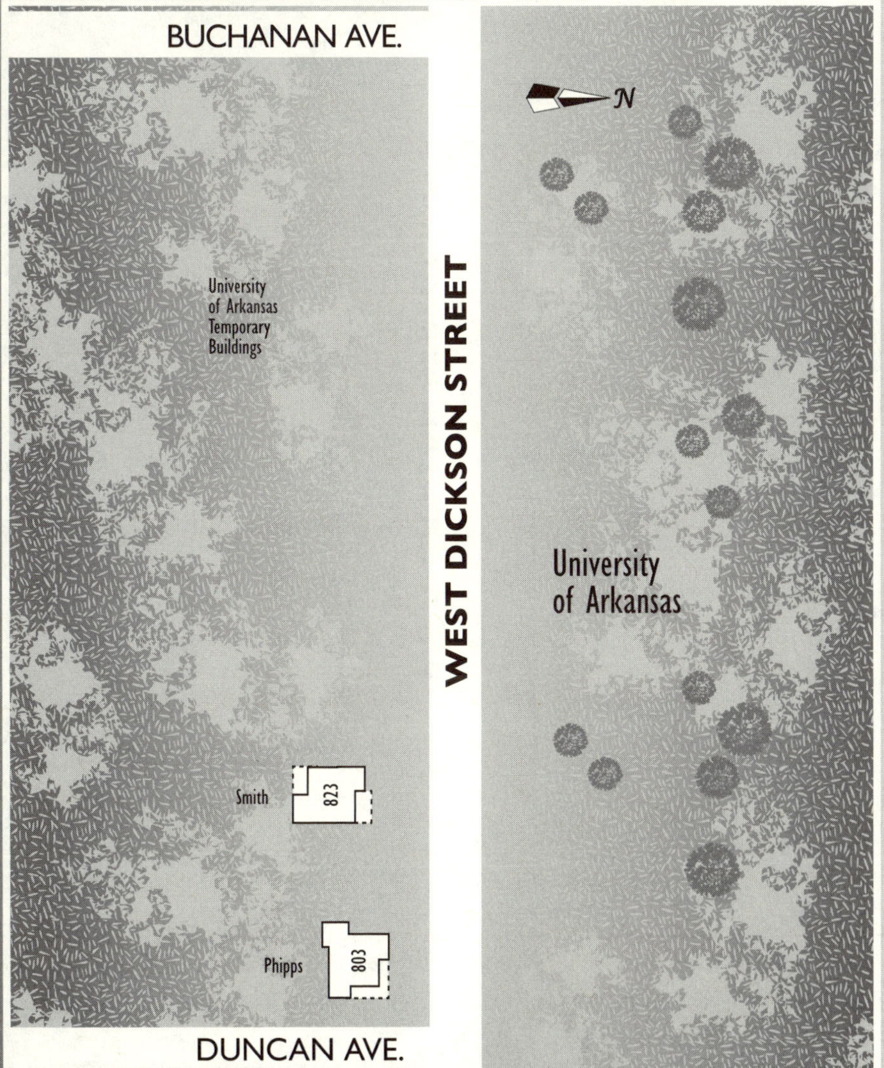
BUCHANAN AVE.
N
University of Arkansas Temporary Buildings
WEST DICKSON STREET
University of Arkansas
Smith
823
Phipps
803
DUNCAN AVE.

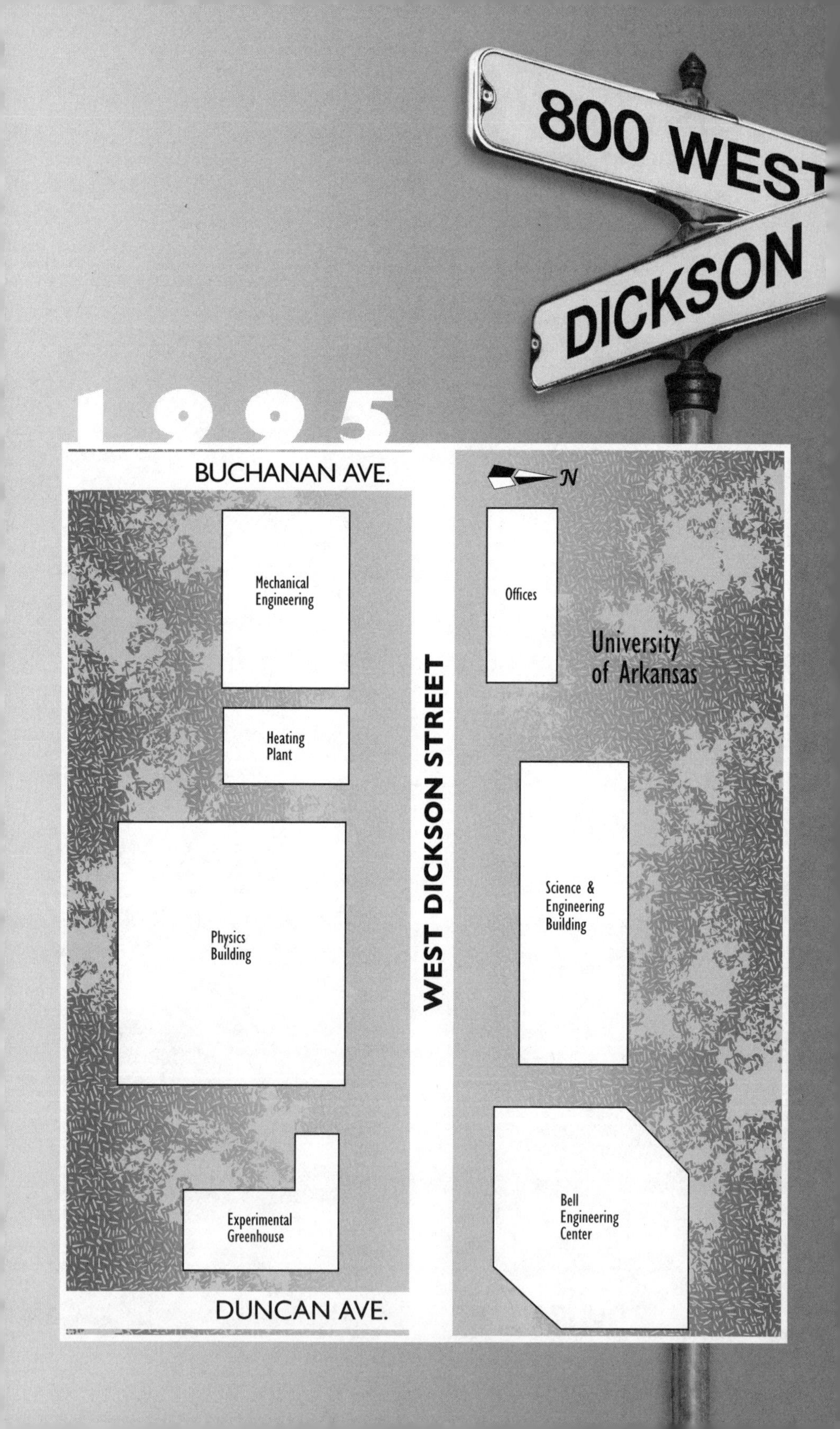
800 WEST
DICKSON
1995
BUCHANAN AVE.
N
Mechanical Engineering
Offices
University of Arkansas
Heating Plant
WEST DICKSON STREET
Physics Building
Science & Engineering Building
Experimental Greenhouse
Bell Engineering Center
DUNCAN AVE.

800 BLOCK

Dickson Street goes downhill one last time toward the University of Arkansas in the 800 block before turning uphill in the 900 block. Until the 1890s the McIlroy family, residents of the 1000 block of West Dickson, owned the mostly undeveloped property on the south side of the street. For many years after 1871 the north side was the southern boundary of the University of Arkansas campus. Until the 1940s the south side of the street contained three boarding houses. Not much information could be located on the residents or houses in this block.

803 WEST DICKSON

Thomason

W. T. and Fannie Thomason lived at 803 West Dickson Street between 1892 and 1929. Their home was on the southwest corner of Dickson and Duncan, the present location of a University of Arkansas greenhouse. Born in 1827, Thomason was a state representative for Washington County during the 1870s and a part of the 1890s. He died in 1909. Mrs. Thomason died in 1929, while visiting her daughter, Annie Dunlap, in Mississippi. Mrs. Dunlap was the wife of C. L. Dunlap, who had been a photographer and associate of Julius H. Field in Fayetteville in the early 1900s. The Thomasons were members of First Baptist Church.

Phipps

James U. Phipps and his wife, Rhea Duncan, also owned the house at 803 West Dickson. They operated it as a boarding house between 1944 and 1955. Born in 1896, Phipps was a veteran of Word War I. He was a laboratory technician at the Veterans Administration Hospital. James and Rhea Phipps were members of Central Methodist Church.

Jessie James Lauderdale

Jessie James and Anna Marie Lauderdale lived at 803 West Dickson Street between 1961 and 1972 and at 901 West Dickson between 1956 and 1961. Born in Missouri in 1900, Lauderdale was a U of A Physical Plant worker. The Lauderdales at one time were also owners of the Nook Cafe at 407 West Dickson. Mr. Lauderdale died in 1970. In 1976 Mrs. Lauderdale moved to 220 East Dickson, where she lived until 1986.

811–843 WEST DICKSON

Not much is known about the residents or houses at 811 and 843 West Dickson. However, as one would expect in a university town, these houses were run as student boarding houses. In the late 1940s and early 1950s Mrs. Fraser ran the house at 811 West Dickson.

Fraser Boarding House ad, 1950

Engineering Hall, 1926

University of Arkansas Buildings

Around 1947 the University of Arkansas began purchasing property on the south side Dickson Street. The first residence to be demolished was at 843 West Dickson, near Buchanan Avenue. The university placed several prefabricated temporary buildings on the site. In time the U of A acquired the remaining properties on the block. In 1951 the U of A constructed the present Physics Building at 823 West Dickson. It was enlarged, remodeled, and upgraded in 1993 and 1994. In 1956 the U of A built a heating plant at 841 West Dickson. Since 1964 the Mechanical Engineering Building has been on the southeast corner of West Dickson and Buchanan, where the temporary buildings once stood. In 1976 the U of A purchased the Lauderdale house at 803 West Dickson, the last remaining residence in the block, demolished it, and put up an experimental greenhouse.

Bell Engineering Center, 1995

Science-Engineering, 1995

Streetlight at Duncan and Dickson, 1940s and 1995

Greenhouse and Bell Engineering, 1995

Physics Building, 1995

Heating Plant, 1956

Old Geology Building, 1995

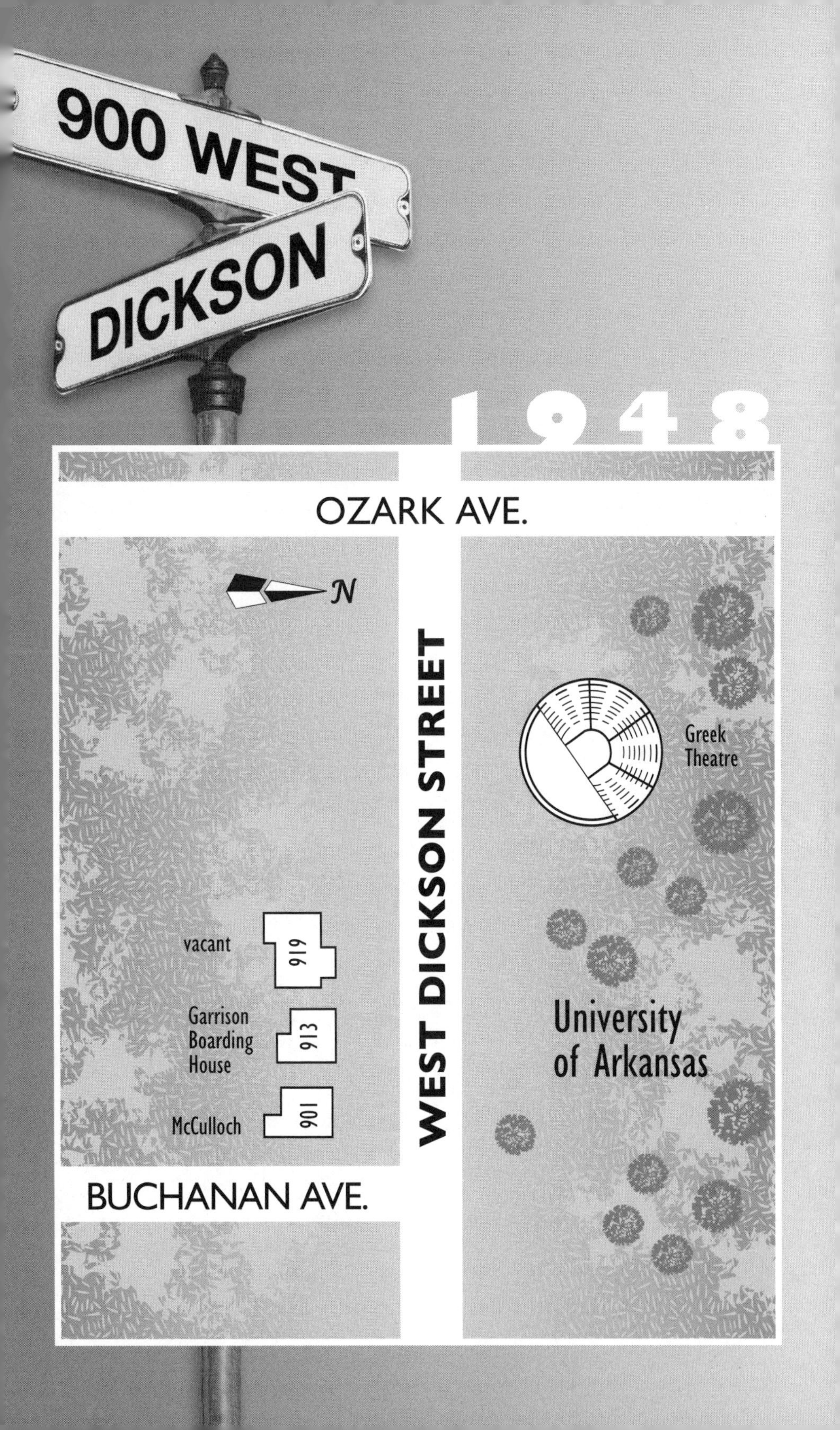
900 WEST
DICKSON
1948
OZARK AVE.
N
WEST DICKSON STREET
Greek Theatre
vacant
919
Garrison Boarding House
913
McCulloch
901
University of Arkansas
BUCHANAN AVE.

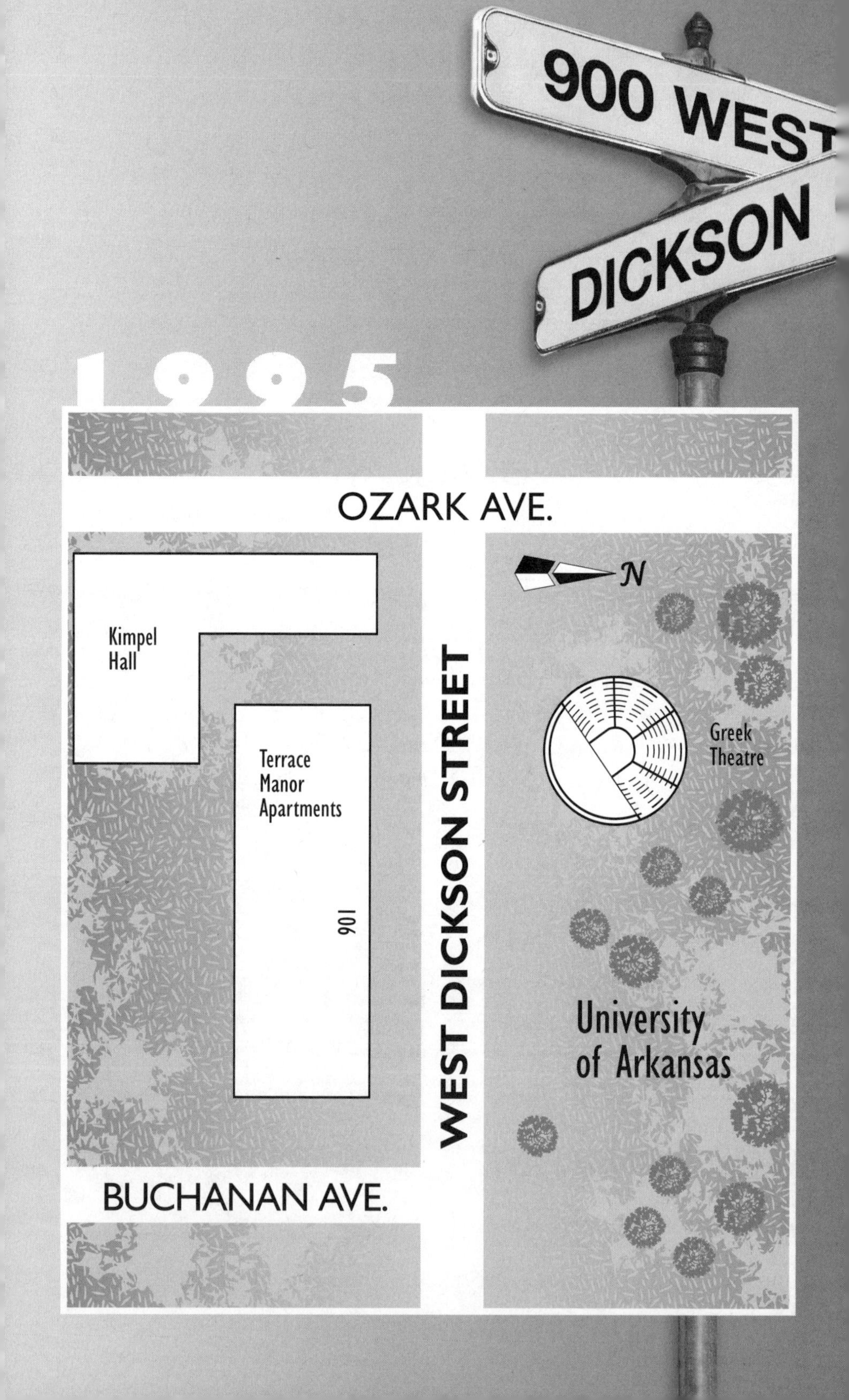
900 WEST
DICKSON
1995
OZARK AVE.
N
Kimpel Hall
Terrace Manor Apartments
901
WEST DICKSON STREET
Greek Theatre
University of Arkansas
BUCHANAN AVE.

900 BLOCK

Dickson Street makes its final uphill climb toward the U of A in the 900 block. The McIlroy family, living in the 1000 block, also owned the undeveloped property on the south side of this block until the early 1900s. Around 1907 three residences were constructed. As with the 800 block, information about the residences and residents of the 900 block is scanty.

901 WEST DICKSON

Campbell

James R. Campbell and his wife, Nicie Clouse, operated a boarding house at 901 West Dickson Street between 1920 and 1936. Their house was on the southwest corner of Buchanan and Dickson, the site of the University of Arkansas's Terrace Manor Apartments, demolished in 2005.

913 WEST DICKSON

Garrison

Alvin J. and Clara Garrison lived at 913 West Dickson Street between 1926 and 1959 and ran a boarding house at 901 West Dickson between 1940 and 1945. Born in 1867, Garrison was employed by the physical plant department of the University for more than twenty years. He was a member of First Christian Church and the Modern Woodmen of America. Mr. Garrison died in 1949. Born in 1871, Mrs. Garrison was a member of Central Methodist Church. She lived here until 1959.

919 WEST DICKSON

Allen

The Dan M. Allen family lived at 919 West Dickson between 1916 and 1930. Born in Mississippi in 1873, Allen moved to Arkansas in 1879 and to Fayetteville in 1894, where he was associated with the Pierce Oil Company. During the early 1900s he was assistant cashier of the McIlroy Bank & Trust Company. During the 1910s and 1920s he was prominently identified with real estate interests in Fayetteville. In 1914 he was elected representative to the Arkansas General Assembly, where he served until 1917. For two years he was also treasurer of the University of Arkansas. Allen was first married in 1896 to his neighbor, Kate McIlroy, who died in 1902. His second wife was Lottie Fitzgerald, a native of Little Rock. Allen was a member of Central Presbyterian Church and of the Modern Woodmen of America. Both of his wives were members of St. Paul's Episcopal Church. Between 1949 and 1950, the Girls' 4-H Club occupied the former Allen home.

919 West Dickson, 1949

Terrace Manor Apartments

Between the 1940s and 1960s the residences in the 900 block were used primarily as boarding houses for University of Arkansas students. Around 1965 the University of Arkansas purchased the properties at 901, 913, and 919 West Dickson and demolished them to put up the Terrace Manor Apartments, the home of many students and new faculty at 901 West Dickson. These in turn were razed in 2005 to make way for academic buildings.

Kimpel Hall

The south side of the 900 block is also the location of Kimpel Hall, which has been at the southeast corner of Dickson and Ozark since 1969. This building, first known as the Communications Center, was named in honor of University of Arkansas English professor Ben Kimpel. In addition to English and Communications, Kimpel Hall houses the Drama, Foreign Language, and Journalism Departments. Walter J. Lemke, a longtime resident of East Dickson, founded the journalism department in 1930, and it was named in his honor in 1988.

Terrace Manor Apartments , 2000

Kimpel Hall, 1969

above: *Ben Kimpel bust, 1995*

right: *Looking east from Kimpel Hall after snowstorm, 1988*

Chi Omega Greek Theater

In 1930 the national Chi Omega Fraternity, a women's organization, presented the outdoor Greek Theatre to the University, where Chi Omega was established in 1895. Located on the north side of Dickson Street, it has been the site of numerous student ceremonies, rallies, and concerts. It can accommodate three thousand people. The theatre is said to be an almost exact replica of an amphitheater built at the foot of the acropolis in Athens, Greece, almost 2500 years ago. The fourteen columns that form the backdrop of the theatre represent the first fourteen members of Chi Omega. The words Knowledge, Intelligence, Courage, Culture, Integrity, and Enlightenment, meant to represent the ideals of the University and of Chi Omega, are inscribed across the back of the theatre.

Chi Omega Greek Theatre, 919 West Dickson (rear), 1930s

Chi Omega Greek Theatre Renovation, 1995

Chi Omega Theatre
Kent State Protest

On Friday evening, May 8, 1970, University students burned an effigy of President Richard Nixon at the Chi Omega Greek Theatre. The next morning, seven hundred fifty people marched down Dickson to the Fayetteville square protesting the shooting at Kent State University of demonstrators against the Viet Nam war and the American invasion of Cambodia. In an apparently unrelated incident, there was a small fire at the Marine Corps Recruiting Station at 316 West Dickson earlier that morning. Fayetteville Fire Chief Burl Skelton said that although the Marine Corps and Navy Recruiting Stations, which shared space in the same building, had been the subject of an earlier protest, there was no evidence linking the fire to the May 9 anti-war demonstration.

Chi Omega Renovation

Since its construction in 1930, the theater has been renovated several times, most recently in 1994–1995 to celebrate the centennial of Chi Omega's founding.

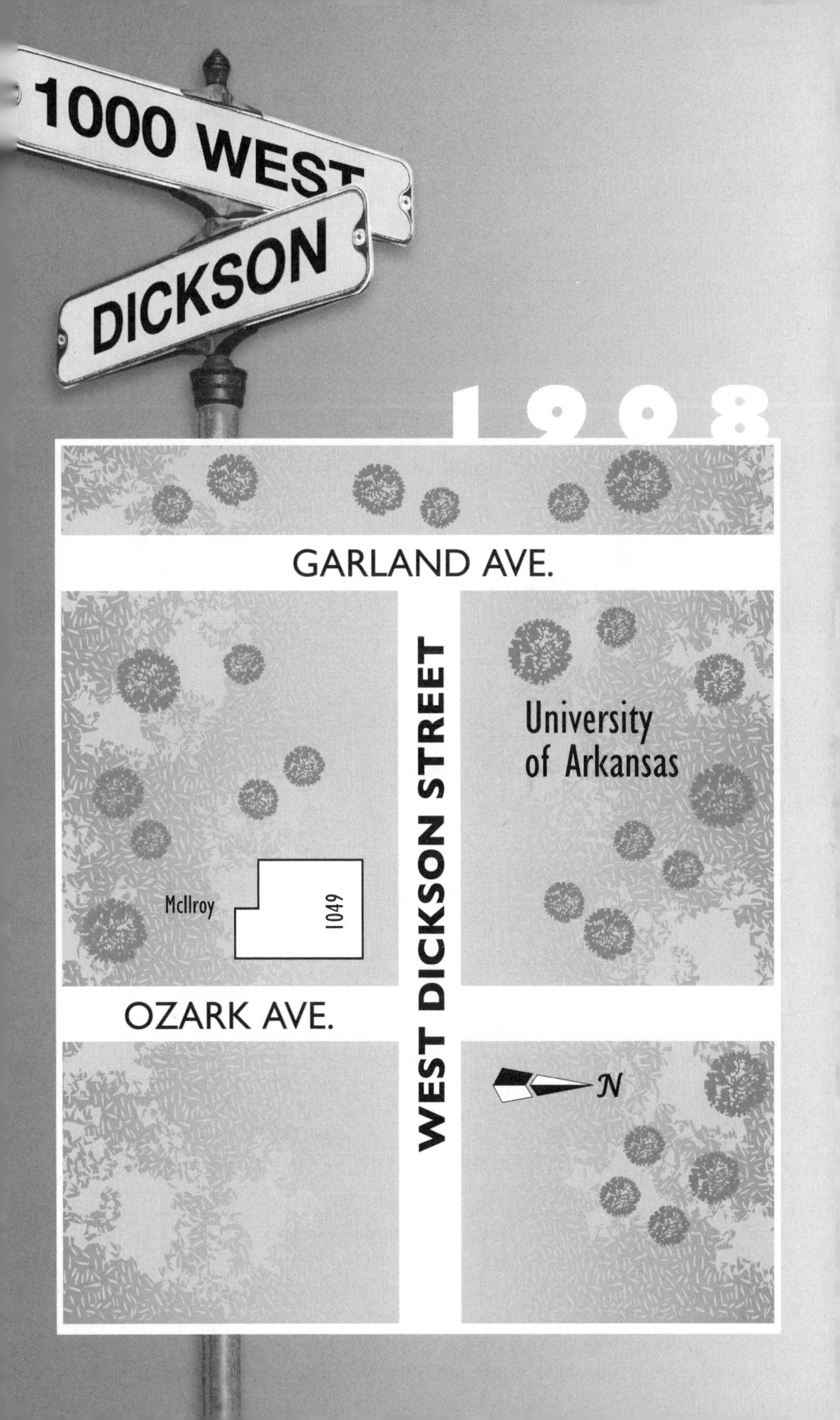
1000 WEST
DICKSON
1998
GARLAND AVE.
WEST DICKSON STREET
University of Arkansas
McIlroy
1049
OZARK AVE.
N

1000 WEST
DICKSON

1995

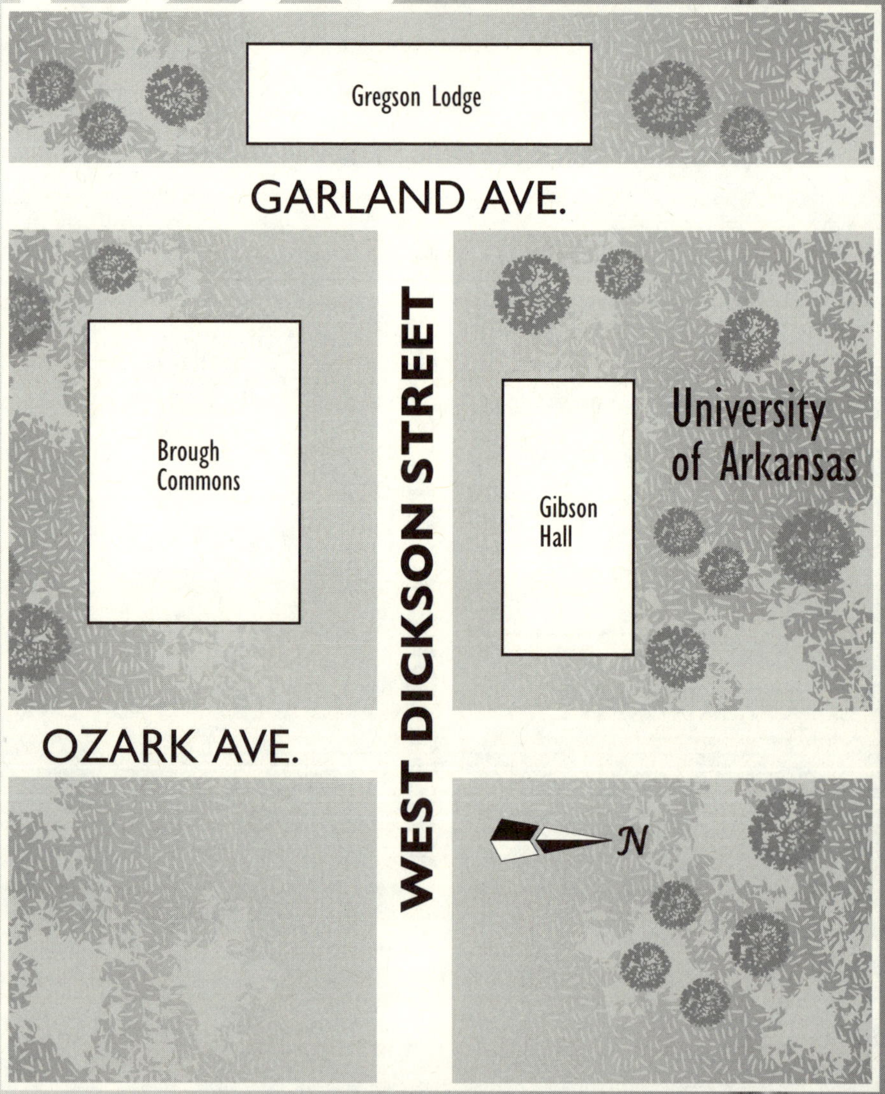
Gregson Lodge
GARLAND AVE.
Brough Commons
WEST DICKSON STREET
Gibson Hall
University of Arkansas
OZARK AVE.
N

1000 BLOCK

The 1000 block is the last, or, depending upon your perspective, the first block of Dickson Street. It is situated on top of the hill on which the University of Arkansas was established in 1871. For most of its history, the 1000 block has been associated with the McIlroy Family, the Sigma Alpha Epsilon Fraternity, and the University of Arkansas.

U of A aerial photograph (note boarding houses on south side of Dickson), 1947

1049 WEST DICKSON
McIlroy

William McIlroy owned the property in this block until his death in 1886. Born in North Carolina during the War of 1812, he moved to Madison County, Arkansas, in 1838 with his wife Mrs. Eliza Jane Russell, a native of Kentucky. Around 1855, they moved to Fayetteville, where McIlroy established a small mercantile. In 1864, Mrs. McIlroy died and in 1865, William McIlroy married Martha Brooks, a native of Tennessee. In 1871, he sold a large portion of his farm to the State of Arkansas for the establishment of a land-grant college in Fayetteville. Originally known as Arkansas Industrial University, it became the University of Arkansas in 1899. In 1872, McIlroy established McIlroy Bank & Trust Company, which, until it was purchased by the Arvest Bank Group, was the oldest bank in Arkansas. In addition to the mercantile and banking business, William McIlroy was at one time Road Overseer for the Boston Mountain District.

William and Martha Brooks McIlroy

After Mrs. Martha McIlroy's death in 1896, their son James Hayden McIlroy and his wife Sarah Ann Rhea took possession of the property. Born in 1868, J. H. McIlroy was president of the McIlroy Bank & Trust Company until his death in 1939. McIlroy organized the Industrial Finance Company, was a commissioner for construction of the Washington County Courthouse in 1904, and was on the paving district responsible for paving the Fayetteville square. In addition, McIlroy was at one time an associate of George W. Donaghey, who built several buildings on the University of Arkansas campus and later served the state as governor.

James Hayden "J. H." McIlroy

Around 1871 the McIlroys built a large house on what became the southwest corner of Dickson and Ozark, and is now the corner of Dickson and McIlroy. Around 1900 they enlarged the house considerably and lived there until 1908, when they began renting the house as a residence hall for student groups. Between 1908 and 1922 the Sigma Chi Fraternity rented the house. In 1913 part of the house was occupied by Catholic girls attending the university and by their sponsors, the Sisters of the Incarnate Word, a Catholic order from Mexico. During the summer months, the McIlroys leased rooms to tourists visiting the Arkansas Ozarks. According to a brochure published in 1911 by the Frisco Railroad, this house was "one of the finest buildings in the city . . . Baths, city water, billiard room . . . Livery charge is 25c per person. Rates, $1.50 per day, $9.00 per week, $35.00 per month."

1049 West Dickson, 1926

Sigma Chi Fraternity

In 1908 the Sigma Chi Fraternity rented the McIlroy house. They occupied it until 1922. Founded at Miami University of Ohio in 1855 Sigma Chi installed the Omega Omega Chapter at the University of Arkansas campus in 1906. Between 1902 and 1906, prior to becoming a chapter, this organization was known as the Indian Club. It was primarily social in nature.

Sigma Alpha Epsilon Fraternity

Sigma Alpha Epsilon House, 1940s

In 1923 the Sigma Alpha Epsilon Fraternity purchased the McIlroy house. They occupied it until 1954. Founded in 1856 at the University of Alabama, the Sigma Alpha Epsilon Fraternity established the Alpha Upsilon Chapter at the University of Arkansas in 1893. Like Sigma Chi, Sigma Alpha Epsilon was also a social fraternity. With the exception of the Kappa Sigma Fraternity at 711 West Dickson, the Sigma Alpha Epsilon Fraternity was on Dickson Street longer than any other fraternity.

Brough Commons

Between 1954 and 1958 the vacant McIlroy house fell into disrepair. In 1958 the University demolished the house and began construction of a two story dining hall for University students living in nearby residence halls, especially Gregson Hall, whose cafeteria had become seriously overcrowded. When it opened in 1959, Brough Commons (named after Arkansas Governor Charles Hillman Brough, who was once a U of A professor) could accommodate twelve hundred students per meal with five serving lines capable of serving six to eight people per minute per line. The dining hall had forty full-time employees and sixty student assistants.

Brough Commons, 1970s

Razorback Hall

Razorback Hall was built in 1944 on the north side of Dickson across from Brough Commons. As the name implies, it was at one time home to the University's male athletes. It was renamed Gibson Hall in honor of James L. Gibson, Director of Housing, after his death in 1981. It has been used as a general-occupancy residence hall since, and a small building at the east side houses the Multi-Media Resource Center.

END OF DICKSON

Gregson Lodge

Dickson Street ends at Gregson Lodge, a men's dormitory. Built in 1948, the hall was named for William Sedgewell "Pop" Gregson, who was chaplain and secretary of the University chapter of the YMCA from 1919 to 1946. Gregson Hall, which was renovated in 1991–1992, is, perhaps accidentally, one of the most photographed landmarks on West Dickson, since many westward-looking panoramic shots of the street capture the dormitory at the top West Dickson Street.

Looking west at Gregson Lodge, 1970s

Gibson Hall, ca. 1944

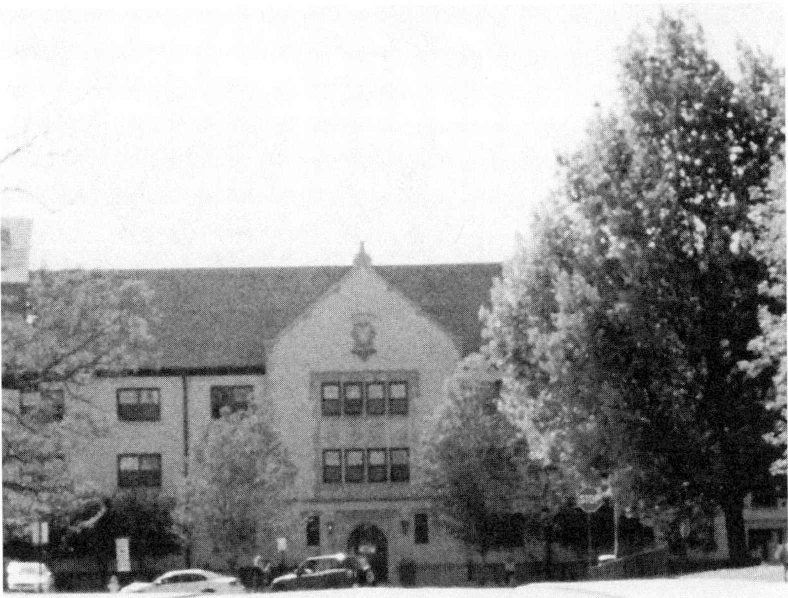

Gregson Lodge, 2000

Dickson Street from Old Main, 1962

CONCLUDING REMARKS

I finished writing the first version of *Once Upon Dickson* in 1994. But circumstances delayed its publication. In addition to experiencing the loss of loved ones, I started a new job. After that, restoration of a 1907 craftsman house so monopolized my time and resources that I could not undertake the final steps toward publication, especially obtaining quality reproductions of the hundreds of images I had collected.

In 2001 I decided I needed to really finish the book. However, I thought it necessary to update my information to include the year 2000. After compiling another six years of information on then rapidly-changing Dickson Street, I turned to long-time University of Arkansas librarian Ethel Simpson for help. She has been of enormous assistance in terminating this book. In addition to navigating the publishing world, she located additional historic images that were not available when I did my original research. Had it not been for Simpson's assistance, many images of 1980s Dickson Street would not have appeared in the book. It turns out that the delay in publishing has actually been a blessing in disguise.

After reflecting upon Dickson Street's history, it has become apparent to me that for most of its history, Dickson Street has been changing. Many generations, including my own 40 something generation, have had to deal with the loss of "their Dickson Street." Since beginning this project in the late 1980s, West Dickson has been transforming itself into an entertainment district, catering not to the student population as it did in the late 1970s and early 1980s, but to a broader spectrum of population, including students. Today the Walton Arts Center and the many clubs and restaurants are West Dickson's main drawing force, just as the Frisco Railroad and businesses such as Kelley Brothers Lumber, Woodruff's Laundry and Ozark Grocer were the drawing force until the 1960s and 1970s.

In the ten plus years since originally finishing this book, many historic buildings have undergone exciting facelifts, including Collier Drug, the Shipley Baking Company, Bates Brothers Market (Swingin' Door/ Ozark Brew Pub), George's Majestic Lounge and the UARK Bowl. There are some new buildings, too, including the Three Sisters Building,

Bordino's and the Underwood Lofts, currently under construction. There is even a new residence at the upper end of East Dickson! Although saddened by the fact that Dickson Street has become too expensive for many students and local residents alike, I am excited that Dickson Street remains a street on which fond memories intermingle with vibrant change.

AFTERWORD: DICKSON STREET IN THE FUTURE

Daniel Hintz
Former Executive Director, Fayetteville Downtown Partners

"Change has a considerable psychological impact on the human mind. To the fearful it is threatening because it means that things may get worse. To the hopeful it is encouraging because things may get better. To the confident it is inspiring because the challenge exists to make things better."

—King Whitney Jr.

Dickson Street elicits a palpable passion in people. Many consider it an icon of Fayetteville's history and a bellwether of the city's future. Stories of youthful adventures sneaking into Kelley Brother's Lumber Yard or hanging out at the Frisco Drugstore are mixed with more recent memories of events at the Walton Arts Center or wild nights at Brewski's Draft Emporium or Roger's Recreation Hall.

Regardless of the era in which this street is experienced, one thing has remained a constant throughout Dickson Street's life—change. Entertainment venues, urban-style clothiers and award-winning restaurants are sprouting up where lumber yards and railroad stations once stood. High-end condominium living is now de rigueur, and the small bungalows that dot the downtown landscape are being discussed with nostalgia.

Festivals like Bikes, Blues and BBQ and the expanded Fayetteville Arts Festival, while they offer experiences unique in the region, are not without controversy. But these events, along with Springfest, Mardi Gras and others, contribute to the changing landscape of downtown, and in particular of Dickson Street.

In 2004, Dover Kohl and Associates were hired by the City of Fayetteville to create a 350- acre Downtown Master Plan. Following a series of public charrettes, or community design sessions, and a multitude of meetings spanning more than two years, the City Council passed the Downtown Master Plan in late 2006. The plan redefined much of the City's Unified Development Code for the area and actually redrew what had historically been the downtown area. This plan represents an exciting vision for the next phase in the history of Dickson Street.

Regardless of the facelifts, history, controversy and debates, Dickson Street remains the heartbeat of Fayetteville and the crown jewel of the city's past, present, and future.

APPENDIX I: OCCUPANT INVENTORY NORTH SIDE

NORTH OLIVE AVENUE AT EAST DICKSON STREET

432 East: *(Masonic Block 15, Lot 1)*

1868–1996: see 404 East Dickson
1996–2000: Jeremy Hess

404 East: *(Masonic Block 15, Lot 1)*

1868–1884: William McGarrah estate
1885–1895: Thomas M. Gunther
1895–1904: James and Margaret Pittman
1904–1957: Harvey D. and Jennie M. Wilkinson (constructed ca. 1904)*
1958–1996: William R. and Rita Ferrell
1996–2000: Delmar O. and Carol J. Duerr

356 East: *(Masonic Block 16, Lot 4)*

1868–1958: see 404 East Dickson Street
1959–1985: Lois C. Glass (constructed ca. 1959) *
1986–1987: Marla Crider
1988–1996: Thomas L. Jackson
1996–1998: Patrick Mardulyn
1999–2000: Sarah Bunch

318 East: *(Masonic Block 16, Lot 4)*

1868–1894: Thomas and Sarah McGarrah Williams
1895–1918: James M. and Margaret Pittman
1919–1944: Henry and Nettie M. Bossemeyer (constructed ca. 1919) *
1945–1948: Melvin M. Collier
1949–1953: Franz Adler
1954–1956: James Donthett
1957–1975: Edward J. & Maxine Englehart
1976–1978: Ewell Tunnell
1979–1980: Liz Ensmiager
1981–1982: Jack R. Atwood
1982–2000: house converted into apartments

---

* Asterisks denote successive structures at the same address.

*=first building; **=second building, etc.

Corner Willow & Dickson (304 North Willow):

1868–1921: see 318 East Dickson
1921–1937: Almond H. and Hattie E. Osborn (constructed ca. 1921) *
1938–1941: vacant house
1942–1949: James E. Critz
1950–1963: Mrs. Rachel I. Yancey
1964–1969: Powell M. Rhea
1970–1971: M. C. Plummer
1971–1972: Robert Lamphear
1973–2000: house converted into apartments

NORTH WILLOW AVENUE AT EAST DICKSON STREET

228 East: (Masonic Block 17, Lot 4)

1868–1929: see 222 West Dickson Street
1929–1936: Vine Q. Blumenberg (constructed ca. 1929) *
1937–1939: James M. Phillips
1940–1943: Castro Robertson
1944–1974: Roy A. and Adortha Scott
1975–1976: Tillman H. Malone
1976–1977: Rhonda S. Carroll
1978–1984: Grant Hall
1985–1989: Daniel B. Levine
1990–2000: Constance Clack

222 East: (Masonic Block 17, Lot 4)

1868–1884: Thomas W. and Sarah McGarrah Williams
1884–1903: Harvey D. and Annette Wood
1903–1949: Eugene W. and Fannie Shuford (constructed ca. 1903) *
1950–1952: Mrs. Mary B. Clark
1953–1955: Mrs. Eva Frederick
1956–1969: Mrs. Lula A. Bush
1970–1984: Herman and Lula A. Greathouse
1985–1986: Glenda Baird
1986–1987: Cathy Rankin
1988–2000: house converted into apartments

220 East: (Masonic Block 17, Lot 4)

1868–1903: see 222 East Dickson Street
1903–1920: J. Austin Shelton (constructed ca. 1903) *
1921–1922: Martha D. Guinn
1923–1970: Ben and Bessie McConnell
1970–1971: vacant house
1971–1972: Doyle C. Shackleford
1972–1975: Maria M. Guess

1976–1986: Anna Marie Lauderdale
1987–1990: vacant house
1991–1993: Teresa A. Masters
1994–1998: Leah Ruth Henningsen
1998–1999: Mariah Shea
1999–2000: Karen Peschka

218 East: *(Masonic Block 17, Lot 3)*

1868–1884: Alf L. and Josie Williams
1884–1904: Harvey D. and Annette Wood (residence at 306 Washington Avenue)
1904–1911: Clint and Jimmie Conner (constructed ca. 1904)*
1911–1936: Jeff and Clementine C. Conner
1937–1938: Roy Williams
1939–1942: Jack Phillips
1943–1953: John R. Sample
1954–1955: Euel A. Bridenthal
1956–1976: John K. and Archie Nell Woodruff
1977–1978: Don W. Gore
1979–1986: Jerry K. Harden
1986–1987: vacant house
1988–1989: H. Kulish
1990–1993: Connie S. Stapleton
1993–1995: Michael A. and Holly V. Paul
1996–1997: vacant house
1998–2000: house converted to apartments

210 East: *(Masonic Block 17, Lot 3)*

1868–1941: see 218 East Dickson Street
1942–1956: Giles E. and Harriet M. Ripley (constructed ca. 1942) *
1957–1971: Rolla H. and Mabel A. Clinehens
1972–2000: Jim R. and Kathy Logue

NORTH WASHINGTON AVENUE AT EAST DICKSON STREET

NW corner Washington & Dickson (305 N. Washington)

1868–1888: see 118 East Dickson Street
1888–1890: Judge B. J. Brown (constructed ca. 1888) *
1890–1903: Clifton and Fannie Gray
1904–1965: John Robert and Mary L. Harris
1965–1976: Hadley Harris Hodson
1976–1983: Richard and Pamela T. Dean
1984–1987: house converted into apartments
1988–2000: Roger E. and Jessie Koeppe

118 East: *(Masonic Addition Block 18, Lots 4–5)*

1868–1873: Joseph & Rebecca Davis (constructed ca. 1853 by Jonas Tebbetts)*
1873–1920: Charles W. and Serena Walker
1920–1936: Charles W. and Lorie H. Appleby
1937–1939: Colonel C. F. and Jessie Armstead
1940–1966: Parris R. Green
1967–2000: Washington County Historical Society

NE corner College & Dickson (304 North College Avenue)

1868–1888: see 118 East Dickson Street
1888–1950: John A. and Lena B. Reed *
1950–1960: Mrs. Morgan McMichael
1961–1963: John A. Reed, Jr.
1964–1967: vacant house / vacant lot
1968–2000: Southwestern Electric Power Company (constructed ca. 1968) **

NORTH COLLEGE AVENUE AT EAST DICKSON STREET

SE corner College & Dickson (303 North College Avenue)

1868–1876: unknown (former location of Fayetteville Female Seminary)
1877–1884: W. H. Ladd *
1885–1889: James A. Ferguson rent house
1889–1894: J. H. Drummond
1895–1906: J. P. and Virginia Hight
1906–2000: First Baptist Church (first church completed in 1908); (present church completed in 1960) **

20 East: *(County Court Block 10, Lot 6)*

1868–1876: unknown
1877–1889: James A. Ferguson
1889–1894: J. H. Drummond
1895–1924: Dr. J. P. and Virginia Hight rent house *
1924–1948: First Baptist Church parsonage
1948–2000: First Baptist Church office and education building (constructed in 1948; expanded in 1995) **

18 East: *(County Court Block 10, Lot 6)*

1868–1894: see 20 East Dickson Street
1895–1939: Jeff & Nannie Williams (Sigma Phi Epsilon Fraternity in 1920–1921)*
1940–1941: Zenas W. Ford
1941–1942: Carl B. Nix
1943–1946: P. L. Hathcock rent house
1946–1947: Jacob E. Gilstrap
1947–1978: Max F. McAllister, physician

1979–1984: Pettus & Johnson
1985–1991: First Baptist Church daycare (original Williams house moved in 1991)
1991–2000: parking lot

HIGHLAND AVENUE AT WEST DICKSON STREET

NW corner Highland & Dickson

1868–1898: see 2 West Dickson Street
1898–1953: Central Methodist Church (completed in 1899) *
1953–2000: see 2 West Dickson Street

2 West: (County Court Block 9, Lot 16)

1868–1892: Sarah Dickson (constructed ca. 1847 by Joseph L. Dickson) *
1892–1900: John L. Buchanan
1900–1931: Andrew C. and Katherine Hamilton
1932–1933: Phi Mu Sorority
1933–1937: Mrs. M. O. Cornett "Ma Cornett"
1938–1939: vacant house
1939–1950: Mrs. Virgie Millsap
1950–2000: Central Methodist Church (constructed 1950–1953) **

6 West: (County Court Block 9, Lot 16)

1868–1903: see 2 West Dickson
1903–1936: Charles H. and Ella Bell *
1936–1943: John P. Scott
1944–1948: Mrs. Katherine Gibson
1949–1953: Kappa Alpha Fraternity
1953–1955: Alpha Tau Omega Fraternity
1956–2000: Central Methodist Church Youth Center (constructed 1956) **

12 West: (County Court Block 9, Lot 15)

1868–1892: see 14 West Dickson Street
1892–1899: W. T. Nesbitt *
1899–1944: Davis F. and Lula A. McMillan **
1945–1961: Mr. and Mrs. Lee Poore
1962–2000: United States Post Office (constructed 1962; opened 1963) **

14 West: (County Court Block 9, Lot 15)

1868–1877: rent house (constructed pre-1840 by Moses Campbell) *
1877–1888: Noah P. and Lucy Jane Gates
1889–1892: J. W. Lipsey
1893–1902: Julius F. and Ida Howell
1903–1961: Central Presbyterian Church (completed in 1906) *
1962–2000: see 12 West Dickson Street

ST. CHARLES AVENUE AT WEST DICKSON STREET

100 West: (Watson Subdivision Block 8, Lot 14)

1868–1877: T. Murray Campbell
1878–1908: Clementine Watson Boles (skating rink at this location ca. 1900–1908) *
1908–1924: Citizen's Laundry **
1924–1949: Dyke Lumber Company (309 St. Charles Street) ***
1950–2000: Collier Drug Store (constructed 1949–1950) ****

200 West: (Watson Subdivision Block 8, Lot 14)

1868–1877: T. Murray Campbell
1878–1883: Clementine Watson Boles
1883–1904: B. F. "Frank" and Angeline Smith *
1904–1907: Mrs. Emma Roll
1907–1915: Eagert and Margaret Williams
1916–1931: Rex House, boarding house
1931–1934: Mrs. Minnie C. Bryant
1935–1937: William Fritts
1938–1964: Coca-Cola Bottling/Fayetteville Ice Company (constructed 1938) **
1965–1976: Southwest Printing Company
1977–1978: Southwest Furniture and Sleep Shop
1979–1991: Frame House & Gallery
1992–1993: vacant building
1993–1994: Downstream Outdoor Outfitters
1994–1995: vacant building
1995–1999: Passages
1999–2000: One of a Kind Imports

202 West: (County Court Block 8A, Lot 13)

1868–1877: W. H. Ladd
1877–1882: J. C. Thompson
1883–1897: B. F. "Frank" and Angeline Smith
1897–1909: Jack L. and Eva J. Maguire *
1909–1918: Add N. and Addie Cole rent house
1919–1924: George W. and Nancy H. Irby
1925–1929: Vine Q. Blumenberg
1930–1939: Hubert H. Bean
1940–1943: unknown
1944–1945: Will Hatfield
1946–1948: Wilburn P. Durnal
1949–1953: K. Porter Rouse
1954–1976: vacant house/vacant lot
1977–1983: Southwest Printing Company (constructed 1977) **
1982–1983: Couch Printing Company

1984–1990: vacant building
1991–1993: Downstream Outdoor Outfitters
1993–2000: U. S. Pizza Company

206 West: *(County Court Block 8A, Lot 12)*

1868–1907: see 204 West Dickson Street
1907–1909: Jack L. and Eva J. Maguire (constructed ca. 1907) *
1909–1920: Add N. and Addie Cole
1921–1928: Mrs. A. P. Houston
1929–1931: Adolph W. Loden
1931–1933: Mrs. Flossie Barnes
1934–1945: Maria Dressmaking Shop
1946–1970: Gerald and Estelle Baker Boarding House
1971–1976: Don Lee's Beauty Salon
1977–1984: New Music Store
1985–1987: vacant house
1988–1990: Abaft Jewelers
1991–1997: vacant house
1997–1998: James Cooper
1999–2000: M. Smith

214 West: *(County Court Block 8A, Lot 10)*

1868–1892: see 216 West Dickson
1892–1905: William and E. E. Wade
1906–1915: Add N. and Addie Cole rent house
1916–1920: Florence Mullen
1920–1922: W. Thaddeus and Mary E. Gabbert
1923–1925: G. W. Dunnaway
1926–1929: Maple Inn
1929–1930: Oscar W. Bass
1930–1931: Phi Mu Sorority
1932–1933: U of A Football Home
1934–1936: Oscar W. Bass
1937–1939: Future Farmers of America annex
1939–1949: Carl A. and Bessie Smith
1950–1957: Jesse Garrett Rooming House
1958–1970: house converted into apartments
1971–2000: vacant lot/parking lot

216 West: *(County Court Block 8A, Lot 9)*

1868–1870: H. A. Vindiver
1871–1877: T. Murray Campbell
1877–1892: W. L. Nolen *
1892–1905: William and E. E. Wade rent house
1905–1912: Byron and Mary McAllister

1912–1926: J. M. Wilson
1927–1928: vacant house
1929–1930: Miller J. Tillman
1931–1933: Herschel Powers
1934–1937: Mrs. Grace D. Calvin
1937–1942: J. Howard Durnell
1943–1945: vacant house / vacant lot
1946–1955: King's Food Market (constructed 1946) **
1956–1961: Fayetteville Paint & Wallpaper Company
1962–1971: Waggoner's Bakery
1972–1976: Office Services Insurance Office Supply
1977–1978: Ruby Begonia's Dining House
1979–1998: Grill restaurant
1999–2000: Three Sisters complex

224 West: (County Court Block 8A, Lot 8)

1868–1892: see 216 West Dickson Street
1892–1918: John P. and Nancy Scott *
1918–1947: O. K. Hotel
1948–1961: house converted into apartments
1962–1998: vacant lot / parking lot
1999–2000: Three Sisters complex

248 West: (County Court Block 8A, Lot 8)

1868–1946: see 224 West Dickson Street
1947–1973: Laundry-Mart, Grover Thomas, proprietor (constructed 1947) *
1973–1998: Restaurant on the Corner
1999–2000: Three Sisters complex

ROLLSTON AVENUE AT WEST DICKSON STREET

300 West: (County Court Block 7A, Lot 6)

1868–1931: see 304 West Dickson Street
1932–1933: Needham's Food Market (constructed 1932) *
1933–1945: King Food Market
1945–1952: Goff Brothers IGA Food Store
1952–1955: Consumers IGA Market # 2
1955–1968: Ragsdale Carpet Cleaning
1969–1988: D-Lux Restaurant Recreation Room
1989–2000: 1936 Club bar & restaurant

302 West: (County Court Block 7A, Lot 6)

1868–1932: see 304 West Dickson Street
1932–1941: Alice's Beauty Shop (constructed 1932) *
1941–1944: Jane's Beauty Shop

1945–1959: Gingham Girl Beauty Shop
1960–1962: Chatter Box Beauty Shop
1963–1968: Lewis and Rada Beauty Saloon # 2
1969–2000: see 306 West Dickson

304 West: (County Court Block 7A, Lot 6)

1868–1892: T. Murray Campbell & Family
1892–1905: W. L. Gregg *
1905–1911: William and Rebecca Bishop Boarding House
1912–1917: Hotel Texas
1917–1924: Iowa Rooms
1924–1929: Collins Boarding House
1929–1931: vacant house / vacant lot
1932–2000: see 300 West Dickson Street

306 West: (County Court Block 7A, Lot 6)

1868–1910: see 304 West Dickson Street
1911–1913: Linton's Shoe Shop *
1913–1922: Fashion Shop, clothing
1922–1931: Maria Dressmaking Shop
1932–1934: Chew and Chat Sandwich Shop
1934–1997: D-Lux Restaurant (constructed 1936–1937) **
1998–2000: New Berlin restaurant

CAMPBELL AVENUE AT WEST DICKSON STREET

310 West: (County Court Block 6B, Lot 14)

1868–1892: T. Murray Campbell & Family
1892–1894: N. J. Tillman
1894–1912: J. C. Mitchell rent house *
1913–1926: vacant lot
1925–1926: Henry J. Rochier, jeweler
1927–1931: U of A Shoe Store **
1932–1938: Marathon service station ***
1938–1940: Lion service station
1941–1946: O.K. Taxi & Transfer
1947–1964: Jug Wheeler's Drive-In (constructed 1947) ****
1964–1969: George's Derby Drive-In
1970–1997: Holsum Thrift Store
1998–2000: vacant building

314 West: (County Court Block 6B, Lot 14)

1868–1900: see 310 West Dickson Street
1901–1908: C. J. Lester & Son's grocery *

1908–1912: First Class Tailoring
1913–1926: Bear State Oil Company **
1926–1929: Continental Oil Company
1929–1931: A. B. Smith Tires
1932–1934: Hugh Campbell's restaurant
1935–2000: see 310 West Dickson Street

316 West: (County Court Block 6B, Lot 13)

1868–1892: T. Murray Campbell & Family
1892–1894: N. J. Tillman
1894–1908: J. C. Mitchell rent house (constructed ca. 1894) *
1908–1919: City Bakery
1919–1937: Star Grocery (house split into two and enlarged ca. 1913–1919) **
1938–1939: Pense's Grocery
1939–1941: Gateway Creamery Company
1942–1946: Hometown Cafe
1946–1947: T. Benjamen Ward, optician
1948–1949: Acme Typewriter Exchange
1950–1961: Fount Richardson and William J. Butt, physicians
1962–1963: David L. Walker, physician
1963–1965: Robert B. Burnham, engineer
1966–1973: U. S. Navy Recruiting Office
1973–1978: U. S. Marine Recruiting Office
1979–1984: Editype Business Services
1985–1986: Fayetteville Food Exchange
1987–1988: Citizens and Philosophers
1988–1994: Puttin' On the Ritz clothing
1994–1996: vacant building
1997–1999: Play It Again Sam's restaurant
1999–2000: Doe's

318 West: (County Court Block 6B, Lot 13)

1868–1908: see 316 West Dickson Street
1908–1932: City Bakery (house split into two and enlarged ca. 1913–1919) **
1933–1939: Snappy Service Grocery
1939–1941: unknown
1942–1946: Dept of Agriculture, Production & Marketing Division
1946–1952: Hampton's Army & Navy Store
1953–1955: Fayetteville Relief Association
1956–1957: vacant building
1958–1967: Brown & Deskin Accountants
1968–1969: Office Services, Inc. printers
1970–1978: U.S. Army Recruiting Office
1979–1987: Dickson Street Book Shop
1988–1990: Fayetteville Martial Arts Academy

1991–1995: Kindred Spirits gift shop
1995–1996: Guido's North restaurant
1997–2000: see 316 West Dickson Street

320 West: (County Court Block 6B, Lot 12)

1868–1903: see 324 West Dickson Street
1903–1910: McCormick Meat Market *
1910–1925: Arkansas Meat Market
1926–1928: Stapes Barber Shop and Beauty Parlor **
1929–1931: Southland Tire & Battery Company
1932–1934: Radio Service Company
1935–1939: Razorback Lunch
1940–1941: Potter's Hatchery
1941–1956: Tri-State Sales Company
1957–1971: vacant building
1971–2000: see 324 West Dickson Street

324 West: (County Court Block 6B, Lot 12)

1868–1895: T. Murray Campbell and Family
1895–1924: Northwest Arkansas Lumber Company *
1924–1965: Kelley Brothers Lumber Company
1966–1968: vacant building
1969–1971: Dennis Home Furniture
1971–1971: Oldham's Furniture Company
1972–1973: vacant lot
1973–1979: Minute Man/Speakeasy restaurant (constructed 1973) **
1980–2000: Jose's Mexican Restaurant

326 West: (County Court Block 6B, Lot 11)

1868–1892: see 324 West Dickson Street
1892–1903: John P. Scott (combination boarding house and commercial building) *
1903–1905: Mrs. Nellie Gorsuch's boarding house and groceries
1906–1908: plumber
1909–1913: Lyons Trading Company
1913–1918: vacant building
1919–1923: Shooting Gallery soft drinks
1924–1932: Walker Second Hand Store
1932–1940: Fayetteville Shoe Shop
1941–1965: see 324 West Dickson Street
1966–2000: vacant building/parking lot

328 West: (County Court Block 6B, Lot 11)

1868–1907: see 326 West Dickson Street
1908–1917: W. B. Wright's shoe repair & Tony White's Shine Parlor*

1918–1925:	Vanity Shop
1925–1931:	Davis Barber Shop
1931–1940:	Fowler's News Stand
1941–2000:	vacant lot/parking lot

400 West: (County Court Block 6B, Lot 11)

1868–1892:	T. Murray Campbell & Family
1892–1903:	vacant building *
1903–1906:	J. W. Cunningham's shoe store (also sold bicycles)
1907–1917:	Fuller Footwear
1918–1919:	Tony White's Shine Parlor
1919–1924:	Mrs. Mabel Jeffery's variety store
1925–1930:	Campbell's cafe
1930–1945:	U of A Cafe
1946–1957:	O. K. Taxi Co.
1957–1966:	Ft. Smith Times-Record Drop Station
1967–1978:	vacant building
1979–1981:	Flag Fair
1982–1983:	vacant building
1984–1985:	Seahorse Trading Post
1986–1994:	vacant building
1994–2000:	parking lot

402 West: (County Court Block 6B, Lot 10)

1868–1892:	T. Murray Campbell & Family
1892–1896:	vacant lot
1897–1904:	McClanahan & Williams grocery and feed store *
1905–1911:	Whitten, Gollaher and Company general merchandise
1912–1918:	Hudson Hardware
1919–1921:	Collegian Tailor
1922–1975:	Fashion Shop Cleaners (constructed 1925) **
1976–1979:	Record Ranch
1980–1982:	Fonzarelli's Pizzeria
1983–1984:	Chelsea's Fish & Chips/Substation Restaurant
1985–1987:	Little Italy
1988–1993:	vacant building
1994–1995:	Jackson's Cajun Restaurant
1995–1996:	vacant building
1996–1999:	Layla's Restaurant
1999–2000:	vacant building

404 West: (County Court Block 6B, Lot 9)

1868–1896:	see 402 West Dickson Street
1897–1910:	DeLuxe Barber Shop *

1910–1911: Shooting Gallery, tobacco and cigar shop
1912–1918: Model Barber Shop
1918–1926: W. B. Wright's Electric Shoe Shop (constructed 1925) **
1927–1928: Richard's Cafe
1929–1931: City Plumbing Company
1931–1935: vacant building
1935–1983: Hob Nob Liquor Store
1984–1985: The Dugout/The Get Away club
1986–1990: Lilly's Restaurant and Bar
1991–1992: vacant building
1992–1993: Great Arts Gallery
1994–2000: see 402 West Dickson Street

404½ West: (County Court Block 6B, Lot 9)

1868–1906: see 406 West Dickson Street (part of Southern Hotel grounds)
1907–1925: Citizen's Bank (constructed 1907) *
1926–1928: Henry J. Rochier, jeweler
1929–1931: vacant building
1931–1945: Ozark Barber Shop
1946–1953: G & R Cafe *
1953–1957: White's Barber Shop
1958–1959: Western Quality Meat Company
1960–1963: Arkansas Printing and Duplicating Service
1964–1966: Moses Studio
1967–1977: Dawn's Flowers
1978–1981: Fun Place
1982–1983: Razorback Pub
1984–1985: Dugout/Get Away club
1986–1991: Lily's Restaurant and Bar
1992–1993: Anna's Coffee House
1994–2000: see 402 West Dickson Street

406 West: (County Court Block 6B, Lot 9)

1868–1882: T. Murray Campbell & Family
1883–1884: Mrs. Fane *
1886–1890: Lone Star Hotel
1890–1903: Southern Hotel
1903–1929: New Southern Hotel **
1929–1930: Main Croquet Parlor (vacant lot used for croquet playing ?)
1931–1937: vacant lot
1938–1947: Eat Shop (constructed 1938) ***
1947–1951: Bill's Recreation Club
1952–1954: Dutchie's Recreation Parlor
1955–2000: Roger's Recreation Hall

408 West: (County Court Block 6B, Lot 9)

1868–1892: see 406 West Dickson Street
1892–1897: restaurant *
1897–1903: confectionary
1903–1904: W. E. Dowell's meat market
1904–1910: Dever Brothers Furniture
1910–1911: Scott Dining Room
1911–1915: Collegian Tailor
1916–1917: Dickson Street Grocery
1917–1918: Flowershop Corona
1919–1929: Fayetteville Shoe Shop & Tony White's Shine Parlor
1929–1934: vacant lot
1934–1936: Supreme Food Market (constructed 1934) **
1937–1939: Kroger Grocery & Baking Company
1940–1943: Lee's Snooker Parlor
1943–1947: Bill's Recreation
1948–1954: G. W. Shirley and Son, plumbers
1955–1963: Fayetteville Air Reserve Center
1964–1986: Acme Typewriter Exchange / Business Equipment Center
1986–1989: Northwest Office Equipment
1989–2000: vacant building

410 West: (County Court Block 6B, Lot 9)

1868–1897: T. Murray Campbell & Family
1897–1899: Bates Brothers Market (constructed ca. 1897) *
1899–1904: Gallaher & Cunningham's confectionery and restaurant
1904–1918: J. L. Mitchell & Company
1918–1928: Simmons Brothers
1929–1931: Razorback Toggery
1932–1934: Supreme Food Market
1936–1939: Jimmy's College Inn, restaurant
1940–1966: Wheatley's Shoe Service
1967–1993: vacant building
1993–1994: Naturally Blue variety store
1994–1998: Gallery on Dickson Street art gallery
1998–2000: see 412 West Dickson Street

412 West: (County Court Block 6B, Lot 9)

1868–1892: T. Murray Campbell & Family
1892–1897: vacant building *
1898–1900: S. Wilcox's boot & shoe repair
1900–1904: Shuler Brothers' groceries
1904–1910: J. W. Randall's grocery
1911–1917: Kandy Bob's / Kandy Don's confectionery (constructed ca. 1911) **
1918–1920: Liberty Hardware

1921–1925: U of A Cafe
1925–1926: Campbell's Cafe
1926–1928: College Cafe
1929–1948: Tony Chiabotti's Shine Parlor
1949–1951: Taylor's Typewriters
1952–1953: vacant building
1954–1959: Irwin Jewelers
1960–1961: Razorback Lock & Key Shop
1962–1963: Drake's TV Service
1963–1965: Agency Art Association, commercial photography
1966–1973: Razorback News Stand
1974–1990: vacant building
1991–1993: Sidney's silkscreens
1993–1995: vacant building
1995–1997: Emerald coast coffee house
1997–2000: Common Grounds coffee house

412 A West: (County Court Block 6B, Lot 9)

1868–1927: see 412 West Dickson Street
1927–1931: Red Ball Transfer & Storage Company
1932–1933: Nu Way Barbecue Restaurant
1934–1940: Fayetteville Welfare Board
1941–1951: Fowler's Fruit and News Stand
1951–1954: Carmen's News Stand
1955–1965: Razorback News Stand
1966–1969: Agency Art Association, commercial photography
1970–1971: vacant building
1971–1983: Dream Merchant gift shop
1984–1985: Special Effects clothing
1985–1987: vacant building
1988–1991: Crossbrooks Graphics
1992–1993: Sidney's silkscreens
1993–1994: vacant building
1995–2000: see 412 West Dickson Street

414 West: (County Court Block 6B, Lot 9)

1868–1891: T. Murray Campbell & Family
1891–1892: Shultz & Son's steam laundry *
1893–1906: William Lilly's bakery
1907–1921: E. C. Gollaher's grocery (constructed ca. 1911) **
1921–1925: Peal's Cash Grocery
1925–1942: Citizen's Bank/Fulbright Investment Company
1943–1956: Student Cleaners
1957–1964: Pyper Company children's clothing
1965–1969: Paul's Recreation Club

1970–1972: Brave New World men's clothing store
1973–1991: Dream Merchant gift shop (Dream Merchant annex 1973–1983)
1992–2000: Melody's Choices gift shop

416 West: (County Court Block 6B, Lot 9)

1868–1892: T. Murray Campbell & Family
1889–1905: Whitten & Myers, feed store *
1906–1910: Model Cleaning Works
1911–1920: DeLuxe Barber Shop (constructed ca. 1911) **
1920–1922: City Plumbing Company
1922–1931: Manhattan Cafe
1932–1935: Wright's Shoe Repair Shop
1935–1940: American Shoe Shop
1941–1946: Johnson Plumbing & Heating Company
1946–1964: Hometown Cafe
1965–1974: Manor House Restaurant
1974–1978: Quincy Jones haircutters
1979–2000: Fantasy Island Haircutters

418 West: (County Court Block 6B, Lot 7)

1868–1891: T. Murray Campbell & Family
1892–1897: grocery & feed store
1897–1911: O. K. Merchant Barber Shop
1911–1918: Palace Drug Store (constructed ca. 1911) *
1918–1921: U of A Cafe
1921–1925: U of A Candy Kitchen
1926–1934: Silverman Brothers Jewelers No. 2
1934–1939: Hodge's Cafe
1940–1975: Beulah Lee Beauty Shop
1976–1995: Rock Bottom Book Store
1995–2000: Condom Sense

420 West: (County Court Block 6B, Lot 7)

1868–1891: T. Murray Campbell & Family
1892–1901: vacant building *
1901–1911: Live and Let Live Drugstore
1911–1915: O. K. Merchant Barber Shop (constructed ca. 1911) **
1916–2000: U of A Barber Shop

422 West: (County Court Block 6B, Lot 7)

1868–1891: T. Murray Campbell & Family
1892–1908: W. M. Lehman's meat market and restaurant *
1908–1911: Kandy Dan's (constructed ca. 1911) **
1912–1918: Cardinal Confectionery
1918–1954: Palace Drug Store

1955–1957: Chemell Store Inc., cosmetics
1958–1959: U of A Cafe
1960–1966: vacant building
1967–1993: Library Club
1993–2000: Chester's Place

424 West: (County Court Block 6B, Lot 7)

1868–1892: T. Murray Campbell & Family
1892–1904: vacant lot
1904–1909: Depot Cafe *
1910–1911: Royal Cafe
1911–2000: see 422 West Dickson Street

426 West: (County Court Block 6B, Lot 6)

1868–1892: W. H. Rhea estate
1892–1904: vacant lot
1904–1955: Bates Brothers Market (constructed 1904) *
1956–1958: vacant building
1959–1961: Washington County Farmer Mutual Fire Insurance Company
1962–1965: Southwest Printing Company
1966–1967: Rustler steak house
1967–1970: Bill & Lil's steak house
1971–1980: Swinging Door
1981–1984: White Water Tavern
1985–1987: Reunion Station
1988–1992: vacant building
1992–2000: see 430 West Dickson Street

428 West: (County Court Block 6B, Lot 6)

1868–1892: W. H. Rhea estate
1892–1904: vacant lot
1904–1913: Cardinal Confectionery (constructed 1904) *
1913–1918: Tillar's/Cozy Cafe
1919–1923: University Barber Shop
1923–1926: Oscar & Britt's Shaving Parlor
1927–1931: W. B. Wright's Shoe Repair Shop
1932–1943: Razorback Toggery
1944–1961: Dixie Radio and Supply Company
1961–1967: vacant building
1967–1971: Bill & Lill's Lounge
1972–1975: Rock Bottom Used Book Shop
1976–1977: Camera Shop
1978–1979: Record Exchange
1979–2000: see 426 West Dickson Street

430 West: *(County Court Block 6, Lot 6)*

1868–1892: W. H. Rhea estate
1892–1898: groceries (constructed ca. 1892) *
1899–1904: Bates Brothers Market
1905–1927: Frisco Drug Store
1928–1931: Hodge's Cafe
1931–1937: Cardinal Drug Store
1937–1962: U. S. Post Office university station
1963–1969: Pizza House
1970–1978: Home Life Insurance Company
1979–1981: vacant building
1982–1984: A Place For Everything
1985–1990: vacant building
1991–1992: Wes's Bar-B-Q
1992–2000: Ozark Brewing Company (business opened in 1994)

WEST AVENUE AT DICKSON STREET

510 West: *(County Court Block 6A, Lot 1)*

1868–1880: see 524 West Dickson Street
1881–1990: Frisco/Burlington Northern Railroad yards
1990–2000: Bank of Fayetteville Train Bank (restored in 1990) *

512 West: *(County Court Block 6A, Lot 1)*

1868–1880: see 526 West Dickson Street
1881–2000: Frisco/Burlington Northern/Arkansas & Missouri Railroad depot (current depot constructed 1925) ***

ST. LOUIS AND SAN FRANCISCO RAILWAY

518 West: *(County Court Block 6A, Lot 1)*

1868–1898: see 526 West Dickson Street
1905–1907: Lewis Brothers' newsstand (constructed ca. 1905) *
1907–1921: Champion's news stand
1921–1928: Tony's
1929–1937: Varsity Shop confectionery
1938–1939: Varsity Beauty & Dressmaking Shop
1940–1945: College Smart Shoppe, ladies clothing
1946–1951: Arcade, men's store
1952–1961: Lloyd's Western Shop
1962–1983: House of Books
1984–1985: Uncle Sam's Safari Outfitters
1986–1987: vacant building
1988–1989: Twelve Winds karate school
1990–1995: Whimsicals Gallery & Gifts

1995–1997: Arkansas Craft Gallery
1997–2000: vacant

522 West: *(County Court Block 6A, Lot 1)*

1868–1946: see 526 West Dickson Street
1946–1961: Barrett Quality Shop (constructed 1946) *
1962–1963: Gregg's Cafeteria
1964–1965: Stevo's Pizza
1966–1970: Gregory's, men's clothing
1971–1974: Mister Tux, formal wear
1975–1976: Purvis Goods sporting goods
1977–1978: Luv's Hallmark Shop
1978–1979: vacant building
1980–1984: Second Time Around clothing store
1985–1987: Monogram Fashions
1988–1989: World Wide Travel
1990–1991: Hunkerin' Hog bookstore
1992–1994: Simmons & Company hair styling
1994–1999: Widespread Bagel
1999–2000: vacant building

524 West: *(County Court Block 6A, Lot 1)*

1868–1937: see 526 West Dickson Street
1937–1948: College Beauty Shoppe (constructed 1937) **
1948–1963: Stape's Beauty Shop
1964–1968: Mr. D's Beauty Salon
1969–1971: vacant building
1972–1977: Forty Acres Imports
1978–1984: Abaft Jewelers
1985–1986: Jones Jewelers
1987–1988: Mind-Body Harmonics Inc., stress reduction
1988–1991: vacant building
1992–1993: Stephanie's Balloon & Variety
1994–2000: see 526 West Dickson Street

526 West: *(County Court Block 6A, Lot 2)*

1868–1874: George W. Reed
1875–1895: Oliver C. and Virginia S. Gray *
1895–1919: Augustus B. and Sophia Lewis
1919–1927: William J. and Elizabeth Hawkins
1927–1933: Linn L. Lewis rent house
1933–1936: vacant house / vacant lot
1937–1939: Varsity Shop restaurant (constructed 1937) **
1940–1942: vacant building

1943–1944: Bill & Belle Cafe
1945–1947: vacant building
1948–1958: Stape's Barber Shop
1959–1974: City Barber Shop
1975–1976: Nelson Leather Company
1977–2000: Flying Possum Leather

540 West: *(County Court Block 6A, Lot 2)*

1868–1964: see 546 West Dickson Street
1965–1988: Christian Science Reading Room *
1989–1991: Classic Cuts barber shop
1992–1993: Alpha Omega Software
1994–2000: see 546 West Dickson Street

546 West: *(County Court Block 6A, Lot 2)*

1868–1936: see 526 West Dickson Street
1937–1944: Varsity Cafe (constructed 1937) *
1945–1952: Top Hat Antique Shop (constructed 1945) *
1953–1973: Fayetteville Floor Company
1974–1980: Dickson Street Dry Goods
1980–1982: McNatural's Cafe
1983–1994: Polly's Cafe
1994–1995: French Quarter Cafe
1995–2000: Asasi Japanese Restaurant

GREGG AVENUE AT DICKSON STREET

604 West: *(Reed's Subdivision Block 1)*

1868–1954: see 612 West Dickson
1955–1971: Piggly Wiggly supermarket (constructed 1955) **
1971–1972: Spee-Dee Supermarket
1973–1976: vacant building
1977–1978: Wild Willie Ray's clothing
1978–1982: vacant building
1982–2000: Hobby Craft

606 West: *(Reed's Subdivision Block 1)*

1868–1955: See 612 West Dickson Street
1955–1964: vacant lot
1964–1969: Stan's Coin Operated Laundry (constructed 1964) **
1969–2000: University of Arkansas Coin Operated Laundry

608 West: *(Reed's Subdivision Block 1)*

1868–1955: See 612 West Dickson Street

1955–1974: Mobil Service Station (constructed 1955) **
1975–2000: Mr. Tux tuxedo rentals

612 West: (County Court NE/NW Sec 16, Lot 3)

1868–1897: George W. Reed (constructed in 1851 by A. M. Wilson) *
1897–1925: Mary J. Reed
1925–1951: Lina X. Reed
1951–1954: vacant house
1954–2000: see 604–624 West Dickson Street

624 West: (Reed's Subdivision Block 1, Lot 4)

1868–1954: see 612 West Dickson Street
1954–1981: Palace Drug Store (constructed 1952) **
1982–2000: Campus Book Store

632–644 West: (Reed's Subdivision Block 1, Lot 6)

1868–1946: See 612 West Dickson Street
1947–1976: Jim Benton/Razorback Bowling Alley (constructed 1947) *
1976–2000: Boardwalk Shopping Center

626 West: (Reed's Subdivision Block 1, Lot 7)

1868–1940: see 612 West Dickson Street
1940–1942: Mrs. Carrie Lee Bivens Boarding House *
1943–1957: UARK Annex Boarding House
1957–1961: Metcalfe House furnished rooms
1962–1964: Fidelity Union Life Insurance (constructed 1962) **
1965–1967: Johnson Hardware
1968–1978: Jet Inn Ice Cream Parlor
1978–1979: Acapulco Dan Tanning Salon
1980–1987: Kinkos Copies
1988–1996: Wooden Nickel Sportswear
1995–2000: Abaft Jewelers

628 West: (Reed's Subdivision Block 1, Lot 7)

1868–1947: see 626 West Dickson Street
1947–1951: U of A Record Shop (constructed 1947) *
1951–1979: Metcalfe Record Shop
1980–1981: Economy Optical
1982–1987: Editype Business Services
1988–1994: Perfumery
1994–1995: Gallery on Dickson
1996–2000: Where Too clothing store

648 West: (Reed's Subdivision Block 1, Lot 8)

1868–1947: see 626 West Dickson Street

1948–2000: University Lutheran Church (completed in 1950) *

Arkansas Avenue at Dickson Street

University of Arkansas Buildings on Dickson Street

700 Block:

Engineering Hall, constructed in 1926

800 Block:

Bell Engineering Center, constructed in 1986
Science Engineering Building, constructed in 1964
Geology Building, constructed in 1947

900 Block:

Chi Omega Greek Theatre, constructed in 1930

1000 Block:

James L. Gibson Residence Hall, constructed in 1937
Gregson Lodge, constructed in 1948 (end of street facing east)

APPENDIX II: OCCUPANT INVENTORY SOUTH SIDE

NORTH OLIVE AVENUE AT EAST DICKSON STREET

405 East: (Masonic Addition Block 22, Lot 3)

1868–1870: Washington Lodge No. 1 (owned)
1871–1900: James and Margaret Pittman (constructed ca. 1871) *
1901–1904: vacant house
1905–1954: Benjamen F. Campbell
1954–1987: James and Mary Gregory
1987–1990: vacant house
1991–1997: Bryan Meldrum
1997–2000: house converted to apartments

401 East: (Masonic Addition Block 22, Lot 3)

1868–1923: see 405 East Dickson Street
1923–1984: Joseph H. and Virginia D. Campbell (constructed ca. 1923) *
1985–1991: Karina Barrentine
1992–1995: rent house
1996–2000: Steve and Jennifer Meldrum

231 East: (Masonic Addition, Block 22, Lot 2)

1868–1870: Washington Lodge No. 1 (owned)
1870–1877: Benjamen J. and Sallie J. Gaines
1877–1895: Thomas A. and Ophelia Reynolds
1895–1898: William T. Hodges
1899–1919: Reverend C. D. and Josephine D. Cheatam (constructed ca. 1899) *
1920–1931: John W. McMurray
1931–1933: Rolland H. Waters
1934–1937: George and Margaret Bowen
1938–1971: Walter J. and Marie E. Lemke
1972–1984: Harold P. Finn
1985–1994: Terry L. McCormack
1994–2000: Richard and Jennifer Alexander

229 East: (County Court NW 1/4 of 15–16–30, Lot 11)

1868–1882: unknown
1883–1891: Thomas Jennings
1892–1898: John B. Cox
1899–1919: William V. Stoffer *
1920–1923: Zed C. and Anna Layson

1924–1945:	Add and Clara Rife
1945–1963:	Mrs. Mary T. Goss
1963–1976:	house converted into apartments
1977–2000:	vacant lot/parking lot

223 East: *(County Court NW 1/4 of 15–16–30, Lot 10)*

1868–1882:	unknown
1883–1891:	Thomas Jennings
1891–1896:	Charles Dale
1896–1898:	J. W. Butler
1899–1910:	C. L. Benbrook *
1911–1935:	Mary D. Shelton, private school at this residence
1936–1942:	Jesse R. and Sarah Watson
1943–1944:	Lynn T. Shelton
1945–1959:	Earle W. Bates
1960–1967:	Mrs. Laura E. Forbes
1968–1969:	Herbert C. Lucand
1970–2000:	vacant lot/parking lot

215 East: *(County Court NW 1/4 of 15–16–30, Lot 9)*

1868–1877:	Thomas and Sarah McGarrah Williams (McGarrah house burned ca. 1877)
1877–1885:	Thomas Jennings
1885–1947:	Reverend Nathaniel M. and Beatrice Ragland **
1947–1951:	Fred Burris
1952–1961:	vacant house
1962–2000:	Fayetteville Public Library (constructed ca. . 1962) ***

207 East: *(Van Hoose/Van Winkle Block 1, Lot 1)*

1868–1877:	Thomas W. and Sarah McGarrah Williams
1877–1899:	James H. Van Hoose
1900–1915:	Caleb C. and Sarah Conner *
1916–1938:	Hosea L. and Edna C. Williams
1939–1940:	Leo J. Adams
1941–1959:	James W. Cain
1960–1962:	vacant lot
1962–1982:	MedArk Clinic (constructed ca. 1962) **
1983–1988:	Fayetteville Pediatric Clinic
1989–2000:	Fayetteville Public Library addition

205 East: *(Van Hoose/Van Winkle Block 1, Lot 1)*

1868–1877:	Thomas W. and Sarah McGarrah Williams
1877–1898:	James H. Van Hoose
1898–1911:	Jeff and Clementine C. Conner *

1911–1924: Jimmie H. Conner (widow of Clint Conner)
1924–1955: Robert L. Kane
1956–1959: vacant house
1960–2000: vacant lot/parking lot

201 East: (Van Hoose/Van Winkle Block 1, Lot 1)

1868–1877: Thomas W. and Sarah McGarrah Williams
1877–1898: James H. Van Hoose
1899–1926: Albert C. and Olive McAdams *
1926–2000: vacant lot/parking lot

129 East: (Van Hoose/Van Winkle Block 2, Lot 1)

1868–1897: see 240 North College Avenue
1897–1920: Sarah Gregg *
1920–1947: Thomas G. and Dove Long
1948–1954: house converted into apartments
1955–1956: Mrs. Emma Palmer
1956–1965: Herbert C. Lucand
1966–1967: Emiko Sakurai
1967–1968: William R. Cain
1969–1970: vacant house
1970–1971: Gail Hopper
1971–1972: M. L. Morgan
1972–1973: Jewell D. Ridenhour
1974–1981: house converted into apartments
1982–2000: vacant lot/parking lot

127 East: (Van Hoose/Van Winkle Block 2, Lot 2)

1868–1904: see 240 North College Avenue
1905–1915: Robert "Rod" and Nell Murchison *
1916–1926: George W. and Myrtle Calaway
1927–1928: T. J. Titus
1929–1930: Millard F. Jarnagan
1931–1972: Eugene E. Murphy
1973–2000: vacant lot/parking lot

125 East: (Van Hoose/Van Winkle Block 2, Lot 3)

1868–1904: see 240 North College Avenue
1905–1907: Mrs. Dresbach
1908–1915: Mrs. Minnie Butler *
1916–1962: George W. and Metta H. Parsons
1963–1964: John Martenson
1965–1967: Stanley E. Stephenson
1968–1969: vacant house

1970–1972: Washington County Economic Opportunity Agency
1973–2000: vacant lot/parking lot

123 East: (Van Hoose/Van Winkle Block 2, Lot 4)

1868–1904: see 240 North College Avenue
1905–1916: Dr. A. I. Moore *
1917–1918: Sam Nunnelly
1919–1941: Mrs. Cener S. Hight
1941–1965: Wilson G. Chamblee
1966–1969: Thomas A. Carter
1970–1971: Mrs. Gloria Crawford
1971–1972: John Locke Early Childhood Development School, Bruce and Edna Baker
1973–2000: vacant lot/parking lot

119 East: (Van Hoose/Van Winkle Block 2, Lot 4)

1868–1934: see 123 East Dickson Street
1934–1936: Joseph R. Gerberich
1937–1940: Lawlis L. Jones
1941–1945: unknown
1946–1949: vacant house
1950–1953: Eilene C. VanGuilder
1954–1955: Reverend Arthur L. Leake
1956–1957: Weldon M. Harnes
1958–1959: Paul H. Harder
1960–1963: vacant house
1964–1968: All List Realty
1969–1970: vacant house
1970–1971: Gary's Art I, beauty salon
1971–1972: Robert Adkins
1972–2000: vacant lot/parking lot

se cr College & Dickson (240 North College Avenue)

1868–1877: LaRue Harrison * (original house moved 1904)
1877–1896: James H. Van Hoose
1896–1904: R. S. Mitchell
1905–1916: John C. Futrall
1917–1955: Charles Mortimar and Beulah Lawson (house constructed ca. 1922) **
1955–1962: vacant house
1962–1984: Cadillac Ranch used car lot ***
1984–1985: vacant lot
1986–1990: First South Savings and Loan Building (constructed ca. 1985–1986) ****

1990–2000: Washington County Courthouse (occupation commenced 1992)

NORTH COLLEGE AVENUE AT EAST DICKSON STREET

SW Corner College & Dickson (241 North College Avenue)

1868–1895: Julius Linn Duke *
1896–1901: W. B. Bentley
1902–1908: C. A. Reese
1909–1945: Birton N. and Hallie Wilson
1946–1949: Jack M. Holt
1950–1951: vacant house
1951–1977: Lion Oil Company service station (constructed ca. . 1951) **
1978–1979: vacant building
1980–2000: Jerry's restaurant

19 East: (Original Block 1, Lot 7)

1868–1927: see 241 North College Avenue
1928–1930: Esther Hudson *
1931–1933: Allen K. Joyce
1934–1949: Henry B. and Fannie Walker
1950–1961: vacant lot
1962–1983: Paul Young, architect (constructed ca. 1962) **
1984–1986: First South Savings and Loan project office
1987–2000: Estes, Estes, and Grambling, attorneys

17 East: (Original Block 1, Lot 6)

1868–1871: C. M. Duke
1871–1922: George and Jane M. Riverscomb
1923–1927: vacant lot
1928–1930: Nymph Studio Dancing *
1931–1967: Mary C. Bateman
1967–1984: apartment house
1984–2000: St. Paul's Episcopal Church playground

se cr East & Dickson (244 North East Avenue)

1868–1871: C. M. Duke
1871–1922: George and Jane M. Riverscomb *
1923–1937: St. Paul's Episcopal Church rent house
1938–2000: vacant lot/St. Paul's Episcopal Church playground

NORTH EAST AVENUE AT DICKSON STREET

5 West: (Original Block 2, Lot 1)

1868–1879: Mrs. S. R. Pratt

1880–1905: W. H. Whitlow *
1906–1925: George W. and Minerva Rattenbery *
1925–1973: Alcuin P. Eason
1974–2000: vacant lot/parking lot

11 West: (Original Block 2, Lot 2)

1868–1877: O. P. Massey
1878–1884: George T. Lake
1885–1944: Henry K. and Katherine Wade *
1945–1948: vacant house/vacant lot
1949–2000: Hathcock Building (240 Block Street constructed ca. 1948–1949) **

NORTH BLOCK AVENUE AT DICKSON STREET

101 West: (Original Block 3, Lot 1)

1868–1906: Seneca and Isabella Sutton (house built by Charles W. Deane ca. 1836) *
1906–1927: Otey and Edith Miller, physician (235 Block Street) **
1927–1955: Richard M. and Nell Miller (235 Block Street)
1955–1956: vacant lot
1957–1996: Texaco Gas Station (constructed ca. 1957) ***
1996–2000: vacant building

115 West: (Original Block 3, Lot 1)

1868–1922: Mary and Belle Sutton, "Sutton Sisters" *
1923–1927: vacant house
1927–1930: W. H. Spencer **
1931–1933: Mrs. Jessie D. Rogers
1933–1968: George W. and Margaret S. Lee
1969–2000: vacant lot/parking lot

121 West: (Original Block 3, Lot 2)

1868–1925: George and Margaret H. Sutton *
1925–1945: Sutton Apartments (home of Phi Mu Sorority in 1926–1930)
1945–1968: Watson Mortuary
1969–2000: vacant lot/parking lot

151 West: (Original Block 3, Lot 2)

1868–1971: see 121 West Dickson Street
1972–1973: The Shack restaurant (constructed ca. 1972) *
1974–1981: Ozark Mountain Smokehouse
1982–1983: Shrimp and Stuff, restaurant
1984–1988: vacant building
1989–2000: Pettus & Company, realtors

NORTH CHURCH AVENUE AT WEST DICKSON STREET

203 West: (Original Block 4, Lot 2)

1868–1875: H. W. Wallace *
1876–1881: James A. and Nancy Ferguson
1882–1887: John and Martha Gilbert
1887–1923: Gilbert Hotel / Gilbert House
1923–1934: Midway Hotel
1934–1936: vacant house
1937–1938: H. H. Taylor
1938–1939: Future Farmers of America House # 1
1939–1940: Oscar Nordyke Boarding House
1940–1941: Midway Cooperative House
1942–1945: vacant house / vacant lot
1946–1973: Holland Brothers Locker Plant (constructed ca. 1946) **
1974–1975: vacant building
1976–1986: King Pizza
1987–1994: see 215 West Dickson
1994–2000: Ozark Natural Foods

215 West: (Original Block 4, Lot 2)

1868–1936: see 203 West Dickson Street
1937–1939: Pettigrew Milk Company *
1940–1952: Pasteurized Milk Company
1952–1964: College Club Dairy
1965–1981: vacant lot
1982–2000: Ozark Mountain Smokehouse (constructed ca. 1982) **

227 West: (Original Block 4, Lot 1)

1868–1945: see 241 West Dickson Street
1946–1969: Sines Body Shop (constructed ca. 1946) *
1970–1971: vacant building
1972–1973: Pizza International
1974–1976: Poor Richard's
1977–1978: Notchy's
1978–1979: Omar's
1979–1983: Landing Strip
1984–1994: vacant building
1994–2000: Downstream Outdoor Outfitters

241 West: (Original Block 4, Lot 1)

1868–1875: H. W. Wallace
1876–1919: James A. and Nancy Ferguson *
1920–1922: James R. and Edna Jewell
1923–1933: Sidney J. and Mollie Graham

1934–1936: Mrs. Ona Coxsey
1937–1964: Conoco (Continental Oil Company) Service Station (constructed ca. 1937) **
1964–2000: Dickson Street Liquor

NORTH LOCUST AVENUE AT WEST DICKSON STREET

303 West: (Original Block 5, Lot 1)

1868–1884: T. J. Blakemore
1885–1893: Cazort Brothers Lumber Company *
1894–1911: John C. Mitchell (constructed ca. . 1894) **
1912–1915: W. W. Chapman
1916–1918: M. E. Smith
1919–1922: Hodge House
1923–1956: rent house (tenant changed each year; too numerous to list all occupants)
1957–1963: Mrs. Dora Stapleton
1964–1978: rent house (tenant changed each year; too numerous to list all occupants)
1979–1983: Old House Gallery art gallery
1984–1986: vacant house
1987–1991: Badge Clothing
1992–1993: Architectural Resources
1993–1994: Johnny Rich Antiques
1994–1995: Puttin' On the Ritz clothing
1996–1997: vacant building
1997–2000: rent house

305 West: Original Block 5, Lot 1)

1868–1948: see 303 West Dickson Street
1948–1950: Kandy Kitchen (constructed ca. . 1948) **
1951–1958: Morse sewing machine and vacuum cleaner company
1959–1960: Girl Scouts of America
1960–1962: vacant building
1963–1972: Russell J. Brophy, public accountant
1973–1974: vacant building
1975–1976: Andrew Kilgore Photographs
1976–1977: Silversmith
1978–1981: vacant building
1982–1983: D's Distributors drugs
1983–1984: vacant building
1985–1986: Captured Moments videography
1987–1988: Village Family Hair Care
1988–1989: Village Center yarn
1990–1991: Elaine's Business Services

1992–1993: Bill Anderson, attorney
1993–1995: Sweet Times Cafe
1995–1996: Kumbya gift shop
1996–1997: Little Shop of Horrors
1998–2000: vacant

307 West: (Original Block 5, Lot 2)

1868–1947: see 303 West Dickson Street
1948–1951: Fayetteville Plumbing and Heating Company (constructed ca. . 1948) **
1952–1953: Morse sewing machine and vacuum cleaner company
1954–1965: Farmers Insurance Group
1965–1966: Camille's Ladies Ready to Wear
1967–1975: Razorback Barber Shop
1976–1985: Hair House barber shop
1986–1987: Vintage Collectibles
1988–1989: vacant building
1990–1995: Village Shoppe, beauty salon
1995–1997: Salon FX
1997–2000: Wildflower Hair Piercing Salon

309 West: (Original Block 5, Lot 2)

1868–1884: T. J. Blakemore
1885–1921: Cazort Brothers Lumber Company *
1921–1931: Read's Plumbing Heating Tinners (constructed ca. 1925) **
1931–1936: Republic Printing Company
1937–1972: Fayetteville Business College
1973–1975: vacant building
1976–1991: see 309 A and 309 B West Dickson Street
1992–1995: Workhorse Computers
1996–2000: see 309 A and 309 B West Dickson Street

309 A West: (Original Block 5, Lot 2)

1868–1975: see 309 West Dickson Street
1976–1978: Furniture Restorations **
1979–1980: Meg's Yarn Shop
1980–1981: D's Distributors drugs
1982–1983: A Leaf of Gold
1984–1985: Elements Workshop jewelry manufacturers
1986–1991: Unique Designs flowers and gifts
1992–1995: see 309 West Dickson Street
1996–1998: vacant building
1999–2000: S. L. Davis

309 B West: (Original Block 5, Lot 2)

1868–1975: see 309 West Dickson Street
1976–1978: Second Time Around clothing **
1979–1985: Fayetteville Open Channel
1986–1987: Photographers' Cooperative
1988–1991: Workhorse Computers
1992–1995: see 309 West Dickson Street
1996–1997: vacant building
1997–1999: Claudia's Boutique
1999–2000: Smoothie King

311 West: (Original Block 5, Lot 3–5)

1868–1884: see 309 West Dickson Street
1885–1926: Cazort Brothers Lumber Company
1927–1929: vacant lot
1929–1933: Hight Roofing Company *
1934–1936: vacant building/vacant lot
1937–1996: Shipley Baking Company (constructed ca. 1936–1937) **
1997–2000: Bakery on Dickson retail complex

313 West: (Original Block 5, Lot 5)

1868–1932: see 311 West Dickson Street
1932–1989: Esso/Exxon Service Station (constructed ca. 1932) *
1990–1996: Kerr-McGee Service Station
1997–2000: Bakery on Dickson retail complex

323 West: (Original Block 5, Lot 6)

1868–1976: see 325 West Dickson Street
1977–1978: vacant building
1979–1984: Record Exchange
1985–1987: Puttin' On the Ritz, clothing
1988–2000: see 325 West Dickson Street

325 West: (Original Block 5, Lot 6)

1868–1884: T. J. Blakemore
1885–1922: Cazort Brothers Lumber Company *
1922–1961: Vickers Cleaners & Dyers (constructed ca. 1922) **
1961–1976: Woodruff's Cleaners and Laundry
1977–1979: vacant building
1980–1982: University Cycle
1983–1985: Faith Evangelical Presbyterian Church
1986–1987: A. B. C. Antiques
1988–2000: Dickson Street Book Shop

NORTH SCHOOL AVENUE AT WEST DICKSON STREET

401 West: *(Original Block 6, Lot 1)*

1868–1912: see 403 West Dickson Street
1913–1943: Winchester's Cash Grocery *
1944–1944: Shamblin's grocery
1945–1946: Val's grocery
1947–1950: Davidson's Food Store
1951–1964: Ideal Mattress Company
1965–1966: Electronics Service Company
1967–1969: American Collection Service
1969–1977: Burger Chef **
1978–1987: Mountain Man Supplies Pawn Shop
1988–1989: vacant building
1990–2000: see 495 West Dickson Street

403 West: *(Original Block 6, Lot 1)*

1868–1877: Wilburn D. Reagan
1877–1889: A. S. Gregg
1890–1893: George Blakely
1894–1898: Joel Waterman
1899–1900: J. P. Woolsey
1901–1904: James S. Bates
1904–1908: Oscar L. Champion
1909–1912: Edward Green
1913–1955: Scott Hotel (lobby closed in 1955); (2nd floor of Scott Hotel operated as rooming house until 1969) *
1956–1960: Lela's Beauty Shop
1960–1969: Dixie Cream Do-Nut Shop
1969–1989: vacant lot
1990–2000: see 495 West Dickson Street

405 West: *(Original Block 6, Lot 2)*

1868–1912: see 403 West Dickson Street
1913–1921: Gholsen and Campbell's "Quick Lunch" Cafe *
1921–1923: Nickens Brothers Cafe
1923–1927: Mrs. Bates' Women's Shop
1928–1931: Blodgett Nut Company
1932–1936: vacant building
1937–1939: W.P.A. Sewing Room
1940–1944: unknown
1945–1954: Sellers & Irwin Jewelers
1955–1964: Top Flite Travel Service
1964–1969: Arkansas Printing and Duplicating Service

1969–1989: vacant lot
1990–2000: see 495 West Dickson Street

407 West: (Original Block 6, Lot 2)

1868–1923: see 409 West Dickson Street
1924–1935: LaNier Cleaners *
1935–1937: Binder's Photo Studio
1937–1943: Student Cleaners
1944–1947: Midwest Tire Mart
1948–1963: Acme Typewriter Exchange
1964–1965: Yellow Cab Company
1965–1972: Jim and Ann's Nook Cafe
1973–1974: vacant building
1975–1976: Friends & Other Peoples / Circle of Friends clothing
1977–1978: Surfside Records
1978–1987: Camera Shop
1988–1989: vacant building
1989–2000: see 495 West Dickson Street

409 West: (Original Block 6, Lot 2)

1868–1877: Wilburn D. Reagan
1878–1903: A. S. Gregg, Sr. rent house (house constructed ca. 1897) *
1903–1939: Boyle Rooms
1940–1946: vacant house / vacant lot
1947–1965: Nook Cafe **
1966–1967: Shirley and Sons
1967–1968: Wheatley's Shoe Service
1969–1977: Ken's Pizza Parlor ***
1978–1987: Bullseye Pizza Pub
1988–1989: vacant building
1989–2000: see 495 West Dickson Street

417 West: (Original Block 6, Lot 4)

1868–1877: Wilburn D. Reagan
1878–1891: A. S. Gregg, Sr.
1891–1919: Henry and Mary Grother (house constructed ca. 1897) *
1919–1923: Robert T. and Margaret E. Pierce
1924–1928: Davis Rooms
1929–1931: Mrs. Anna Rice
1931–1936: O. K. Taxi and Transfer Company **
1936–1965: Cities Service Station
1966–1972: Yellow Cab Company
1973–1974: Shuler-Town Dari Freez
1974–1978: vacant building

1979–1982: Schlotzsky's Sandwich Shop
1983–1986: vacant building
1987–1988: Nearly Famous restaurant
1988–1989: vacant building
1989–2000: see 495 West Dickson Street

441 West: *(Original Block 6, Lot 5–6)*

1868–1877: Wilburn D. Reagan
1878–1883: A. S. Gregg
1883–1922: Grother's / Frisco Hotel *
1923–1940: Simpson-Mintum Company Building **
1941–1957: Wester Motor Company & Service Station
1958–1959: Baldwin Piano Company
1960–1961: vacant building
1962–1984: Fayetteville Linen Supply
1985–1987: Cintas Linen and Supply
1988–1989: vacant building
1989–2000: see 495 West Dickson Street

495 West: *(Original Block 6, Lots 1–6)*

1868–1989: see 401–441 West Dickson Street
1990–1991: vacant lot
1992–2000: Walton Arts Center (constructed ca. 1990–1992) ***

NORTH WEST AVENUE AT DICKSON STREET

509 West: *(Original Block 7, Lot 1)*

1868–1873: C. L. Duke
1874–1882: D. Y. Ellis
1883–1907: Fayetteville Grocer Company (constructed ca. 1883; enlarged 1901) *
1907–1954: Ozark Grocer Company
1954–1968: McCord-Ozark Co. Wholesale Grocery Company
1969–1974: Ruble Transfer and Storage
1975–1991: vacant lot
1992–2000: parking lot

ST. LOUIS AND SAN FRANCISCO RAILWAY

519 West: *(Original Block 7, Lot 2)*

1868–1917: see 521 West Dickson Street
1917–1926: Hodges Cafe *
1927–1947: Majestic Cafe (constructed ca. 1926–1927) **
1947–2000: Majestic Lounge / George's

521 West: (Original Block 7, Lot 2)

1868–1873: C. L. Duke
1874–1875: D. Y. Ellis
1875–1905: Lewis & Sharp, general merchandise *
1906–1911: Depot Meat Market
1912–1913: Pullman Cafe
1913–1917: vacant lot
1918–2000: see 519 West Dickson Street

525 West: (Original Block 7, Lot 2)

1868–1875: C. L. Duke
1875–1898: Augustus B. Lewis
1898–1905: Sweitzer Wagon Company *
1905–1933: Sandford & Son, machinists and welders **
1934–1947: vacant lot
1947–1949: Razorback Cab Company ***
1950–1956: vacant building
1957–1959: Oliver Chaplejewski, veterinarian
1960–2000: vacant lot/parking lot

GREGG AVENUE AT DICKSON STREET

601 West: (County Court SE/NW 16, Lot 1)

1868–1881: George W. Reed
1881–1901: James H. Williams
1901–1906: Evins-Wilson Grocery Company (constructed ca. 1901) *
1907–1922: Goddard Grocer Company
1923–1925: Eclipse Electric Shop
1925–1937: U. S. Post Office university station
1927–1936: Griffin Grocery
1937–2000: see 603 West Dickson Street

603 West: (County Court SE/NW 16, Lot 1)

1868–1922: see 601 West Dickson Street
1923–1925: Arkansas Seed & Nursery Company
1926–1927: Red Ball Transfer & Storage Company
1927–1936: Griffin Grocery
1937–1939: Drake & Hargis wholesale grocers
1939–1948: Vita-O-Ray Milling Company
1949–1959: Stump Furniture Company
1959–1984: Polk's Furniture Discount House
1985–1990: vacant building
1991–1995: Bancroft and Tabor clothing
1995–1996: vacant building
1997–2000: Sound Warehouse

607 West: (County Court SE/NW 16, Lot 1)

1868–1881: George W. Reed
1881–1923: James H. and Louisa A. Williams *
1923–1942: Naomi J. Williams
1942–1953: Hattie E. Williams
1954–1957: vacant lot
1958–1986: Gulf Service Station (constructed ca. . 1958) **
1987–1997: University Auto Service
1997–2000: vacant building/parking lot

611 West: (County Court SE/NW 16, Lot 1)

1868–1881: George W. Reed
1881–1919: James H. and Louisa A. Williams rent house *
1919–1928: Mrs. Susie L. Williams
1928–1931: Mrs. Virgie Millsap
1932–1933: Mrs. Ollie M. Gorham
1934–1936: L. L. Lewis, Sr.
1937–1939: Charles A. Ford
1940–1945: Mrs. Ione Leaming
1946–1949: Hubert A. Hopper
1950–1953: William F. Sonneman
1954–1955: vacant house
1956–1959: Eddie Brantes
1960–1965: vacant lot
1966–2000: Underwood's Jewelers Building (constructed ca. 1964–1966) **

617 West: (County Court SE/NW 16, Lot 1)

1868–1881: George W. Reed
1881–1919: James H. and Louisa Williams rent house
(house constructed ca. 1897) *
1919–1920: Roy H. and Mary R. Vickers
1920–1924: Otis E. and Ina I. Hays
1924–1930: O. W. Williams
1931–1934: Walter W. Heflin
1935–1936: Mrs. Edna Ervin
1937–1942: Wilson Studios
1943–1944: Guy Miles
1944–1945: H. O. Burrough
1945–1953: Richard W. Burke
1954–1963: Gale Gray
1964–1965: Mrs. Opal Drake
1966–2000: see 611 West Dickson Street

623 West: *(County Court SE/NW 16, Lot 2)*

1868–1884: George W. Reed
1885–1897: T. P. Harrison *
1897–1903: C. J. Jones
1903–1919: Lucius Lewis rent house
1919–1931: William B. and Mira Deatherage
1932–1934: William R. Cannaday
1935–1936: Mrs. J. O. Gates
1937–1940: Mrs. Alice V. Austin
1940–1941: Fayetteville Electric Company
1941–1942: Zenas W. Ford Boarding House
1943–1945: N. V. Drake
1945–1946: vacant house / vacant lot
1947–1954: Campus Bookstore (constructed ca. 1947) **
1955–1956: vacant building
1956–1957: College Jewelry
1957–1965: Underwood's Jewelry
1966–1968: University Tailor Shop
1969–1974: Studio Northwest Gifts
1975–1986: World Wide Travel
1987–2000: Editype Business Services

625 West: *(County Court SE/NW 16, Lot 2)*

1868–1946: see 623 West Dickson Street
1947–2000: UARK Court Apartments (rear of building, 623–641 constructed ca. 1947) **

641 West: *(County Court SE/NW 16, Lot 2)*

1868–1946: see 623 West Dickson Street
1947–1977: Campus shop, clothing store (constructed ca. . 1947) **
1978–1980: Tennis Hog
1981–1995: Borealis Specialized Baggage
1995–1996: vacant building
1997–2000: Uncle Sam's Pack Shack

643 West: *(County Court SE/NW 16, Lot 2)*

1868–1940: see 653 West Dickson Street
1941–1952: Harkey's Feminine Fashions (constructed ca. 1940) **
1953–1960: Dixie Cream Do-Nut Shop
1961–1972: University Shop, clothing
1973–1976: Pearce's Collegiate Store
1977–1978: Balfour Sporting Goods
1979–2000: Best Sports

647 West: *(County Court SE/NW 16, Lot 2)*

1868–1940: see 653 West Dickson Street
1941–1981: UARK Theatre (constructed ca. 1940) **
1982–1986: vacant building
1987–1988: Rubbersouls Shoe Store
1989–1990: vacant building
1991–1997: Decades vintage clothing & Kaylin's antiques
1997–1998: Inner Garden
1999–2000: U-ARK Theatre rentals

653 West: *(County Court SE/NW 16, Lot 2)*

1868–1884: George W. Reed
1885–1902: T. P. Harrison *
1903–1908: Jesse W. and Mary J. Goddard
1909–1914: Frank D. and Dora Coffey
1915–1920: William B. and Maude Putnam
1921–1923: J. W. Webb
1924–1926: Tau Alpha Phi Fraternity
1927–1928: Joe N. Wills
1929–1930: vacant house
1930–1933: Jobe W. Franklin
1934–1936: Mrs. Flora M. Richey
1937–1940: Waggoner Boarding House
1941–1968: Campus Grill (constructed ca. 1940) **
1969–1987: Arkansas Book Store
1987–1995: Kinkos Copies
1995–1997: vacant building
1997–2000: Arkansas Book Exchange

NORTH UNIVERSITY AVENUE AT DICKSON STREET

703 West: *(County Court SE/NW 16, Lot 5)*

1868–1896: George W. Reed
1897–1898: G. M. Hagood *
1898–1903: W. A. Crawford
1903–1908: James W. Kuykendall
1909–1915: Millard F. Croxdale
1916–1925: Oscar M. and Margaret L. Henderson
1926–1927: Kappa Kappa Gamma Sorority
1927–1928: G. N. Jordan
1929–1933: Sigma Nu Fraternity
1934–1938: Tau Epsilon Phi Fraternity
1939–1940: Zenas W. Ford Boarding House
1941–1942: Future Farmers of America House # 1

1942–1943: Oscar Nordyke Boarding House
1944–1946: Lena Lewis Sharp Boarding House
1946–1949: Erie Hardy Boarding House
1950–1953: house converted into apartments
1953–1956: Ardean Falwell Boarding House
1956–1964: Alton H. Tedford Rooming House
1965–1991: First National Auto Bank (constructed ca. 1965) **
1992–1995: Worthen National Bank
1995–1997: Boatmen's Bank
1997–2000: Bank of America

711 West: (County Court SE/NW 16, Lot 5)

1868–1896: George W. Reed
1897–1903: Charles Bell *
1903–1904: Lt. Frank Ellis
1904–1921: William A. and Allie L. Cornwell
1921–2000: Kappa Sigma Fraternity (present house constructed ca. 1929–1930) **

717 West: (County Court SE/NW 16, Lot 5)

1868–1896: George W. Reed
1897–1905: T. B. Whitehead *
1906–1923: Oliver P. and Hattie J. McDonald
1924–1939: Kappa Alpha Fraternity
1940–1944: Future Farmers of America House
1945–1946: Joel F. Hembree
1947–1975: house converted into apartments
1976–2000: parking lot

725 West: (County Court SE/NW 16, Lot 5)

1868–1896: George W. Reed
1897–1900: John W. Baker *
1900–1961: John F. and Mary A. Mulrenin
1962–2000: vacant lot/parking lot

735 West: (County Court SE/NW 16, Lot 6)

1868–1896: George W. Reed
1897–1902: S. A. Pleasants Boarding House *
1902–1919: Mrs. Mary C. Moore Boarding House
1919–1925: Harrison A. and Mabel Hale
1926–1928: Mrs. W. W. Griffith
1929–1931: Mrs. Fannie P. Northcross
1931–1933: Mrs. Ruth M. Porter

1933–1961: Julius H. and Minnie B. Field
1962–2000: vacant lot/parking lot

743 West: (County Court SE/NW 16, Lot 7)

1868–1896: see 747 West Dickson Street
1897–1906: Charles D. McIlroy Boarding House *
1907–1918: Len Lewis, Jr. Boarding House
1919–1922: Sally E. Bassett
1923–1925: Dean Bradford and Stella Knapp
1925–1957: James A. and Dove English
1958–1962: Mrs. Telee Robinson
1963–2000: vacant lot/parking lot

747 West: (County Court SE/NW 16, Lot 7)

1868–1886: William McIlroy
1886–1892: James H. McIlroy
1892–1896: William Shreve
1897–1902: Charles D. McIlroy Boarding House *
1903–1926: Thomas C. and Ruth Poor
1926–1949: Oscar L. and Merle Champion
1950–1965: rent house (tenant changed each year; too numerous to list all occupants)
1966–1975: Francesca Apartments (constructed ca. . 1966) **
1976–2000: University of Arkansas (various offices)

753 West: (County Court SE/NW 16, Lot 8)

1868–1896: see 747 West Dickson Street
1897–1922: Dr. John C. and Haseltine Keeney *
1923–1925: Theta Phi Delta Fraternity
1926–1931: Lamda Chi Alpha Fraternity
1931–1937: Sigma Pi Epsilon Fraternity
1938–1940: Theta Kappa Nu Fraternity
1940–1949: 4-H Club (Girls)
1949–1959: Sigma Pi Epsilon Fraternity
1960–1961: William D. McGahey Boarding House
1962–1964: John T. Babb Boarding House
1964–1965: James Pershall
1966–1968: Robert Adkins
1969–1974: vacant house
1975–2000: vacant lot/parking lot

763 West: (County Court SE/NW 16, Lot 9)

1868–1896: see 747 West Dickson Street
1897–1908: George A. Cole *

1909–1953: Lena Lewis Sharp (home of Kappa Kappa Gamma Sorority, 1932–1933)
1953–1959: Christian Church Student Center
1960–1961: Mrs. Carrie L. Hewgley
1962–1969: Theta Tau Fraternity
1970–1974: vacant house
1975–2000: vacant lot/parking lot

NORTH DUNCAN AVENUE AT DICKSON STREET

803 West: (County Court SW/NW 16, Lot 10)

1868–1892: William McIlroy
1892–1929: W. T. and Fannie Thomason *
1929–1933: vacant house
1934–1937: Mrs. C. L. Dunlap
1938–1939: Walter J. Bates
1940–1941: O. R. Waggoner Boarding House
1942–1943: vacant house
1944–1955: James U. and Margaret Phipps Boarding House
1956–1957: Mrs. Mary E. Onwiler
1960–1961: Effie L. McGahey Boarding House
1961–1972: Jim J. and Anna M. Lauderdale
1973–1974: Steve Martin
1975–1976: William M. Crow
1977–2000: University of Arkansas (Greenhouse constructed ca. 1977–1978) **

811 West: (County Court SW/NW 16, Lot 10)

1868–1900: see 803 West Dickson Street
1901–1919: S. B. Crozier *
1920–1926: George E. Miller Boarding House **
1926–1928: Harrison A. and Mabel Hale
1929–1933: Thomas J. Sargents
1934–1936: Mrs. Mamie Wilson
1937–1944: Andrew and Viola E. Combs
1944–1946: Miss Toka Henry Boarding House
1947–1948: Gerald Smith
1949–1955: Mrs. Zula Fraser
1956–2000: University of Arkansas (Physics Building constructed ca. 1955–1956; expanded 1993–1994) ***

841 West: (County Court SW/NW 16, Lot 10)

1868–1956: see 823 West Dickson Street
1957–2000: University of Arkansas (Heating Plant constructed ca. 1957) **

843 West: (Shreve Addition Lots 1–6)

1868–1892: William McIlroy
1886–1892: James H. McIlroy
1892–1905: William F. Shreve
1905–1917: Miss Abbie Neal
1917–1929: Jessie R. and Martha A. Loving *
1929–1931: Mrs. Nellie Broyles
1932–1933: James M. Parish
1934–1937: Mrs. Nicie Campbell
1938–1942: Thomas A. Green
1943–1944: Clifton Wade
1944–1946: George Crook
1946–1947: vacant lot
1947–1963: University of Arkansas (Temporary Buildings) **
1964–2000: University of Arkansas (Mechanical Engineering Building constructed ca. 1964) ***

BUCHANAN AVENUE AT DICKSON STREET

901 West: (University Addition, Block 1, Lots 10–15)

1868–1886: William McIlroy
1887–1907: James H. McIlroy
1907–1915: Helen E. Croxdale *
1916–1920: Theodore F. Jones
1920–1936: James R. and Nicie Campbell
1937–1939: George P. McLemore
1940–1945: Alvin J. and Clara A. Garrison Boarding House
1946–1948: Richard B. McCulloch
1949–1951: James T. Kell
1952–1961: vacant house
1961–1964: Marvin Kemp
1965–2000: University of Arkansas (Terrace Manor Apartments constructed ca. 1965) **

913 West: (University Addition, Block 1, Lots 7–9)

1868–1907: see 901 West Dickson Street
1907–1915: Mrs. Lina McNamara *
1916–1920: Henry L. and Elizabeth M. Paisley
1921–1924: James H. and Etta Farley
1924–1925: F. E. Worrell
1926–1959: Alvin J. and Clara A. Garrison Boarding House
1960–1961: Mrs. Aggie McClelland
1962–1964: Lee Lum
1965–2000: see 901 West Dickson Street

919 West: (University Addition, Block 1, Lots 1–6)

1868–1907:	see 901 West Dickson Street
1907–1915:	Sam A. Clark *
1916–1930:	Dan M. and Lottie Allen
1931–1936:	vacant house
1937–1942:	Joseph W. Webb
1943–1944:	Lawrence Little
1944–1946:	Mrs. Arlin Jones
1946–1948:	vacant house
1949–1950:	Girls 4-H House
1950–1952:	Vol W. Hannah
1953–1961:	Aggie McClelland Boarding House
1962–1963:	Hallie Bundrick Boarding House
1964–1968:	vacant lot
1969–2000:	University of Arkansas (Kimpel Hall constructed ca. 1967–1969) **

OZARK AVENUE AT DICKSON STREET

1049 West: (University Addition, Block 2, Lot 1)

1868–1886:	William McIlroy
1887–1908:	James H. McIlroy *
1908–1923:	Sigma Chi Fraternity
1923–1954:	Sigma Alpha Epsilon Fraternity
1954–1958:	vacant house / vacant lot
1959–2000:	University of Arkansas (Brough Commons constructed ca. 1958) **

GENERAL SOURCES

CENSUS RECORDS

U. S. Census, 1870–1920

CITY & TELEPHONE DIRECTORIES

Fayetteville City Directory (Polk's and others), 1904–2000 (incomplete).

Southwestern Bell Telephone Directories, 1923–2000.

GENERAL HISTORIES

Arkansas and Its People, a History, 1541–1930. David Y. Thomas, editor. New York: The American Historical Society, 1930.

Arkansas State Gazetteer and Business Directory. Detroit, MI: R. L. Polk & Co., 1884–1913.

Brown, Kent R. *Fayetteville: A Pictorial History.* Norfolk and Virginia Beach, VA., Donning Company, 1982.

Campbell, William S. *One hundred years of Fayetteville, 1828–1928.* Fayetteville, Ark.: W.S. Campbell, c1928.

Centennial history of Arkansas. Dallas T. Herndon, editor. Chicago, Little Rock, S. J. Clarke Publishing Co., 1922.

Flashback. Fayetteville: Washington County Historical Society.

Hale, Harrison, University of Arkansas, 1871–1948. Fayetteville, University of Arkansas Alumni Association, 1948.

Leflar, Robert Allen, *The First One Hundred Years: Centennial History of the University of Arkansas.* Fayetteville, University of Arkansas Foundation, c1972.

Reprint of the Washington County section of Goodspeed's Benton, Washington, Carroll, Madison, Crawford, Franklin, and Sebastian Counties, Arkansas history. Siloam Springs, Ark., J. R. Huff, 1978.

Reynolds, John Hugh, and David Yancey Thomas, *History of the University of Arkansas.* Fayetteville, The University, 1910.

Rural Directory of Washington County. Fayetteville, Fayetteville Printing Company, 1921–1923.

Simpson, Ethel C. *Image and Reflection: A Pictorial History of the University of Arkansas.* Fayetteville, University of Arkansas Press, 1990.

Brochures and pamphlets on Fayetteville, Fayetteville businesses, and churches from the Arkansas Collection, University of Arkansas Libraries, Fayetteville.

MAPS

Copy of the official map of the city of Fayetteville, Washington Co., Ark. / Drawn by S. B. Robertson. [Fayetteville, Ark., 1884.]

Atlas of Washington County, Arkansas, Compiled Drawn and Published from Official Records, Personal Examinations and Surveys / by Gordon V. Skelton , 1894.

Plat book of Washington County, Arkansas, compiled from county records and actual surveys. Des Moines, Iowa, Northwest Publishing Co., 1908.

Sanborn Fire Insurance Maps of Fayetteville, 1886–1940. New York, Sanborn Map Company, 1885–1951.

NEWSPAPERS

Arkansas Sentinel, 1876–1919

Fayetteville Daily Leader, 1929–1931

Fayetteville Democrat, 1869–1937

Grapevine, 1970–1990

Nightflying, 1980–2000

Northwest Arkansas Times, 1937–2000

Obituary Index at Grace Keith Genealogy Library, Fayetteville Public Library, for many family histories for which no other published sources are available.

TAX RECORDS

Washington County Real Estate Tax Records, 1868–1945

UNIVERSITY OF ARKANSAS PUBLICATIONS

Arkansas Alumnus, later retitled *Arkansas*

Cardinal , *Razorback* yearbooks

University Weekly (student newspaper), 1907–1921

Arkansas Traveler (student newspaper), 1921–2000

SPECIAL THANKS TO INFORMANTS WHO PROVIDED DETAILS ABOUT BUSINESSES & RESIDENCES

Helen Brannen

John Burrow

Dave & Belva Clark

Tom Clark

Morris Collier

Ellen Compton

Mike Dameron

Dawn DeLong

Joe Fennel

Mary Jo Godfrey

Barbara Hale

Mary Hinton

Herbert Holcomb
Charles V. Kappen
Grace Keith
Roger Koetter
John Lewis
Joan Lines
Dr. Max McAllister
Ed McCormick
Susan Shelton McRae
Stephanie Meehan
Dorothy Metcalfe
Mary Margaret Morton
Wendel & Sarah Nothdurft
Forrest Poorman
Wally Scranton
Frank Sharp
Curtis Shipley
Ethel Simpson
Bette Stamps
Ann Sugg
Bill Underwood
Bruce Walker
Lina Hayes Watson
Ron Woodruff
Sandy Young

SPECIAL THANKS TO THESE INSTITUTIONS AND THEIR STAFFS:

Fayetteville Public Library (Grace Keith, Helen Brannen, Mary Jo Godfrey)

Grapevine writers Joe Neal and Stephanie Eifling Meehan, who wrote extensively about Dickson Street in the 1980s

Shiloh Museum of Ozark History (Bob Besom, Marie Demeroukas, Manon Wilson, Susan Young,)

Special Collections Department, University of Arkansas Libraries (Andrea Cantrell, Michael Dabrishus, Tom Dillard, Geoffery Stark, James Wilhelm)

Washington County Assessor's Office (Sue Phillips, Lee Ann Kizzar)

Washington County Circuit Clerk's Office (Alma Kohlmeyer, Kathleen Harness)

Washington County County Clerk's Office (Marilyn Edwards, Karen Combs)

Washington County Judge's Office (Charles Johnson, Roger Haney, John Gibson)

Washington County Historical Society (Pete Jordan)

IMAGE CREDITS

Citations are to the General Sources, p. 375. Read: page number in this book, location of image on page (top, bottom, middle, left, right), source, specific location of image.

KEY: Shiloh = Shiloh Museum of Ozark History. Citations are to specific collections and items

Special Collections= University of Arkansas Libraries, Special Collections Department. Citations are to specific collections

Front jacket: (l) Special Collections, Ida Barr Scrapbook; (r) top to bottom: *Razorback, see* p. 75; Special Collections, *see* p. 226; Shiloh, *see* p. 155; photo by author

4 photo by author

7 Special Collections, Picture Collection # 1878;

8 (t) Shiloh, Steve Meldrum Collection (S-2007–54);8 (m) Campbell, p. 89; (b) Shiloh, Steve Meldrum Collection (S-2007–54)

9 (t) Special Collections, Washington County Historical Society Papers; 9 (b) *Razorback,* 1953, p. 173

10 photo by author

13 photo by author

14 photo by author

17 Special Collections, Lemke Photos # 20

18 (t) Shiloh, Washington County Historical Society Collection (P- 3881); (b) Special Collections, Lemke Photos # 19

20 (t) Campbell, p. 61; (b) Brown, p. 111

21 (t) Special Collections, Agnes L. Reagan Papers; (b) Brown, p. 100

22 photo by author

25 Special Collections Picture Collection # 4311n

26 Campbell p. 79

27 (b) Special Collections, Washington County Historical Society Papers; 027 (l) *Northwest Arkansas Times,* 08/06/1953, p. 2; (r) Shiloh, Washington County Historical Society Collection (P- 2051)

28 Special Collections, Washington County Historical Society Papers

29 (t) Special Collections, Washington County Historical Society Papers; (b) courtesy of Susan Shelton McRae

30 (t) Special Collections, Picture Collection # 703; (b) photo by author

35 courtesy of Washington County Historical Society

36 (t) Lemke, *Walker Family Album,* 1964; 036 (b) Campbell, p. 89

37 (b) Special Collections, Washington County Historical Society Papers; (l and r) courtesy of Steve Jones

38 Campbell, p. 79

39 (t) photo by author; (b) *Flashback,* October, 1964, cover

40 *Flashback,* August, 1967, p. 42

41 (t) photo by author; (l) *Flashback,* August, 1961, cover; (r) *Flashback,* August, 1961, cover

42 *Flashback,* February, 1966, p. 6

43 courtesy of Julie Smith Bonds

44 photo by author

45 (t) Campbell, p. 109; (b) *Flashback,* August, 1968, p. 21

46 (t) Campbell, p. 97; (b) *Northwest Arkansas Times,* 11/12/1968, p. 10

47 photo by author

51 (l) courtesy of Joan Lines; (r) Special Collections, Picture Collection # 4310n

52 *Fayetteville Democrat,* 03/15/1889, p. 1
53 Reynolds and Thomas, p. 539
54 *Northwest Arkansas Times,* 10/31/1951, p. 3
55 (t) photo by author; (b) courtesy of Bryan Walker
56–57 Shiloh, Bob Besom Collection (S-82–199–10)
58 photo by author
59 photo by author
60 Frisco Lines, *Summer Days in the Ozarks,* 1911, p. 22
61 Shiloh, Bruce Vaughan/McQuaid Collection (S-79–4-63A)
62 (t) Special Collections, Picture Collection # 4629p; (b) First Baptist Church, *History of First Baptist Church, 1857–1966, cover*
63 photo by author
69 *Fayetteville Democrat,* 07/22/1922, p. 3
71 *Fayetteville Democrat,* 08/29/1933, p. 3
72 Fayetteville Chamber of Commerce, *Fayetteville,* 1941, cover
73 *Northwest Arkansas Times,* 09/18/1952, p. 11
74 *Special Collections , vertical file clipping of Grapevine,* 04/05/1978, p. 1
75 *Razorback,* 1977, p. 43
76 *Grapevine,* 09/26/1979, p. 3
77 *Razorback,* 1980, p. 49
78 *Razorback,* 1983, p. 17
79 *Arkansas Times,* 09/1986 (John Watson photo), p. 48
80–81 *Grapevine,* 09/30/1988, p. 8
81 *Northwest Arkansas Times,* 03/27/1994, p. 6
85 Campbell, p. 109
87 Shiloh, Maggie Smith Collection (S-83–92–23)
88 Central Methodist Episcopal Church, *History of Methodism in Fayetteville,* 1907 p. 2
89 (t) Central Methodist Episcopal Church, p. 16; (b) courtesy of author
90 Reynolds and Thomas, p. 421
91 *Razorback,* 1917, n.p.
93 (t) Central Presbyterian Church, *Centennial Celebration,* 1930, cover; (b) photo by author
94 Shiloh, General Photograph Collection (S-83–92–24)
95 Shiloh, Washington County Historical Society Collection (P-3214a)
96 (t) Campbell, p. 79; (b) Shiloh, Washington County Historical Society Collection (P-381)
97 (t) Campbell, p. 33; (b) photo by author
101 Campbell, p. 7
103 photo by author
104 *Northwest Arkansas Times* 10/24/1957 p. 6
105 (t) *Razorback,* 1928, p. 291; (b) *Southwestern Bell Telephone Directory,* December 1946, yellow p. 2
106 Shiloh, Washington County Historical Society Collection (P-1180)
107 Shiloh, Clyde Widders Collection (S-88–144–32)
108 Polk, R. L., *City Directory of Fayetteville, Arkansas,* 1957, yellow p. 26
110 *Northwest Arkansas Times,* 04/24/1950, p. 3
111 courtesy of Collier Drug
112 courtesy of Collier Drug
115 Shewmaker, C. D. *City Directory of* Fayetteville, 1920–1921, p. 7
116 *Razorback,* 1939, p. 267
117 (t) *Northwest Arkansas Times,* 11/01/1952, p. 27; (b) *Northwest Arkansas Times,* 08/21/1970, (Ken Good photo), p. 1
118 *Northwest Arkansas Times,* 11/15/1937, p. 5
119 (t) *Southwestern Bell Telephone Directory,* 1962, yellow p. 40; (b) photo by author
120 (t) photo by author; (b) Special Collections, *Grapevine* Papers (unprocessed collection)
121 (t) Campbell, p. 79; (b) Shiloh, Peter Harkins Collection (S-90–194–43)
122 *Southwestern Bell Telephone Directory,* 1954, yellow p. 6

123 (t) Special Collections, William Simeon Campbell Papers; (b) *Arkansas Traveler,* May 1, 1974, p. 15
124 *Fayetteville Democrat,* 04/22/1937, p. 11
125 photo by author
126 (t) courtesy of James E. Duncan (also in Frisco Lines, 1916, p. C.); (b) *Northwest Arkansas Times,* 6/03/1944, p. 6
127 (t) *Northwest Arkansas Times,* 10/20/1938, p. 8; (b) photo by author
128 photo by author
129 (t) *Southwestern Bell Telephone Directory,* June 1928, yellow p. 9; (b) photo by author
130 (t) *Razorback,* 1931, n.p.; (b) Special Collections, *Grapevine* Papers (unprocessed collection)
131 (t) courtesy of Sarah Nothdurft; (b) *Nightflying,* March 1981, "back p."
132 (t) Brown, p. 114; (b) *Razorblade,* February 1954, p. 19
133 photo by author
134 (t and b) courtesy of Sarah Nothdurft
135 Special Collections, *Grapevine* Papers (unprocessed collection); Razorback, 1955, p. 5
139 Campbell, p. 61
140 photo by author
141 (t) Campbell, p. 109; (b) Shiloh, Betty Mohney Collection (S-86–73–15)
142 courtesy of James S. Chase
143 (t) *Northwest Arkansas Times,* 08/24/1946, p. 11A; (b) photo by author
144 photo by author
145 (t) *Razorback,* 1923, p. 340; (b) courtesy of Ron Woodruff
146 (t) courtesy of Ron Woodruff; (b) *Northwest Arkansas Times,* 12/30/1969 (Ken Good photo), p. 1
147 (t) photo by author; (b) Campbell, p. 29
148 Special Collections, *Grapevine* Papers (unprocessed collection)
149 Shiloh, Washington County Historical Society Collection (P-2725)
150 (t) *Northwest Arkansas Times,* 11/19/1937, p. 4; (b) Polk, R. L., *City Directory of Fayetteville, Arkansas,* 1947, yellow p. 8
151 (t l) *Southwestern Bell Telephone Directory,* December 1941, yellow p. 5; (t r) *Southwestern Bell Telephone Directory,* 1962, yellow p. 21; (b l) *Southwestern Bell Telephone Directory,* 1949, yellow p. 48; (b r) University of Arkansas Campus Directory, 1968–69, p. 55
152 *Northwest Arkansas Times,* 06/01/1937, p. 5
153 (t) Special Collections, *Grapevine* Papers (unprocessed collection); (b) courtesy of Sarah Nothdurft
154 (t) *Rural Directory of Washington County,* 1922, p. 69; (b) *Southwestern Bell Telephone Directory,* December 1945, yellow p. 31
155 (t) Shiloh, Springdale Morning News Collection (S—87–261–3); (b l) *Southwestern Bell Telephone Directory,* 1958, yellow p. 83; (b r) *Southwestern Bell Telephone Directory,* 1965, yellow p. 147
156 photo by author
157 (t) *Southwestern Bell Telephone Directory,* December 1927, cover; (b) *Razorback,* 1922, p. 335
158 Special Collections, *Grapevine* Papers (unprocessed collection)
159 (t) *Cardinal,* 1909, p. 238; (b) American Guidebook, 1945, p. 8;
160 Stewart & Weeks, *City Directory of Fayetteville, Arkansas,* 1904, n. p.
161 (t) *Razorback,* 1936, n. p.; (b) *Northwest Arkansas Times,* 05/09/1942, p. C4
163 (l) Arkansas Traveler, 09/26/1975, p. 3; (r) *Northwest Arkansas Times,* 02/08/1973, p. 10
164 (t) *Razorback,* 1982, p. 491; (b) photo by author

170 (t) photo by author; (b) *Southwestern Bell Telephone Directory,* May 1926, yellow p. 4
171 *Frolic,* January, 1948, p. 16
172 *Razorback,* 1977, p. 42
173 (t) *Fayetteville Democrat,* 06/10/1909, p. 1; (b) *Razorback,* 1922, p. 330
174 Special Collections, *Grapevine* Papers (unprocessed collection)
175 (t) Frisco Lines, *Summer Days in the Ozarks,* 1911, p. 28; (b) *Arkansas Times,* September, 1986, p. 49
177 *Northwest Arkansas Times,* 05/06/1947 (Ed Puska photo), p. 1
178 *Northwest Arkansas Times,* 04/04/1968 (Ken Good photo), p. 1
179 *Southwestern Bell Telephone Directory,* 1955, p. 85
180 (t) *University Weekly,* 02/17/1916, n.p.; (b) *Fayetteville Democrat,* 06/12/1922, p. 2D
181 (t) *Cardinal,* 1915, n. p.; *Razorback,* 1920, p. 255, *Razorback,* 1922, p.320; (b) *Frolic,* May, 1948, p. 3
182 (l) *Frolic,* January, 1948 p. 15; (r) Special Collections, *Grapevine* Papers (unprocessed collection)
183 Special Collections, *Grapevine* Papers (unprocessed collection)
185 (t) Shiloh, Washington County Historical Society Collection (P-3854B); (b) Shiloh, Washington County Historical Society Collection (P-3854A)
186 (t) photo by author; (b) *Northwest Arkansas Times,* 03/23/1946, p. 5
187 *White Mule,* 1925, p. 25
188 *Southwestern Bell Telephone Directory,* 1957, yellow p. 17
189 (t) *Cardinal,* 1912, p. 227; (b) Special Collections, *Grapevine* Papers (unprocessed collection)
190 (t) Shiloh, Washington County Historical Society Collection (P-2596A) (b) Shiloh, Washington County Historical Society Collection (P-2596B)
191 (t) *Razorback Directory,* 1943–1944, p. 29; (b) *Cardinal,* 1906, p. 209
192 (t) *Cardinal,* 1912, p. 229; (m) *Southwestern Bell Telephone Directory,* June 1928, cover; (b) *Razorback,* 1917, n.p.
193 photo by author
194 (t) courtesy of author; (b) photo by author
195 *Northwest Arkansas Times,* 04/30/1955
196 (t) Special Collections, Folklore Class Reports, Sue Dunlavy, "Shuler Town." Spring, 1962; (b) courtesy William Bates Cobb
197 (l) *Northwest Arkansas Times,* 06/17/1968, p. 8; (r) *Arkansas Traveler,* 09/19/1975, p. 5
198 Shiloh, Peter Harkins Collection (S-90–194–84)
199 courtesy of Peter Tooker
200 *Razorback,* 1980, p. 50
202 *Razorback,* 1980, p. 51
203 (t) Special Collections, *Grapevine* Papers (unprocessed collection); (b) *Cardinal,* 1906, p. 210
204 (t) Special Collections, *Grapevine* Papers (unprocessed collection); (b) Special Collections, Folklore Class Reports, 1959, "Stories of Fayetteville"
205 photo by author
206 photo by author
207 (t) Shewmaker, C. D., *City Directory of* Fayetteville, 1920–1921, p. 188; (b) Shiloh, Washington County Historical Society Collection (P-340)
208 (t) Shiloh, Washington County Historical Society Collection (P-2446); (b) *Fayetteville Democrat,* 3/27/1931, p. 5
209 *Nightflying,* September 1981, p. 2
210 Special Collections, *Grapevine* Papers (unprocessed collection);
211 (t) *Northwest Arkansas Times,* 02/28/1946 (Ed Puska photo), p. 1; (b) *Rural Directory of Washington County,* 1926, p. 13

212 (t) *Darkhorse,* 11/01/1979, p. 6; (b) Polk, *City Directory of Fayetteville, Arkansas,* 1947, yellow p. 4

213 (t) *Southwestern Bell Telephone Directory,* 1961, yellow p. 73; (b) Special Collections, *Grapevine* Papers (unprocessed collection)

215 (t) Shiloh, Washington County Historical Society Collection (P-3826 p. 50); (b) *Razorback,* 1920, p. 174

216 Special Collections, *Grapevine* Papers (unprocessed collection)

217 courtesy of Richard Black

218 photo by author

219 photo by author

226 (t) Special Collections, Picture Collection # 3690; (b) Special Collections, Picture Collection # 1644

227 (t) *Fayetteville Democrat,* 09/19/1918, p. 3; (b) Special Collections, Picture Collection # 3629

228 *Northwest Arkansas Times,* 09/18/1965 (Woodruff & Carl photos), p. 9

229 (t and m) photos by author; (b) courtesy of Bank of Fayetteville

230 (t) *Arkansas Engineer,* III, 2, 1922–23, [back cover] ; (b) *Razorback,* 1920, p. 257

231 (t) *Northwest Arkansas Times,* 05/31/1962, p. 2; (b) Special Collections, *Grapevine* Papers (unprocessed collection)

232 (t) *Southwestern Bell Telephone Directory,* 1949, yellow p. 24; (b) Reynolds and Thomas, p. 466

233 (t) Shiloh, Washington County Historical Society Collection (P-1733); (b) Special Collections, Picture Collection # 3887

234 Shiloh, Steve Meldrum Collection (S-2007–54)

235 (t) *Northwest Arkansas Times,* 01/24/1939, p. 5; (b) *Southwestern Bell Telephone Directory,* 1941, yellow p. 5

236 photo by author

237 (t) Special Collections, *Grapevine* Papers (unprocessed collection); (b) *Southwestern Bell Telephone Directory,* 1954, yellow p. 31

238 photo by author

239 (t) *Washington County in Pictures and Prose,* 1940, p. 13; (b) *Fayetteville Democrat,* 08/24/1933, p. 5

241 (t) Special Collections, *Grapevine* Papers (unprocessed collection); (b) photo by author

243 Special Collections, Picture Collection # 4096

244 (t) *Razorback Directory,* 1951–1952, cover; (b) Special Collections, Ethel Simpson Papers (unprocessed collection)

245 photo by author

247 (t and b) *Northwest Arkansas Times,* 10/16/1969 (Ken Good photos), p. 1, 2

248 (map), *Flashback,* November, 1957, cover

251 Campbell, p. 61

252 *Northwest Arkansas Times,* 08/11/1949, p. 16

253 (t) Shiloh, General Photograph Collection (S-87–289–13);(b) Shiloh, Washington County Historical Society Collection (P-206)

254 photo by author

255 photo by author

256 *Northwest Arkansas Times,* 11/19/1966, p. 5

257 (t) Frisco Lines, *Summer Days in the Ozarks,* p. 25; (b) Shiloh, Washington County Historical Society Collection (P-2470a)

258 *Arkansas Traveler,* 01/14/1941, p. 3

259 (t) *Razorback,* 1941, p. 321; (b) *Arkansas Traveler,* 02/25/1949, p. 4

261 *Razorback,* 1982, p. 480

262 photo by author

262 (b) *Razorback,* 1970, p. 8

263 *Arkansas Democrat,* 07/01/1934, p. 4B

264 (l) Shiloh, Washington County Historical Society Collection (P-1966); (r) Campbell, p. 7

265 (t) courtesy of Reed descendant,

Cloudcroft, NM; (b) Lemke, Walter J., *Some Old Fayetteville Homes*, 1951, n. p.

266 (t) *Arkansas Traveler*, September 20, 1962, p. 3 (b) *Razorback*, 1957, p. 65

267 *Southwestern Bell Telephone Directory*, 1965, yellow p. 156

268 (t) *Southwestern Bell Telephone Directory*, 1955, yellow p. 28; (b) *Northwest Arkansas Times*, 6/02/1955, yellow p. 18

269 *Northwest Arkansas Times*, 07/31/1957, p. 12

270 photo by author

271 photos by author

272 *Northwest Arkansas Times*, 03/26/1971, p. 37A

273 *Big Picture in Ozarks*, 06/1948, p. 28

274 Benton's Bowling lanes *Northwest Arkansas Times*, 9–28–51

275 photo by author

276 (t) *Razorback*, 1949, p. 295; (b) courtesy of Dorothy Metcalfe

277 courtesy of Dorothy Metcalfe

278 photo by author

279 St. John's Lutheran Church, *Dedication*, 1950

280 photo by author

282 (t) *Northwest Arkansas Times*, 10/15/1971 (Ken Good photo), p. 1; (b) *Ozark Mountain These Times*, 2/12/1971, p. 1

285 *Razorback*, 1952, p. 22

286 (t) photo by author; (b) *Razorback*, 1983, p. 14

287 *Razorback*, 1932, n.p.

288 Polk, R. L., *City Directory of Fayetteville, Arkansas*, 1968, yellow p. insert

289 photo by author

290 (t) *Razorback*, 1928, p. 261; (b) photo by author

291 (t) *Plat of Washington County, Arkansas*, 1908, photographs insert; (b) *Razorback*, 1940, p. 118

292 Special Collections, Field Photos # 93

294 *Razorback*, 1928, p. 275

295 *Razorback*, 1956, p. 340

296 (t) *Razorback*, 1969, p. 319; (b) photo by author

297 photo by author

302 *Arkansas Traveler*, 10/27/1950, p. 5

303 Special Collections, Picture Collection # 1063

304 photos by author

305 (t) Special Collections, Picture Collection # 1090; (b) photo by author

306 photos by author

307 (t) Special Collections, Picture Collection # 1226; (b) photo by author

312 *Razorback*, 1949, p. 291

313 (t) photo by author; (b) Special Collections, Picture Collection # 5042

314 photos by author

315 (t) Special Collections, Picture Collection # 1151;315 (b) photo by author

319 Hale, Harrison, *University of Arkansas, 1871–1948*, p. 61

320 (l) Washington County Historical Society, *Bulletin # 48*, p. 15; (r) Washington County Historical Society, *Bulletin # 48*, p. 3

321 (t) Washington County Historical Society, *Bulletin # 48*, p. 15; (b) *Razorback*, 1926, p. 254

322 *Razorback*, 1947, p. 249

323 Special Collections, Picture Collection # 1556

324 Shiloh, Joe Neal Collection (S-88–247–3)

325 (t) Special Collections, Picture Collection # 1344; (b) photo by author

326 *Razorback*, 1962, p. 30

INDEX

ANTHONY J. "TONY" WAPPEL

Born and raised in East St. Louis, Illinois, Wappel obtained his A. B. in Political Science from Loyola University of Chicago and his M.P.A. from the University of Arkansas. He has worked for the Special Collections Department of the University of Arkansas Libraries and the Benton County Circuit and County Clerks' Offices. Since 1997 Wappel has been the Archivist & Records Manager for Washington County. He has had a lifelong interest in historic research and historic preservation, having restored two craftsman era houses in Fayetteville. Wappel also has a strong interest in local government, housing, and community development issues.

ETHEL C. SIMPSON

Ethel Simpson has lived in Fayetteville on and off since 1958. Her first date with Vergil Simpson, whom she married in 1959, was for beer at George's. The couple taught in Maryland and Louisiana before returning to Fayetteville in 1969, and she finished a PhD. in comparative literature at the U of A. She worked for thirty years in the Special Collections Department of the University of Arkansas Libraries, where she acquired an extensive knowledge of Arkansas bibliography and literature and supervised the manuscript processing unit of the department. She is the author or editor of many articles and books, including *Image and Reflection, A Pictorial History of the University of Arkansas.* Since her retirement in 2005, Simpson has continued to do research, editing, and writing, especially for the Internet resource known as the *Encyclopedia of Arkansas History and Culture.*